S0-BEI-486

The Gun Digest® Book of SPORTING SHOTGUNS

WITHDRAWN

URBANDALE PUBLIC LIBRARY
3520 86TH STREET
URBANDALE, IA 50322-4056

Edited by

KEVIN MICHALOWSKI

©2005 KP Books

Published by

kp books
An Imprint of F+W Publications

700 East State Street • Iola, WI 54990-0001
715-445-2214 • 888-457-2873

Our toll-free number to place an order or obtain
a free catalog is (800) 258-0929.

All rights reserved. No portion of this publication may be reproduced
or transmitted in any form or by any means, electronic or mechanical,
including photocopy, recording, or any information storage and retrieval system,
without permission in writing from the publisher, except by a reviewer who may quote
brief passages in a critical article or review to be printed in a magazine or newspaper,
or electronically transmitted on radio, television, or the Internet.

Library of Congress Catalog Number: 2004098427

ISBN: 0-89689-173-9

Designed by Patsy Howell
Edited by Kevin Michalowski

Printed in the United States of America

ACKNOWLEDGMENTS

When time was short and the pressure was on M.D. Johnson came through with a series of well-written articles that are sure to inform and enlighten everyone who reads them. His work made this book possible.

CONTENTS

INTRODUCTION

Sporting shotguns are, for the most part, the blue-collar workers of the firearms family. Sure, there are some high-end guns out there with fancy wood and delicate engraving, but when you say "shotgun" the vision that most often comes to mind is that of a hard-working field gun. Shotguns do their work from coast to coast without flash or ego. They are there on the trap ranges and the clays courses, in the goose pits, the duck marshes and the upland. We use them all the time without a second thought. This book will help you choose and use these tools better, every time you take them out of the gun safe. Enjoy.

Kevin Michalowski
Editor

A 1970s-era Remington 1100 12-gauge in straight 2-3/4 inch format is a shotgun seldom seen afield these days.

Autoloaders: Yesterday, and Today

By M.D. Johnson

Christmas Day, 1979, and I'm enthusiastically tearing the paper from around a heavy though somewhat small box. Suddenly, the words *16-gauge Dove & Quail* come into view. "Thanks, Pop," I tell my father, who's at the time sitting in his recliner smoking a Camel Light and grinning a grin that would put the Chesire Cat out of business.

It was an odd gift, I thought. Not that I didn't have a 16-gauge, for I was shooting my father's first gun, a 1952 Winchester Model 24 side-by-side. Odd, though, because I had plenty of 16-gauge ammunition on the shelves downstairs. Still, when you're 15 and shot – poorly – as much as I did, another box of shells was always a welcome addition to the stockpile.

"Those are special 16-gauge shells," my Pop said as I went to put the box alongside my stocking full of PEZ dispensers and Hershey Kisses. "Better check 'em out." The grin got bigger. Inside, laying atop the first row of shotshells, was a note written in my father's unmistakable heavy hand. *Look Under The Couch* was all it said. Stumped, I peered under the sofa. A box, long and narrow and a familiar shade of green, immediately caught my eye. With clumsy hands, I hauled the cardboard box out into the light. REMINGTON, the white cursive letters spelled. A shotgun!

Trembling fingers fumbled with tape. Tabs A were pulled none too gently from Slots B and C, and the lid flung wide.

The author's Remington Model 11-87 proved itself worthy during this late-season Ohio goose hunt.

Versatile autoloaders like this Benelli Super Black Eagle are fast gaining popularity, particularly among waterfowlers.

This wasn't just any shotgun; this was a Remington 1100. An autoloader. My autoloader. Walnut stock and blued receiver gleamed in the incandescent glow of my mother's living room. Quickly, I unscrewed the magazine cap and removed the forearm. Gas pistons, O-ring...they were all there, just like on Pop's 12-gauge. Carefully slipping the barrel into place, I reversed the process, inadvertently hitting the silver bolt release on the bottom-side of the receiver. *S-L-I-C-K*, the bolt slammed shut with a welcome metallic chime. "Sounds good, doesn't it, Jake?" My father, master of the understatement. Throwing the autoloader to my shoulder, I swung the gun – my gun! – through an imaginary rooster and slapped the trigger. Somewhere, a ringneck crumpled at the report. Suddenly, PEZ dispensers went forgotten.

That was 26 years ago. Since that Christmas Day in northeastern Ohio, I, along with the rest of the shotgunning community, have seen tremendous changes – many would say improvements – in the design and functionality of the autoloader. Do-It-All guns are the norm today, shotguns that will handle interchangeably any and all ammunition from the lightest 2-3/4-inch shotshells to the largest candlestick 3-1/2-inchers. Gone are the processes of flip-flopping friction rings as in the earliest Browning Auto-5s, or twisting end-caps to switch between light and heavy loads such as had to be done with the Remington Model 58 in the late 1950s.

However, before we get any farther into a history lesson here, let's take a minute and discuss a couple different terms; the definitions for which will serve as the basis for much of that to come. These would include –

Semi-automatic – To be technically correct, the word is *semi-automatic* or *autoloading*, not *automatic*. An automatic firearm – the U.S. military's light machine gun M-60 or the standard infantry weapon, the M-16A1, for example – will continue to fire as long as the trigger is depressed *and* there is a supply of ammunition. Release the trigger or run out of ammunition, and the gun ceases to fire. A semi-automatic firearm, such as the aforementioned Remington Model 1100 or Browning A-5, will fire once with each pull of the trigger; that is, each discharge requires the trigger be released and pulled again. True, such pieces load themselves upon firing, hence the proper use of the term *autoloading*; however, they are not automatics.

Gas-operated – With a gas-operated semi-automatic shotgun, a portion of the gases produced upon ignition of the powder charge are recycled and used to operate the action. Think of a gas-operated autoloader like a steam locomotive. Steam is produced in the boiler. A portion of this steam is used to power the drive wheels via a turbine conversation, while the unused or unnecessary steam is vented off through the stack. In a gas-operated semi-automatic, part of the gases propel the shot cup and its pellets down the barrel. Other gases are directed out of the barrel and rearward via holes, and work elements whose functions are to eject the empty hull and chamber a live round. The primary advantage of a gas-operated autoloader is reduced felt recoil. This is a result that correlates directly to the reduction of gases actually leaving the barrel. The disadvantages? Dirt and other gas-associated fouling enter the gun's mechanism. This is perhaps the most notable. However, and as is the case with recoil-operated semi-automatics, a second topic worthy of note is the importance of such gas guns being firmly seated against the shoulder. Inadequate resistance upon recoil, and there's a good chance that the gun won't cycle.

Recoil-operated – As the name implies, recoil-operated autoloaders rely on the energy produced by the firing of the piece – the recoil – to work the action. Upon firing such a shotgun, the

barrel and bolt travel rearward as a single unit. As it moves, the bolt, with its extractor/ejector, pulls the spent hull from the chamber and tosses it aside. The bolt and barrel then unlock, and the barrel, powered by a spring compressed by the recoil, returns to its original position. Finally the bolt itself,

L to R – Beretta AL390, Benelli Super Black Eagle, and Remington 11-87 (third from left) are favorites among waterfowlers and turkey hunters.

Winchester's Super X2 – a tremendous 3- and 3-1/2-inch option for the waterfowler or turkey hunter.

also powered by a separate spring, strips a fresh shotshell from the magazine carrier and feeds it into the chamber. The advantage of a recoil-operated shotgun is, perhaps obviously, the lack of gas or powder-related fouling. The disadvantages, however, are two and I find them relatively significant. First, recoil-operated shotguns like the A-5 have a *two-step* push; that is, one jolt upon firing, and a second when the barrel/bolt unit slams rearward. Like firing a flintlock rifle, this process does take some getting used to. Secondly, a recoil-operated autoloader, again using

This Washington state drake woodie fell to a Remington 11-87 autoloader that's seen its fair share of use across the country.

the A-5 as an example, must be seated firmly against your shoulder in order for the action to operate; that is, the resistance your body (shoulder) provides is necessary for the gun to function. That said, the revolutionary *inertia recoil design* of Benelli's Super Black Eagle is just the opposite – rather, "the only way," says literature from Benelli USA's website, "to stop a Benelli from cycling is to put the butt against a brick wall; the shotgun must be free to move backward slightly to operate." Here, and upon firing, the whole of the shotgun moves rearward, while a theoretically free-floating bolt assembly remains stationary. Once recoil decreases, kinetic energy stored in a strong spring located between the bolt and a rotating bolt head drives the bolt to the rear, ejecting the spent shotshell. A recoil spring in the stock then, via a linkage and bolt seat assembly, drives the bolt forward where it picks up and chambers a live round. The strong positives here? Such an inertia system is fast, uncomplicated, and, as all of the gases produced are pushed out of the barrel, extraordinarily clean.

Through the ages

In the early part of the 20th century, the venerable inventor and innovator, John M. Browning, brought to the American shooting public what can only be considered a foundation block for the semi-automatic shotgun, the Browning Auto (A)-5. Patented in 1901, the autoloading 2-3/4-inch A-5 afforded unners the opportunity to fire both light and heavy loads; unfortunately, the word *interchangeably* hadn't come into vogue with the A-5 quite yet. Operation of the A-5 was due, in part, to a pair of friction rings tucked away underneath he forearm. Light loads required one arrangement of the rings; heavy oads, a different arrangement. It was inconvenient, certainly, but shooters agreed that it was without question a step in the right direction in terms of autoloader advancement.

This brings us in a round-about manner to a problem inherent with all autoloading shotguns, both old and new, that problem being the regulation of the energy produced by varying loads. Going back to our earlier locomotive example, imagine the work capability of the locomotive engine with the boiler operating at 50 pounds of pressure. That's a light shotshell load. Now, increase that pressure to 200 pounds – a heavy load – and lacking a means by which to regulate the increased pressure, any number of operating parts on the engine run the risk of being literally battered to pieces. In an autoloading shotgun, these *operating parts* would likely include the bolt assembly and the rear of the receiver, although other vital parts – bolt linkages and springs, to name but two – could also be affected. Some way of regulating these increased pressures had to be found. In his A-5, Browning addressed this issue with his friction rings; that is, less friction allowed the lighter loads to cycle the piece, while increased friction helped compensate for the elevated pressures and resulting recoil of the heavier loads. Likewise, gas guns employ a piston or series of pistons designed to automatically adjust the amount of pressure actually diverted and dedicated to operating the action.

A step in the right direction? The A-5 was indeed a step in the right direction; that is, if a shooter wished only to use 2-3/4-inch shotshells *and* he didn't mind partially disassembling the gun to flip-flop the friction rings every time he wanted to switch from light to heavy

A newcomer in the semi-automatic realm, the Mossberg Model 935 handles 3- and 3-1/2-inch shotshells equally well.

Left: Reliable and easy to maintain, the author's Remington 11-87 is one of the more popular autoloading shotguns in the country. Right: Regardless of its maker, any semi-auto must be able to function reliably under any number of weather conditions.

loads or vice versa. Still, the gun was – and still is – a phenomenal success, so much so that other gun makers, including Remington and Savage, produced models of their own using operating systems very similar to Browning's A-5. In the late 1940s, however, Browning and his friction ring-equipped A-5 would take a technological backseat to the folks at Remington, with their introduction of the Model 11-48. A recoil-operated gun, the Model 11-48 allowed gunners to shoot both light and heavy loads interchangeably, *without* first having to make any type of physical adjustment to the shotgun. An advantage, certainly, but it still limited shooters to 2-3/4-inch shells. Fortunately, growth, both literally and figuratively, for autoloaders and their ammunition was just over the horizon.

But first came gas – or rather, gas-operated autoloaders – and it took Sears,

Mossberg's latest addition to the semi-automatic family – the Model 935 3- and 3-1/2-inch.

Roebuck, and Company, with their J. C. Higgins Model 60 to do it. Introduced in the latter part of the 1950s, the Model 60 required no changes should the shooter wish to swap light loads for heavy and back again. An innovation, yes, but the rather bulky M60 never quite caught on. Nor did its offspring, the Model 58, a piece which, while allowing shooters the option of light or heavy loads, did require the user to change settings – "L" for light, "H" for heavy – via a dial incorporated into the magazine cap. A 3-inch magnum version of the Model 58 was even shorter lived, what with its inability to reliably cycle the less powerful 2-3/4-inch rounds.

In 1963 and with the coming of the then-revolutionary gas-operated Remington Model 1100, the door to a new era of autoloading shotguns was opened a bit wider. Like earlier semi-automatics, the Model 1100 relied on a system of gas ports by which the action was operated. Standard (2-3/4-inch) guns had two smaller ports; magnum (3-inch) guns, one larger port. It wasn't perfection, as shooters still had to choose between 2-3/4 and 3-inch. But regardless of what many saw as a minor inconvenience, the Model 1100, with its smooth lines, slim fore-end, and almost universal off-the-shelf fit, immediately garnered a huge following, particularly among the trap and skeet shooting crowd – a fact evidenced when one looks at the more than three million Model 1100s sold during the course of the gun's initial three decades. Hunters, too, enjoyed the Model 1100's reliability and ease of maintenance. With the Model 1100, many thought the search for the Utopian autoloader was coming to a close.

It wouldn't be until the mid-1980s, however, that shotgunners would get their first true glimpse of Nirvana, and from such an unexpected source as Smith & Wesson. Recognized as a builder of fine handguns, S & W, via builders at Howa Machinery in Japan, began importing what they dubbed the Super 12, a semi-automatic 12-gauge capable of handling 2-3/4 and 3-inch shotshells interchangeably…and without any adjustments whatsoever. The secret behind this gas-operated autoloader was an innovative metering system consisting of a lipped (flanged) piston and a strong coil spring. Pressures from light loads would compress the spring a certain amount, thus moving the piston significantly and allowing sufficient energy (gas pressure) to enter the piston chamber, via the gas ports, to cycle the action. Conversely, the coil spring would work against the higher pressures generated by the heavier 3-inch loads. The result would be the flanged piston allowed only a portion of the gases produced to enter the piston chamber. Such an operating system was at the time, and is today, known as a self-metering system.

With this self-metering system in place, it was but a matter of time before other manufacturers jumped on the 2-3/4 and 3-inch bandwagon. And perhaps not surprisingly, it was the folks at

> *The secret behind this gas-operated autoloader was an innovative metering system consisting of a lipped (flanged) piston and a strong coil spring.*

Remington who, with a beefed up big brother version of their earlier success, would emerge as one of the frontrunners in an all-or-nothing battle for semi-automatic supremacy; this time with a winner known as the Model 11-87. Like the Super 12, the M11-87 is self-metering, with a twist. Instead of two gas

Shotgunning editor, Phil Bourjaily, reloads a Mossberg Model 935 during an early September goose hunt in northeastern Ohio.

Remington's 11-87 is an excellent, reliable choice for those seeking a 2-3/4 and 3-inch semi-auto.

ports, the Model 11-87 has four – two in the barrel, and another pair, one on each side of the barrel loop (the steel circle that slips over the magazine tube). A flat steel piston ring affixed atop the barrel loop serves as a secondary valve system. With heavy loads, this ring "opens," allowing additional (unnecessary) gasses and pressure to exit the system via ports in the upper portion of the forearm. In the case of light (low-pressure) loads, this steel ring remains closed, ensuring that the power needed to cycle the action remains within the system. In truth, the Model 11-87 is an elemental and reliable system, though not one without need for routine maintenance. Still, it did offer the shotgunner everything he could hope for, without the inconvenience of knobs, dials, rings, or costly second barrel. Perfection, at last, had been achieved ... for a time.

Enter the 3-1/2-inch 12-gauge. In response to a growing desire among waterfowlers for a 12-gauge shotshell capable of holding higher numbers of large steel pellets O.F. Mossberg and Sons in North Haven, Connecticut, introduced the Model 835, the world's first 3-1/2 inch 12-gauge shotgun. Though a pump-action, the M835 nonetheless started a stampede among shotgun developers back to the drawing board, where it wasn't long before a battery of 3-1/2-inch autoloaders began to emerge. Soon, two standouts became apparent. The first takes shotgunners full-circle back to John Browning, whose Morgan, Utah-based company began building the Gold Series of gas-operated semi-automatics in the opening days of the 1990s. A 3-inch Gold was quickly followed by a 3-1/2-inch model, and hunters took to them almost immediately.

The second, though emerging quietly from the then little-known Italian firm of Benelli, has in recent years taken the auto-shotgunning world by storm. The Benelli *Super Black Eagle*, or SBE, is the 3-1/2-inch cousin to the company's first semi-automatic offering, the 3-inch Black Eagle. Yet unlike the Black Eagle, with its light alloy receiver, the SBE features a slightly heavier all-steel receiver designed so the piece could withstand the 3-1/2-inch batterings for which it was conceived. But it doesn't end there. With its lightning-quick inertia recoil operating system and no powders or residues to foul up its steel innards, the SBE is touted as one of the fastest-shooting, most reliable semi-automatic shotguns, bar none, to ever grace the industry. This, and a menu that includes 2-3/4 to 3-1/2-inch ammunition, leaves no doubt as to why the SBE, unquestionably, ranks high on the popularity scale among the nation's waterfowl and turkey hunters.

The Bottom Line?

Will the perfect autoloading shotgun ever be manufactured? Ask the man who owns and shoots a Super Black Eagle, and chances are he'll say that it already exists. Same with the man who takes afield a Model 11-87 or a Browning Gold. And what of the 60-something waterfowler with the time-worn Model 58? Perhaps in his mind, his piece is as good an autoloader as will ever be produced … and there's a chance he's right.

Perfection, it seems, is in the eye of the beholder. Or in this case, the shooter. That said, technology certainly marches onward, and each season sees new and innovative self-loaders hitting the ranges, the uplands, and the marshes, each a little quicker, a little cleaner, a little lighter, or just a little bit better looking than the previous year's model. Whether it's straight 2-3/4-inch, 2-3/4-

and 3-inch, or everything from 2-3/4-inch up through the candlestick-sized 3-1/2-inchers, today's semi-automatics will handle them all.

The author used a Winchester Super X2 throughout much of the 2002-03 waterfowl season from Canada to Arkansas, and was extremely pleased with the gun's performance.

The author with a sharptail grouse and a prairie chicken taken with a 16-gauge SxS and Kent IMPACT #6 shot on the Nebraska prairie.

Why the 16-Gauge *isn't* Dead

By M.D. Johnson

A sleet-filled, buckshot rain began to drizzle down as I slid off the Ford's front seat and let Maggie, our then 9-year-old black lab, out. Gray muzzled but still full of energy, she immediately began nosing around the sage, shortgrass, and wild rose that surrounded the truck. "I'll be right back," I whispered to my outdoor photographer wife, Julia, who had opted to sit inside the relative comfort of the cab and shoot stills through the window. "Don't miss," she said, the corners of her mouth turning slightly into a grin.

Twenty miles north of the tiny town of Brewster and in the heart of the Nebraska Sandhills, we'd come across a little patch of what looked like ideal prairie chicken ground. What was more, according to our map and the yellow signs on every third or fourth fence post, this particular parcel was public land as well. "Can't hurt to try," I told Maggie as I dropped a pair of tungsten-matrix rounds into the breech of the Model 24 and checked the safety.

The first flush came not by one bird, but by a quintet of grouse that had been picking at the rosebuds. Instinctively, the side-by-side found its way to my shoulder, my thumb already pressing the top safety to the OFF position. Slapping the front trigger, I watched as the lead bird crumpled in a puff of tawny feathers. Out of the corner of my eye,

I could see a flash of black – Maggie! – already on her way to make the first retrieve. A short twist at the waist, and the left barrel's charge of #6s swatted

A Washington state blue grouse and Winchester Model 24 16-gauge were a fine mountain country combination.

The author with a South Dakota rooster taken with a pet Model 24 16-gauge SxS.

Tail-End Charlie and rolled him, unseen, into the dust.

"Thanks, Mag," I said as I took the first bird. Heavy, dark barring on its chest identified it as a chicken. Maggie, back with the second half of the double, returned. "A sharptail!" I said in surprise as I took note of the V-shaped markings on the bird's breast. Typically, we'd been told, prairie chickens and sharptails don't co-mingle. "These must not have minded," I told Maggie as I pocketed the second bird and turned in the direction of the truck and Julie. Behind us, the Sandhills stretched out toward Mother Nature's definition of infinity.

My first ruffed grouse. My first blue grouse. My first whitetail deer. My first rooster pheasant. My first woodcock. My first double on sharptail grouse and prairie chickens. The common denominator here ... each of these animals was killed not with a 12-gauge or a 20-gauge. Nor the birds with a lightweight fancy 28-gauge side-by-side. Instead, they were all taken – whitetail included – with one of the most traditional of bores, the 16-gauge.

The 16-what? That bastard gauge. No, sorry – we don't sell 16-gauge ammunition.

I've heard it all, or practically all of it. And unfortunately, little of what's said today about the 16-gauge is complimentary. With the exception of a handful of upland bird enthusiasts, a small gathering of folk who still talk of and extol the virtues of the 16, there are few who speak nicely of the little gun that's said to carry like a 20-gauge and shoot like a 12.

Fact is, there's very little said, period, about the 16-gauge anymore. Why? Most will tell you that it's due to the simple fact that the 16 has been squeezed into obscurity between the popularity and versatility that is the 3-inch 20-gauge on one side, and the tradition that is the 2-3/4-inch 12-gauge on the other. And in large part, what these folks are saying is correct; that is, to an extent. Yes, the 16 offers a maximum shot charge of 1-1/4 ounces, something both the 3-inch 20 and the 2-3/4-inch 12-gauge handle nicely. And yes, with the 16-gauge, you have a shotgun that is physically heavier than the 20-gauge. And finally, the 16 may not be as versatile in terms of loadings, i.e. shot charges, shot sizes, and velocities,

An Iowa ringneck and the author's 1979 16-gauge Model 1100 autoloader.

Phil Bourjaily and Ike with an Iowa woodcock taken with a 16-gauge Merkel SxS.

as is its only slightly larger brother, the 2-3/4-inch 12-gauge.

So what, then, would be the reasons behind any shooter wanting a 16-gauge? Actually, there are plenty of reasons for the life still pulsing through the veins of this tried-and-true bore as you'll see here as we take a look at – The 16-Gauge: Still kickin' after all these years.

Get an actual 16

The first thing you need to understand about today's 16-gauge is that there are 16s, and then there are 16s. The former here we'll refer to as a *true* 16-gauge; that is, everything about the gun – dimensions, receiver, barrel – is based on the traditional 16-gauge scale. The latter, however, is something altogether different. The Remington Model 870 16-gauge pump, for instance, is little more than a 16-gauge barrel matched to a 12-gauge frame. True, it chambers 16-gauge shotshells; however, this 16-gauge chamber is wrapped in a 12-gauge steel body, and has neither the look nor the feel of a 1952 Winchester Model 24 or 1979-vintage Remington Model 1100. To this end, you might be better off buying and shooting one of the more popular 12-bores.

There are, however, traditional 16-gauge shotguns available in this day and age. Used Winchester Model 12s and 24s, Remington Model 31s, and Browning "Sweet Sixteen" A-5s can be had with a little bit of looking, a feat made remarkably easier thanks to the Internet. Remington's attempt at reintroducing the Model 1100 in 16-gauge produced a 7.25-pound autoloader with a 28-inch barrel that differs little from the 1979 model I currently shoot. Though a special order item, Browning offers their Citori Lightning Feather in a 16-gauge. Ithaca, Merkel, and Rizzini also offer 16-bores in pump-action, side-by-side, and O/U formats, respectively. Parkers and L.C. Smiths in 16-gauge? They're out there, and are as much a part of the shotgunning heritage as is any Maine ruffed grouse or Upper Peninsula timberdoodle.

Availability of 16-gauge guns is but one part of the equation. There must be other factors contributing to the rebirth – or rather, the non-death – of the 16-gauge than simply the existence and availability of firearms. Rest assured, there are, and these reasons include –

Ballistic Superiority: The 16-gauge shot string

To better understand this concept of shot string and why it plays a role in this discussion on the virtues of the 16-gauge, let's think of the 20-gauge as a test tube, and the 16 as an 8-ounce water tumbler. Fill each vessel with BB shot. The shot column in the 20-gauge tube is long and narrow, while the column in the 16-gauge tumbler is short and squatty.

Next, imagine if each column of BBs were propelled from its respective container with the same force. The shot charge emerging from the tube would be correspondingly long and thin, while the other would mirror its short, squatty container. Thanks to Mister Newton's Laws of Physics, both the length of the columns and the distance between the individual BBs becomes greater as distance increases; however, because the column originating from the 16-gauge tumbler starts out shorter, it will also be shorter in comparison to that from the tube at an equal distance. And because it's short, it will also be more dense than will the pattern from the tube at the same distance.

What's all this mean? In a nutshell, a 1-ounce load in the 16 will have a shorter shot string, and thus greater pattern density, than will a one-ounce load in the 20. It's said in some circles that the same 1-ounce charge in the 16 will exhibit greater pattern density than will a 1-1/4 ounce 12-gauge; however, the jury that is ballistics is still out on that one. Why the focus on pattern density? Pattern density

can make all the difference in the world when you're trying to place a fleeing ruffed grouse and your 1-1/8 ounce 16-gauge shot charge at the same point in space at the same time.

Non-toxic options

Three significant events – two natural, and one ammunition related

The author with a pet 16-gauge SxS and "friends" on a grouse hunt in the Nebraska Sandhills. (bottom) The author's Winchester Model 24 double shoots these non-toxics from Kent well for prairie grouse, pheasants, and early season waterfowl.

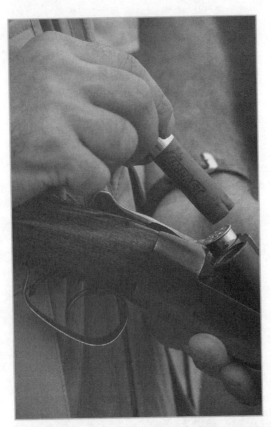

Non-toxics like Kent's IMPACT allow older guns such as the 1952 Winchester M24 to rejoin their owners afield.

– contributed to the decline in the popularity of the 16-gauge. The first came in the late 1970s when bobwhite quail populations in the East and Southeast dropped to historically low levels. Subsequently, the 16-gauge-carrying quail hunters, of which there were many prior to the fall, then too began to wane in number. Contributing to the 16s pseudo-demise was the simple, though very natural and expected, fact that America's hunting public was growing older. Follow-up generations, appear to, have been far more attracted to the popularity and versatility that is the modern 12-gauge, not only in the ammunition selection offered, but in the wide range of firearms currently available.

And finally – 1991, the declaration that all waterfowl hunting would henceforth be conducted with a federally approved non-lead, non-toxic

A 1952 Model 24 SxS – The "perfect" pheasant gun? The author thinks so.

Contributing to the 16s pseudo-demise was the simple, though very natural and expected, fact that America's hunting public was growing older.

> *Fortunately, and while quail numbers remain alarmingly low and the average age of the U.S. hunter continues to climb slowly, this third element – the lack of suitable 16-gauge non-toxic ammunition – has turned the corner for the better.*

ammunition. Initially, shotshell manufacturers hurried to develop and then stock shelves with 12-gauge ammunition. This was quickly followed by a selection of non-toxic rounds in 3-inch 20-gauge, at the time fast becoming a favorite among a growing number of waterfowlers, both young and old. Unfortunately in this rush to supply hunters with suitable alternatives to the traditional lead shotshells, the manufacturers overlooked – or perhaps dismissed – the 16-gauge; in some cases, the omission was complete, and a tidal wave of 16s found themselves relegated to the corner of the closet. Less than a decade later, this non-toxic regulation would in some locales be applied to the hunting of other species – upland birds on state-managed wildlife areas, a prime example – and the drizzle that was the 16's slide into history became a deluge.

Fortunately, and while quail numbers remain alarmingly low and the average age of the U.S. hunter continues to climb slowly, this third element – the lack of suitable 16-gauge non-toxic ammunition – has turned the corner for the better. Today, Federal and Remington both offer a 15/16-ounce steel load for the 2-3/4-inch 16. Filled with either #2 or #4 steel shot, either loading makes an above average choice for ducks over decoys, or for pheasant and grouse-sized birds in most upland style situations. But it's not just steel that's come along. Kent Cartridge currently has available their Impact Tungsten Matrix shotshells in 1-, 1-1/16-, and 1-1/4-ounce loadings for the 16. From personal experience, the 1-1/4-ounce charges of #6 tungsten are remarkable performers on both pheasants and prairie grouse, as well as smaller ducks – widgeon, teal, and wood ducks – at moderate ranges. Likewise, the Bismuth Cartridge Company provides its product in a traditional

1-1/8-ounce charge of either #4 or #6 shot. And should handloading the 16-gauge be an option, hulls, primers, and powders are widely available, while non-toxic shot such as the aforementioned bismuth and the newly-founded Hevi-Shot can be purchased in bulk and dropped into specialized shot cups from Ballistic Products. The excuse that there is simply nothing out there in terms of ammunition is no more.

Lighter than a 12-gauge

What a shotgun physically weighs has been an element of roller coaster concern in terms of the 16-gauge. In the 1950s and 60s, American shotgun manufacturers began to make not only fewer side-by-sides, the traditional format of the 16, but, thanks to alloy receivers, a much lighter 12-gauge piece – lighter even than the traditional 16s. And who would opt for the 16-gauge when a ballistically superior 12 was lighter, thus easier to carry? The death knell for the 16-gauge was certainly walking the bell tower.

In recent years, however, a resurgence in the number of 16-gauge double shotguns being made, both in the U.S. and abroad, has helped swing the scales – literally – more in favor of this so-called little/heavy gun, what with these double-gun styles weighing in, in some instances, a full pound less than their 12-gauge counterparts. Single barrels, too, have enjoyed this trimming down. The Ithaca Model 37 Ultralight 16, with its aluminum receiver, drags the needle down to the 6-pound mark. A matching 12-gauge? Seven pounds.

When a day's hunt is measured in miles, as it often is in the world of the upland bird hunter, 16 ounces can make a tremendous difference, as can the 16s ballistic advantage over the 20-gauge.

Great for beginners

Nowadays when someone speaks of a "great shotgun for young people or ladies," it's more often than not assumed the speaker talks of a 20-gauge. "It's the recoil," they claim. "It's the weight of the gun," says another. Truths? Certainly the 20-gauge does offer the recoil- or weight-conscious – young, female, or otherwise – an advantage over the heavier and harder-hitting 12s; however, what about the 16-gauge?

The truth is, most modern 16s – where here, *modern* can be defined as the reintroduced Model 870 or non-ultralight Model 37 – are within ounces if not identical in weight to their 20-gauge counterparts. In some cases, e.g. the *Ithaca Ultralight* or *Browning Citori Lightning Feather*, the 16-gauge version will actually weigh less than a similar contemporary 20-gauge of the same make and model.

As for recoil, the 16-gauge offers shooters a 2-1/2-dram equivalent, 1-ounce charge, a load that mirrors the most popular 2-3/4-inch 20-gauge shotshell in use today in terms of recoil. Yes, some hunting situations can call for upsized – 2-3/4- to 3-1/4-dram equivalent – 16-gauge loads; however, in high fire volume instances such as trap, skeet, sporting clays, and perhaps dove hunting where this increase in "power" isn't a necessity and where recoil might be most noticeable, there is absolutely no difference between the 16-gauge and the 20. None, that is, except in performance. And here, that hanger-on and thought-to-be-deceased traditionalist, the 16-gauge, proves that now, more than ever, is not the time for a eulogy.

Purchased in 1979, this Remington Model 1100 in 16-gauge has accounted for winged game across the United States.

Courtesy Winchester Ammunition

A swift-winged woodcock through the trees? Or a fleeing ruffed or blue grouse perhaps? Sporting clays can bring it all to life.

Sporting Clays:
Frustration and Reward

By M.D. Johnson

You tell me if this sounds familiar. It's late May; turkey season's over, the weather's nice, and you're headed to your friendly neighborhood sporting clays course where, along with some much-needed practice, you'll have a chance to catch up on all the happenings with your wingshooting brethren. You're fresh, you're encouraged and enthusiastic, and as has been the case in past years, you shoot well on this first outing.

May gives way to June, and June to July. The drive to the clays course and the two-and-a-half hours spent there continue as a weekly ritual; however, the scene is no longer as rosy as it once was. Scores that had previously hovered around the low 70s now are the in low 60s; that is, if you're lucky. Marks in the high 50s aren't unheard now, and – Heaven forbid! – wasn't that a personal low of 53 just last week? What's worse, as your scores tumble, your frustration level rises. By the time August arrives, you're seriously considering changing what you do for entertainment and recreation to something a bit more positive and rewarding. On the course, you walk from station to station like a condemned man trudging his way to the gallows, your mind racing as you analyze this trajectory and calculate that lead. You change your stance, switch guns, go back to church, ring a bell for the Salvation Army … and still your scores continue to slip. The game you once loved, you realize, is no longer enjoyable. In fact, it's downright traumatic. And yet, like an alleyway junkie, you can't seem to stop. You keep going back and back and back …

Gil Ash and his wife and partner, Vicki, feel and know all too well your pain and suffering, for they see it on a daily basis. True, they don't see it personally, though I'm sure there was a time when they weren't as skilled with a shotgun as they are today. These days

Water settings are often used to simulate duck or goose hunting situations.

Courtesy Winchester Ammunition

they host hundreds upon hundreds of students who pass through the doors of their OSP, or as it's known technically, the Optimum Shotgun Performance Shooting School.

Headquartered in Houston, Texas, the Ashes have been shooting sporting clays since 1984, and have been teaching the sport professionally since 1996. Each year, the team works with approximately 2,000 students from all walks of life and of all ability levels at shooting centers, ranges, and courses across the United States. And every year, the Ashes see more than their fair share of shooters get frustrated, both with themselves and with the game in general. So what do these talented instructors do when facing a disgruntled shotgunner with quitting on his mind – the guy who isn't shy about letting the world know that he hates sporting clays, but simply can't seem to stop going?

Gun Digest had an opportunity to sit a spell with Gil Ash, and ask him some pointed questions about what one does when this ordinarily relaxing shooting sport becomes an object of mental contention. Do you give up, or do you get better?

Gun Digest – Gil, describe sporting clays in a paragraph.

Ash – Sporting clays isn't an easy game. It's probably one of the most difficult games out there to master,

Springing teal – targets launched vertically to mimic a pair of flushing blue-wings or green-wings – is a popular but often frustrating station.

simply because there is no give in this sport. In golf, somewhere around 72 is par. In tennis, the net's always the same height. In basketball, the hoop and the court are always the same size. In every sport out there, there are boundaries of the game. The things that makes sporting clays so difficult and at the same time so mystifying and addictive are the numbers of variables in the game. Anything goes. Five different targets thrown in different trajectories, at different distances, and at different speeds with different backgrounds and in different combinations. The number of variables in the game of sporting clays is infinite. That's the beauty and the bitch of it, if you will. It's a fascinating game simply due to the number of variables. You never conquer it. But it can be the most disheartening three or four hours you'll ever experience *if* you don't understand why you're missing.

Gun Digest – But I'm a good shooter in field. Why not on the course?

Ash - The typical good wingshooter develops a gun speed that's commensurate with the bird's speed. These folks are really good shots in the field, but they really don't have a good gun mount. They mount the gun and swing through the bird and pull the trigger. And there's nothing wrong with that in shooting live birds. You can get away with excessive gun speed with live birds because a live bird has something moving on it that's moving faster than you can move the gun barrel, and that's the wings. So your eyes are attracted to the movement of the wings, and as the gun goes through the bird, you can pull the trigger and your eyes stay on the bird.

But in sporting clays, there isn't anything moving on that clay target. And when the typical bird hunter tries

Courtesy Winchester Ammunition

to shoot a sporting clays target like they shoot a live bird, they mount the gun and slash through the target. When they do that, the eye tends to go with the gun – the fastest thing they see – and they tend to miss. And what's worse, they don't know how they missed or why they missed. That's the frustrating part about it.

Gun Digest – You've used a comparison between shotgunners and carpenters in the past. What's that?

Ash – Field hunting and shooting sporting clays are like a framing

While others watch and learn, this shooter tries his hand at a "ruffed grouse."

Ladies represent an ever-increasing segment of the sporting clays society.

Courtesy Winchester Ammunition

A woodland scene, here known as Grouse Ridge, provides a challenging target.

Courtesy Winchester Ammunition

carpenter and a finish carpenter. They still use the same tools, but one has to execute with a little more finesse and feel than the other.

The framing carpenter – he's interested in getting it close enough. He's interested in getting things plumb, but every board he puts into a house is either going to be covered up by sheetrock, paint, or trim. He's putting the skeleton of the house up. If he misses the nail and dents the board, it's not that big a deal. The bird hunter, he's more like the framing carpenter. He can go out and he can slash that gun around, and he can kill some birds.

A finish carpenter – well, what he finishes, people are gonna look at. So he's got to be real careful when he's putting these things together. With the finish carpenter, it's not a game of brute strength. It's a game of finesse and feel, of angles and lines. Everything's got to match up just perfect. The good sporting clays shooter has to have a perfect move and a perfect mount.

He not only has to be able to kill the bird regardless of the trajectory of the course, but he's got to be able to kill the bird wherever he needs to kill the bird in order to set himself up for the second shot.

Gun Digest – Is there a bit more to it than that, this comparison?

Ash – Well, in bird hunting, you never keep score. It's just "Did you get your limit?" It's not – "Did you get your limit in 10 shells?" So because how many shells it took for you to get your limit is never a point of contention, you never realize at what level of proficiency you're operating at in the field. But because sporting clays is shot in groups of 50 or 100, how many "kills" versus how many shots comes into play. Most bird hunters don't realize their lack of proficiency in the field because they don't look at it from the point of – "I got six ducks with 18 shots." It's just "I got a limit." With sporting clays, it's "I got 58 birds, but I shot 100 times." That's the frustration factor.

The guys come into sporting clays – and they're damn good shotgun shooters in the field 'cause they get their limit every time – but when they come in and they start keeping score on how many did you get versus how many times did you shoot, it can be demoralizing in some ways.

Gun Digest – So is it that difficult, this going from the field to the formal sporting clays course *and* being proficient?

Ash - People that come to clay targets from bird hunting have one major problem, and that is excessive gun speed and a sloppy gun mount. Once they understand what the problem is, and once they understand the risks they're putting into their clay target game because of this excessive movement and poor gun mount – and they understand the benefits of changing what they're doing – then change becomes improvement. And everybody wants to improve. Everybody wants to get better at this game. The clay target is not respectful of persons. It doesn't matter if you wear a Timex or a Rolex. When the target's in the air, you have to break it; and if you don't, everybody knows.

Gun Digest – That all said, is there an upside then to this frustration prior to improvement cycle that many seem to go through on the sporting clays course?

Ash - Clay target shooting can show shooters not only where they're missing, but show them why they're missing – and give them an opportunity to improve so they become a better harvester of game birds.

You aren't going to learn to shoot from reading a book, reading an article, or looking at a video. You're going to learn to shoot by going and taking a lesson. Swallow your pride, and go find an instructor. Or find a buddy who's a little bit better than you, and ask him what he's doing. You'll learn that there's something fundamental that you're not doing that's essential for you to break that target. And 99.99 times out of 100, that will be excessive muzzle awareness.

Gun Digest – So time spent on the clays course, even frustrating time, will help me in the field?

Ash - Here's what we see with people who start shooting sporting clays. They think that if they go out and shoot the course, they're practicing. Nothing could be further from the truth. When you go out and shoot the course, you're playing the game. It's no different than me trying to learn to play baseball, but the only time I touch the ball, the bat, and the glove is in a game. I never play catch.

Courtesy Winchester Ammunition

Here, thanks to a well thought out clays course, a shooter practices his moves on a left-to-right mourning dove target.

I never have anyone hit me flies and grounders. I never practice hitting. You have to separate the game, and put it into its component parts. It's a common misconception that you have to shoot the complete course. Shoot, you don't have to do that; just shoot one station. Go to another station. If you're having trouble with right-to-left crossers, go out there and find a station that has right-to-left crossers and shoot a box of shells at it. Go up closer to it, if you can, and shoot it until you can hit it. Then back up a little bit.

Gun Digest – Don't shoot the entire course?

Ash – When you go to a sporting clays course to practice your field shooting, rather than shooting the course – 50 pairs of targets – go to a station that has a bird that looks like the bird you're having problems with, or a live bird you'd shoot in the field, and shoot that as a single. And do that six or eight times. You don't have to shoot pairs. Work on your basic move and mount by shooting single targets. Inevitably, you're going to come to a station on a course with a difficult target, maybe a 40-yard crosser. You're not going to shoot birds at 40 yards in the field, so save your shells and go to

Good manners are never out of place, especially at the gun club.

the next stand. Go to your course and say "Today, I'm going to work on flushing shots." And then do that.

There's only six trajectories in sporting clays – left-to-right and right-to-left crossers, left-to-right and right-to-left quartering birds, birds going up, and birds going down. There's only six. Figure out the ones you can do. And figure out the ones you can't do. And then go to work on them. Start shooting single targets while working on your move and your mount, and try to figure out what it is you have to do to correct the shot. But I'll tell you again, and for hunters, 99 percent of the time they miss the target is excessive muzzle awareness.

Gun Digest – But isn't that a break from tradition, this starting in the middle of course? What would the range operator say?

Ash – The proper thing to do is walk in and introduce yourself to the gun club manager, and say – "You know, I'm having trouble with a right-to-left crosser. Do you have a station out here that has a good, soft, easy right-to-left crosser where I can go and work on that one?" And nine times out of 10, they'll say – "Sure, Station 11 down there. And we have a trapper right here …" Now, what I would tell you is this – an extra five bucks for the trapper will go a long way to get him to go out there and pull that target for you over and over and over again. Good manners are never out of place, especially at the gun club. And it's been my experience that there are very few gun clubs out there that won't accommodate someone who's looking to just go out and shoot one station. Some of them will make you shoot the bird only from the shooting cage; it's just not safe for you to get up in front of the cage and move closer to the bird. That's why I might tell you to go to a skeet field 'cause

Under the watchful eye of his fellow shooters, this shotgunner tries his hand at grouse hunting – sporting clays style.

ou can move up closer to the bird and you can move farther away from the bird.

Sporting clays is a great place to practice wingshooting, but the best place to practice your technique for crossing birds is on the skeet field. It's cheaper, and the birds are easy. The best place to practice on flushing birds is on the trap field. Again, it's cheaper, and it's easier.

Gun Digest – Will practice really make me better on the course?

Ash – I'll ask people – How often are you willing to go and practice? What kind of commitment are you willing to make to become a better wingshooter? And then they'll stutter and stammer, and they'll tell me they can go once a month. Well, that isn't going to cut it. You don't get better going once a month. I'd be lying to you if I said you were. Once we show you what you need to practice, you're going to have to make a concerted effort to go out to the range at least twice a week for three weeks so that it gets into the computer (Translation – the brain). Then after that, once every three weeks or so, just go out and shoot.

Gun Digest – What about shooting lessons? Will they help me on the sporting clays course?

Ash – A bird hunter's money would be better spent if he would go and take a lesson from a qualified and experienced instructor. One or two lessons will give him something to practice when he goes to practice. Otherwise, what will happen is this – He knows he can't hit a right-to-left crosser and he'll go out there and try to practice it, and he keeps doing the same thing over and over and over again. He's practicing how to miss that bird.

There was a time when shooting instruction wasn't in vogue. Today, there are enough people out there who have been through the NSCA (National Sporting Clays Association) course to where you can easily find an instructor who can help you with some basic, fundamental moves. Then you can go out and begin to learn on your own.

Gun Digest – What, Gil, does all this – the practice, the instruction, the frustration – boil down to? Can I get better?

Ash – It's senseless to go out and keep beating your head against a post. If you're not getting any better, you need to take a good, hard look at yourself in the mirror and say – Look, do I want to do this? If I do, what am I willing to commit in terms of time, effort, and funds to get better?

You know, it doesn't take much to get better. You can take a couple of lessons, and with a little effort and some practice – two or three times a month – hell, in a year, you can be shooting in the 70s. It's really easy to get in the mid-60s or low 70s in sporting clays. Getting into the mid-80s to low 90s, that's a difficult, long task. But if someone's going out shooting and they're not getting any better, the worst thing they can do is to keep doing what they're doing *and* expect a different result. Churchill said – Success is moving from one failure to the next with no loss of enthusiasm.

Gil and Vicki Ash's first book, *If It Ain't Broke, Fix It!*, is a most definite read for anyone interesting in lowering their frustration level while simultaneously boosting their scores, whether those numbers be on the sporting clays, skeet, or trap range. Copies are available by calling Optimum Shotgun Performance Shooting School at 800-838-7533; additional information about the OSP facilities and course scheduling can be obtained on-line at www.ospschool.com.

> *But if someone's going out shooting and they're not getting any better, the worst thing they can do is to keep doing what they're doing and expect a different result.*

All shotgunning "schools" need not be formal. Here, Winchester's Kevin Howard studies a student's form during an outdoor writers conference.

Is Shooting School for You?

By M.D. Johnson

Although I'm sure there existed shooting schools during the time I was growing up in northeast Ohio in the mid-1970s, I'd never heard of them. No, I take that back; I had heard of them. They were called the Mick Johnson School of Shotgun Shooting. And the Jim Johnson School. And the Neal Verity School. And the Dzedo Johnson Shooting School. Those men, by the way, were Dad, Uncle, Uncle, and Grandpa.

Back then, school was a place a kid went Monday through Friday until he turned 18. Then he either went to work in one of the steel mills in the Mahoning Valley, or he went to college where he wore scarlet and grey and cheered for the Buckeyes in the horseshoe on Saturday afternoons in the fall. Shotgun shooting was something that he learned at home; or rather, in the field, and not at the hands of a smartly dressed Brit or penny loafer-wearing psychologist who just so happened to be armed with a vintage O/U. Nope, shooting skills were taught, to use the term loosely, by Dad or by Grandpa. Maybe an uncle or the neighbor down the way, if a relative wasn't available. Unless I'm mistaken, instruction back in The Day consisted primarily of very simple rules. One, don't shoot your teacher. Two, keep both eyes open. And three, shoot where the bird's going, not where it's been. End of story ... school's out.

Gun fit back then was simple, too. You put the butt plate or recoil pad in the crook of your elbow, and if your finger reached the trigger ... well, then the gun fit. Back then, there were only two kinds of shooters. Those who hit what they shot at, also known as good shots, and those who couldn't hit the proverbial broad side of a barn from the inside. These were the men that the good shots talked about, and that's just the way it was.

Today, though, the scene is quite different. Shooting instruction – shooting

A "shooting school" can be as informal as a helpful adult and an eager young student.

And before you ask, the answer is a definite no; these courses and clinics aren't attended only by professional or competitive trap, skeet, and sporting clays shooters, but often by the average, everyday hunter in the field – someone who simply wants to leave the ranks of the bad shots *and join the ranks, even if only occasionally, of the* good shots.

schools or clinics, if you will – are quite popular, not to mention quite effective in helping men, women, and children become more efficient shotgunners. And before you ask, the answer is a definite no; these courses and clinics aren't attended only by professional or competitive trap, skeet, and sporting clays shooters, but often by the average, everyday hunter in the field – someone who simply wants to leave the ranks of the *bad shots* and join the ranks, even if only occasionally, of the *good shots*.

A native Texan, Gil Ash, and his wife and teaching partner, Vicki, are what most would call the good shots. Gil, 55, was born in Madisonville, Texas, though he lived most of his life in the Dallas area. He attended East Texas State University where he earned a degree in photography and business. Upon his matriculation, Ash borrowed $300, rented a U-Haul trailer, and as he says "went to Houston to seek his fortune." He started his own commercial photography

business, and the rest, as he says, is history; that is, until his path crossed that of a young lady named Vicki

"I didn't grow up in a very well-to-do family, and my father's boss bought me a Remington Model 1100 16-gauge when I was 14 or 15 years old," remembers Ash. "I shot that gun for years. I took up the game of skeet, and at that time, you couldn't get any reloading components for the 16-gauge. I loved to shoot skeet, so I sold the 16-gauge. I traded it in on a 20-gauge so I could reload for it. This was just about the time Vicki and I started to date.

"Well," he continued, "she started shooting with me, and her Daddy bought her a shotgun and had it cut. And we started hunting together, and we went on a dove hunt. We were sitting by a little pond and I'd missed a few birds, and I said – 'You know. If I had that little 16-gauge, I would have killed that bird.' This is in September and we'd been dating about 30 days. She went down to

This young man shows fine form during a practice day afield.

the gun shop that I traded that gun into and she bought that gun back. She kept it and gave it to me for Christmas. The following August we were married. You might say we had a shotgun wedding. Not the normal shotgun wedding."

That so-called shotgun wedding was in 1975. In the years following the nuptials, the Ashes spent much of time afield, both on the range and hunting a variety of upland birds in their native Texas. It was during this time, too, that the couple found a new addiction – sporting clays. From 1983 through 1987, the Ashes toured much of the United States shooting sporting clays on a competitive level.

"Because we were from out of town and because we won the tournaments," said Ash, "people wanted to know how we did it. We quickly got the reputation for being able to teach people to do it. By the late 1980s and early 1990s, we began to teach more than we would compete. In 1993, I tore a rotator cuff in my shoulder and couldn't shoot. So I began to study how to teach because I wanted to stay involved."

He continued. "In 1992, Vicki won the ladies' division of the national sporting clays championship. We began to teach more, and our teaching schedule began to grow rapidly. Vicki and I are both Level 3 certified NSCA (National Sporting Clays Association) instructors. I was in the first NSCA Level 3 course that was given, and I was one of two out of 12 people who passed it. Vicki was in the third or fourth course."

Perhaps not surprisingly, this love for both the shotgunning sports and teaching eventually lead to the Ashes creating their own shooting school – Optimum Shooting Performance (OSP) of Houston, Texas.

"We teach about 2,000 people a year," said Ash. "Since beginning our business in 1995, we've seen in excess of 4.5 million shotgun shells fired at clay targets and game birds. When you see that much, certain patterns begin to emerge. Certain patterns that create success with a shotgun, and certain patterns that create risk with a shotgun. We began to realize that there is a lot more to shooting a shotgun than just telling people where they missed."

With this educational experience in mind, it seemed fitting that Gun Digest sit with Ash for a spell and talk with him about the whats and whys of the modern shotgun shooting school, not forgetting that one most important question – Is shooting school for me?

Gun Digest: Who are your students?

Ash: Of the 2,000 people that we teach each year, 60 percent of them

Winchester's Kevin Howard provides pointers during an informal shooting school presented at a Midwestern outdoor writers conference.

Perhaps not surprisingly, this love for both the shotgunning sports and teaching eventually lead to the Ashes creating their own shooting school – Optimum Shooting Performance (OSP) of Houston, Texas.

Talented shooter and instructor, Steve Schultz, walks a student through her paces.

will never shoot a tournament or a registered target. They enjoy shooting. They're recreational shooters. And they're hunters. They love to shoot shotguns at clay targets and make noise and break things.

The person we see often is the person who used to shoot a lot when they were growing up. And they were a really

good shot. Now they're 45 to 60. They have some disposable income, they remember how fun hunting used to be, and they want to start hunting again. And they can't hit anything. They go on a corporate dove hunt or they go hunting with their buddies, and they're embarrassed because it takes 'em a box of shells to kill one bird. They come to us saying – 'There's something wrong with my eyes. I've lost my timing. I just can't hit anything anymore.'

When they were a kid, they just looked at a bird and they shot it. Now that they're a success and they've trained their conscious doubt voice to doubt everything they do, they try to look at the gun and they try to check the lead. They're trying make sure the lead is right before they pull the trigger, and when you do that, you're going to miss.

Gun Digest: How about a 'for instance?'

Ash: You're sitting under a tree on a stool picking your nose in a dove field,

A knowledgeable instructor can mean all the difference in the world as you progress through your shotgunning skills.

and someone yells "Over ya!" You look up, mount the gun, shoot, and stone the bird. Then you see one a'coming 200 yards away. You stand up – Gun on shoulder? Check. Cheek on stock? Check. Beads lined up? Check. Boom-boom-boom-damn! That's the difference between conscious and subconscious function. Your focus was on the barrel and not on the bird, and that's why you miss. That's why most people kill their birds on the second shot.

Gun Digest: What about men versus women? Do you see one more often than the other?

Ash: We teach from 10 to 15 percent women. The people that actually come to take a shooting lesson come to learn, male and female. The problem with women is many don't have the upper body strength to hold a shotgun up. Women have to work at two things

in opposite order. First, they have to work on their upper body strength so they can hold a shotgun up long enough to learn. Second and most importantly, women have to develop a timing database.

Women have no timing database. When you were a kid, you played those games that typically have to do with timing; women don't have that. Give me a man who was an athlete in high school or college, and they have a timing database. Our task is to get women to understand the rhythm and timing of shotgun shooting. Get them to develop a good gun mount, and the timing database that's already in their brain can be converted over to shooting a shotgun. A woman has to learn to develop that database AND shoot a shotgun at the same time.

Gun Digest: How does the clinic actually begin?

Sooner or later, they're going to turn around and ask – "Why can't I hit this target?"

Ash: After we watch a student shoot one bird, we'll tell them what their normal score is. What birds they can hit, and what birds they can't hit. This after shooting one shot. And sometimes we can tell these things before they yell PULL. Then we'll take the group over to a target that we know they can't hit, and we'll have everybody in the group shoot five. They'll break five in a row. Then we'll take the person in the group that the group sees as being the least experienced, and we'll have them break five in a row. Then we'll take the person who's reluctant to change – who's missing – and we'll keep feeding them bullets. Sooner or later, they're going to turn around and ask – "Why can't I hit this target?" We call that the teachable moment.

Gun Digest: Gil, talk about instinctive shooting.

Remington's Linda Powell "in the box" with a skilled shooting instructor at a recent Remington shooting school.

Ash: Webster defines instinctive as happening below consciousness. We teach instinctive shooting. Most people look at instinctive shooting on the clays course as you get in the cage, you call pull, you mount the gun, and you shoot at the birds. That's instinctive, but there's no rhyme nor reason for that type of shooting. What we teach is this – You have to move and mount the shotgun precisely. Once you master those mechanics and you master a couple of moves, then regardless of what the bird does in the field, all you have to do in the field is mount the gun, look at the bird, and pull the trigger.

Gun Digest: Can attending a shooting school actually worsen a person's shooting?

Ash: Everything new feels strange until it becomes old. For you to correct your problem, we have to first show you the problem and why it creates risk. Then we have to show you how to practice to eliminate that chink in your armor. Then you must practice it. And once you've practiced it, then you'll become a better shooter.

Your question to me was – Can taking your course screw me up as a shooter? Definitely, because the only way you're going to get better is to change what you're doing. Nobody likes to change because they're afraid of the failure that can come with change. The last thing you should expect when you go take a shooting lesson is for you to end up a great shot because you have to learn what's wrong and how to correct it. THEN you have to correct it, and after you've practiced it, then you become a better shooter.

Gun Digest: Everything I see about shooting schools shouts *formal*. Are formal and shooting school synonymous terms?

Ash: If you're looking for formal, go somewhere else. I wear sandals, running shorts, and a polo shirt. You have to dress with the climate. We're outdoors from 8 in the morning 'til 5 in the afternoon, and if we try to be too formal,

"Here's what you should see," the instructor explains before any live rounds are ever fired.

Shotgunning editor, Phil Bourjaily (left), talks with instructor Steve Schultz during a day-long "school" session.

Sooner or later, we as hunters are going to have to look at our proficiency in the field and look at it for what it is.

you're getting so hot that you can't see by 2 o'clock in the afternoon.

Gun Digest: Will shooting school help me as a hunter?

Ash: Most dramatically. The way it helps you in the field ... one, when you're having a bad day or you miss a shot, you'll know why. But more importantly, people that take instruction shoot more often. They spend more time on the clays range or the skeet range or the trap range, and they practice their moves and they work on their proficiency as a shooter. Therefore when they go to the field, they're more proficient. And if they're more proficient in moving and mounting their gun, they'll spend more time on target focus ... in part because, after a course, they know the importance of target focus. They instantly become better wingshooters.

When we have field hunters come in and they start missing, here's what we tell 'em. We tell 'em to watch three to five birds fly by and don't shoot at 'em. Focus on them. Focus on the heads. Point at 'em with your finger. Realize how slow they're moving. Then when they start shooting at them again, they'll only load one bullet until they break one bird. Then they'll load two. That third shot, you might as well throw it away.

Shooting proficiency is the cornerstone for the ethical harvest of all wildlife. Sooner or later, we as hunters are going to have to look at our proficiency in the field and look at it for what it is. We're going to have to look at what we're doing – how we're shooting – or we're going to have a problem with the anti-hunters.

Gun Digest: Is shooting more often an effective way to improve, or is it simply shooting more often?

Ash: We've done some studies on shooting more often, and we found that the students that we have that do two things – practice what we tell them or teach them to practice, and go to the

Patterning, or Point of Impact training, is the first step in many shotgunning schools.

range at least two times a week for the three weeks following the clinic – they'll retain over 80 percent of what we taught them. The people who don't do these things retain from 25 to 40 percent. These people will retain what we teach them intellectually, but they can't apply it. You can't be thinking about swing mechanics when the bird's in the air. The swing mechanics have to be in the subconscious.

The physical therapists and neurologists tell us that you have to have done something 2,500 to 3,000 times, and done it correctly, before it's embedded in the subconscious. And instinctive shooting is nothing more than subconscious shooting. Now you can be subconscious without good mechanics, and not be a very good shot. But if you have good subconscious mechanics, you're going to be lethal.

Gun Digest: When would you recommend attending a shooting school?

Ash: We recommend that you take a shooting lesson a minimum of 30 days before you're going to go hunting. People come to us three days before they go quail hunting, and they expect us to make 'em a great quail shot. It's not going to happen. We can talk to them about fundamentals and we can help them with their gun mount, but once they go out after we've talked to them and they shoot better and more proficiently, then they want to start four weeks or six weeks out…before next season.

Gun Digest: I'm new to the shooting sports and I don't as yet have a shotgun. Should I purchase before going to a school, or will there be shotguns there that I can use and evaluate?

Ash: We have guns for people to use, but we would recommend prior to coming to an all day clinic, you come spend a

couple hours with us. We'll work on your gun mount; we'll get you into a gun.

As for a gun, it all depends on how much money you want to spend and what kind of commitment you want to make. If you want to spend $500 on a gun 'cause you want to go dove hunting a couple times a year and, with the clinic, you want to be a little more proficient, then maybe a pump-gun or a semi-automatic. Something that's functional in

Phil Bourjaily, right, works with Instructor Gil Ash and a "Try Gun" as part of a recent shotgunning school held in Austin, Texas.

Fit, as Instructor Gil Ash calculates here, is vital to good shotgunning performance.

In order to shoot well, a shotgun must first FIT well.

the field. On the other hand, if you want a nice O/U, nice O/Us go from $1,400 to $140,000. It depends on what you want to spend. We can arrange for you to try different guns before you buy them, but the most important thing we're going to do as teachers is not tell you what you're going to buy, but we're going to educate you in the different types of shotguns that are available – and then you can make your own decision.

Gun Digest: How critical is gun fit to successful shotgun shooting, and what role does that play in a shooting school?

Ash: We do from 150 to 200 gun fits a year. Gun fit is important, to a certain extent. If a gun is too long for an individual or too short for an individual, that's very important. But the quality of the gun fit is tied directly to the ability of the person shooting the gun to move it and mount it consistently. We do two gun fits. We do a complete and thorough gun fit for a person who has a good move and a good mount. Then we have what we call a novice gun fit for someone who cannot move and mount the gun. The novice gun fit is to adjust the pull and pitch, and put a little drop and a little cast in the stock, so that the person can shoot the gun without it hurting them. It's then the person's job to go and shoot the gun a couple thousand rounds, then they'll come back, we'll go to the pattern plate, and we'll finish up the gun fit.

It's like this. If you were to come to me and want me to build you a custom set of golf clubs, but you'd only played golf three times in your life. You don't have the ability to swing the clubs consistently enough to appreciate the nuances that a custom set of clubs provides. You don't swing the clubs consistently enough for me to adjust the shaft length to a 1/16 of an inch. It's the same thing with shotguns. There are some people out there who will tell you that gun fit is the number one priority. It's not. A lot of gun fit problems can be cured with a good gun mount, and I think that any gun-fitter worth his salt would agree with that statement. Vicki and I routinely demonstrate shots with students' guns. We demonstrate them right-handed and we demonstrate them left-handed. The length of pulls on those guns can range from 12.5 inches to 17 inches, but because we have a good gun mount, we can consistently mount the gun well and break those targets so the students can see how to do that.

Gun Digest: What is the most difficult shooting concept, for lack of a better phrase, for your students to grasp?

Ash: Moving the muzzle with the target. Let's say you're shooting at left to right target at 20 yards, and the target takes three of lead. If you move and mount the gun with that bird and the gun's three feet ahead of the bird, but the gun's going twice as fast as the bird – when you pull the trigger, what's going to happen? You're going to shoot ahead of the bird. Now, same scenario, but now the gun's going half as fast as the target. What then? You're going to shoot behind the target.

It's not the lead that's important. It's whether or not the muzzle speed is equal to the bird's speed because then and only then is the right lead the right lead. We call that tempo. Tempo is the most common misconception in shotgunning. People want to get the gun up, run and chase, find the bird, triangulate the lead, and shoot. What ends up happening is the birds appear to fly three times faster than they're really flying.

Watch someone shoot sporting clays. When you're watching, the birds seem to fly slow. Then when you're in the cage, the birds seem to speed up. The engineers call this relative velocity – how fast something appears to fly. We call it visual speed. We're standing on the edge of the highway watching the cars go by at 70 miles-per-hour. They seem to be going awful fast. Now, we get in your pickup truck and we start going 70 miles-per-hour. The traffic seems to slow down.

Gun Digest: Is there a bottom line to shotgunning and shooting schools?

Ash: Shooting is just like putting a new program in your computer. You have to learn about it before you can use it, and before you can do it instinctively. It doesn't matter if it's fly casting or learning to walk ... it just doesn't matter; you have to do it. We sum it up this way. Technical expertise is always preceded by experience. In order to do something well, we must have done it many times.

Gun Digest: What should I expect during a day-long shotgunning clinic with you folks?

Ash: You're going to shoot somewhere between seven and 10 boxes of shells, depending upon the types of targets we're shooting that day. We'll start in the morning and we'll talk to the group. Vicki will divide the people into two groups, and she'll let me know what my group has to work on. She'll take a group, and we'll each start with one fundamental crossing target, probably a simple left-to-right or right-to-left target. You'll walk up to the target and shoot five or six times doing what you normally do. Don't try to impress me; just do what you normally do. I'll make notes on your card, not as to what your perception of the problem is, but what your *real* problem is.

Gun Digest: Large groups? Small groups?

> *If you move and mount the gun with that bird and the gun's three feet ahead of the bird, but the gun's going twice as fast as the bird – when you pull the trigger, what's going to happen?*

Ash: Number? Vicki will take five people, and I'll take five. Five's the magic number. If you take six, they don't get to shoot enough. If you take four, they end up going brain-dead about 3:15. If you take five, they go brain-dead about 4:16, plus or minus a minute. And they're not

Ladies take to shotgunning instruction exceptionally well, and present one of the fastest-growing segments of the shooting sports.

physically tired. They're mentally tired. In a group scenario, you learn more from watching others shoot than you do actually pulling the trigger.

If everyone has a common problem, which they normally do, we'll start to work with the first shooter. Get them to slow down. Look at the bird before they move. Move and mount with the speed of the bird, and hit the bird. Then the next shooter has watched the first, and they're ready. Finally the last shooter, it usually only takes them two or three shots before they're there. Then we go to another target. Eventually, we train these shooters to instinctively react to what the target does.

Gun Digest: And as the day continues?

Ash: About 10:45 to 11:00, it clicks. People begin to understand why they miss when they miss, and why they hit when they hit. Each person will have a unique problem that we will deal with throughout the day. By lunchtime, the people are slapping high fives. They're amazed at how slow the birds are, and they're amazed at how easy the birds are to hit. They're amazed at how much they're been looking at the gun, and how looking at the gun prevents them from being successful.

After lunch, we may pattern the guns on the pattern plates, or we'll talk about gun fit. Then we'll go back to shooting; maybe, some slow targets to give them time to move and mount the gun and be successful. Mid-afternoon, and depending on what the group needs, we might shoot pairs. We might shoot report pairs. We might shoot doubles. If the group's coming along well or they're experienced shooters, we might move back and shoot 40, 50, or 60-yard crossers. We'll get them to believe that they can hit those birds without checking the lead.

Gun Digest: A typical price and timeframe for this instruction?

Ash: In 2005, the price will be $350 a day, plus your targets and your ammo. You can bring your own ammo or you can purchase that at the club. Targets are 30 cents apiece, and you'll end up shooting roughly 200 targets. We typically recommend people, if they can, come for two days. The first day is typically deprogramming; the second day is typically reprogramming. If we know you can only be there for one day, about 2 o'clock in the afternoon we will shift what we're doing for you so as to begin the imprinting phase of our teaching. We'll begin to say things in a different way to you, and we'll begin to point out specific things you need to practice and why you need to practice them.

If this is you, then about 2 o'clock, I'd begin to take you to targets that were your weak points. I would coach you on these targets, and I would emphasize how important it is for you to become a better shooter. For you to conquer the two or three things that I'm pointing out to you. I would tell you how to practice and how often to practice. I'll tell you that if you will do what I'm telling you to do – shoot at least two times a week for the next three weeks, doing this the first week and this the second week and this the third week – this problem we're discussing will go away.

Here, let's shift our focus away from the teacher and speak for a moment to one of OSP's former students, Philip Bourjaily. Currently living in Iowa City, Iowa, Bourjaily, 46, serves as the shooting editor for *Field & Stream*, and as such, along with his passion for English pointers and upland wingshooting, spends more than his fair share of time behind the buttplate of a shotgun. And with that –

Gun Digest: Why would an experienced shooter like you attend a shooting school?

Bourjaily: Why would a major league ball player go to the batting cages or to his batting coach? I'm not saying that I'm at that level of shooting – I'm not – but everybody, regardless of their level of ability, can improve. Everybody goes into slumps. Everybody needs work on the mental end of their game. There's a lot that shooting coaches can do for you.

Gun Digest: And as a hunter? Has *formal* shooting instruction proved effective?

Bourjaily: I've learned a lot. We practiced some long-range shooting at the last OSP clinic I attended. They told me that the secret to long-range shooting is to move the gun very slowly, which seems wrong. But I was able to put that into practice in Canada, and shot geese at ranges that I'd just as soon not reveal.

Gun Digest: How was your personal style of shooting affected by this professional instruction, or was it?

> *We'll begin to say things in a different way to you, and we'll begin to point out specific things you need to practice and why you need to practice them.*

Remington's Linda Powell offers pointers to an eager student during an informal session on the range.

Bourjaily: The two things that the Ashes picked on me for … one was riding targets. That is, staying with the targets too long to make sure my lead was right. The longer you stay with the target, the greater the chance you're going to slow the gun and miss. Like every shooting instructor I've ever worked with has

emphasized, when the gun comes to your cheek and shoulder, that's when you pull the trigger. When you check and double check your lead like I was doing, the only thing that lies down that path are misses and frustration

The other thing, which I was initially surprised about but which made sense once they explained it to me, was that I follow through too much. I have a very conscious push of the gun following the shot, which I'm sure is a habit left over from bird hunting. The Ashes said that what happens here is that the shooter begins relying too much on that exaggerated follow-through in order to get the gun out in front of the target rather than putting the muzzle in the right place the first time. Sooner or later, you will begin to miss if you begin to rely on that conscious follow-through.

One of the things that I got out of shooting with the Ashes, and watching them shoot, is that very good shooters are very economical with their movement. That really impressed me quite a bit.

Gun Digest: Has shooting instruction helped you to improve in the field?

Bourjaily: Perhaps the most significant thing you take away from any shooting lesson is that you learn to diagnose your own misses. You learn to answer the question – Why did I miss? And that's very important to become a better shooter, whether that's on the range or in the field. Yes, clay targets don't have wings that flap and they slow down versus speeding up; still, hitting a moving target is hitting a moving target. There is a lot of carry-over from a clinic to the field.

Gun Digest: And practice after instruction?

Bourjaily: You can go to a clinic and you can shoot really well with someone

Ladies take to shotgunning instruction exceptionally well, and present one of the fastest-growing segments of the shooting sports.

standing at your elbow handing you bullets and telling you what to do, but if you don't follow through and practice, it's all for naught. And you need to practice a specific way or you'll lose a lot of what they'll teach you. And practicing the right way isn't going to the gun club and shooting a couple rounds of skeet. You go to the gun club when there's nobody there, and you shoot a couple boxes of shells at whatever target or targets that give you trouble.

Gun Digest: Is there any type of mental preparation a shooter might want to consider prior to enrolling in a shooting school?

Bourjaily: You need to be ready to admit that you might be doing it wrong. Anybody who has shot as long as you or I have – NOTE: That would be approximately a combined 53 years – has developed bad habits. Instructors would much rather work with someone who has never picked up a shotgun before. It's amazing what they can do with a total beginner. With us, they have to break down the bad habits. What most instructors have told me is that they like to have somebody for two days. The first day is spent breaking the bad habits, and the second day is spent instilling the new ones.

Gun Digest: And as a student, your bottom line on shooting schools?

Bourjaily: These shooting clinics are fun. Taking lessons is just fun, as long as you don't let your ego get in the way. Gil uses a lot of humor and a lot of sarcasm – in a good-natured way – in his clinics, and he keeps it fun. You find yourself doing things that you really didn't think you could do, and that's neat too. You

have to go into these clinics with an open mind and be ready to admit that some of the things you thought were right aren't necessarily right. If you do that, you'll get a lot of benefit out of the lesson.

Shooting Schools: *Where to find 'em*

Unlike days of old when the words *shooting school* and *blood relative* could be used interchangeably, clinics and courses offered by someone other than Pop or Grandpa are showing themselves in great number across much of the United States. Like the Ashes' program, many of these courses can be tailored to fit the needs, schedule, and pocketbook of the individual shooter.

Resources for the prospective student include –

Gil and Vicki Ash
Optimum Shooting Performance
15020 Cutten Rd.
Houston, TX 77070
281-897-0800
www.ospschool.com

Published in Maple Grove, Minnesota, *Black's Wing & Clay Shotgunner's Handbook* is without question the definitive reference manual for everything shotgun, including a tremendous listing of over 90 shooting schools located throughout the country.

Black's Sporting Directories
Ehlert Publishing Group
6420 Sycamore Lane, Suite 100
Maple Grove, MN 55369
800-877-6118 (subscriptions)

Finally, there's the Internet. A quick check using the *Google* search engine revealed 1.36 million returns when I typed in the words *shooting school*. Certainly, there should be something here to fit your needs and your wallet.

Winter crow hunting can be as hot as it is cold.

Off-Season Hunting

By M.D. Johnson

I have a friend – Mister X – who, on the January 11, begins to slowly spiral into a sort of long, drawn out state of withdrawal. You see, the January 11 just so happens to be the day after the last day of pheasant season, and Mister X just so happens to be an avid – no, a rabid – wingshooter. Throughout the spring and into the summer, he languishes in his non-hunting agony, the suffering eased only slightly by periodic trips to the skeet range or to the sporting clays course. "It's just not the same," he cries long-distance into the phone as he again counts the days until September 1 and the coming of dove season. And rail season. And snipe season. And early goose season. And… you see what I mean?

What Mister X, and a whole lot of Mister Xs, doesn't realize is that hunting season doesn't necessarily have to end simply because the state-mandated seasons come to a close. Now, before anyone raises a hand to question my ethics here, let me say just two words – off-season hunting.

Riflemen have long been the envy of wingshooters, in part because the .243-toting individual seldom lacks for something to hunt. There are coyotes and ground squirrels, rock chucks, woodchucks, and prairie dogs. The southern states have their nutria, while the northern climes have their jackrabbits – and they're all fair game to the man who likes nothing better than to shoot small projectiles at things very, very far away.

But what about the shotgunner? Well the truth be known, there are plenty of wingshooting opportunities to be had throughout the whole of the year, aside, that is, from attempting to break fast-flying disks made of baked clay. And with that said, let's take a look at three of the most traditional off-season wingshooting opportunities to be had in the Lower 48.

Crows

For many shotgunners, off-season hunting is all about crows. The truth is, crow hunters can often be as passionate about their sport as the waterfowler or upland bird hunter is about his. And with good reason. Crow hunting can be tremendously challenging, and often combines many of the aspects of more traditionally sought-after species, including the use of decoys and calls, the building of blinds, personal camouflage, scouting and patterning, and lest we forget, the fundamentals of shotgun shooting. Marksmanship, if you will.

In the past, crows were often a target of opportunity. Duck hunters shot at them. Goose hunters shot at them. Rabbit hunters shot at them. As an

> *Crow hunting can be tremendously challenging, and often combines many of the aspects of more traditionally sought-after species, including the use of decoys and calls, the building of blinds, personal camouflage, scouting and patterning, and lest we forget, the fundamentals of shotgun shooting.*

avid squirrel hunter, I spent as much time chasing crows around the treetops with 40-grain .22 Long Rifle rounds as I did bushytails. And as for the summer months, the true heart of the off-season? Well, there were always cornfields and pecan groves to protect from these treacherous thieves.

Today, the situation is a bit different, what with the states permitting the killing of crows only within defined seasons. Typically, these seasons consist of late fall and/or early winter opportunities, roughly from October through January; however, some states do offer spring seasons, while others such as Minnesota set a regular season to begin in mid-July. The best advice here is to consult your state's small game or migratory bird hunting regulations, and then plan accordingly.

Successful crow hunting, like waterfowling, consists of four primary elements. These are location, blinds, decoys, and calling.

Traditionally, crow roosts have been declared voluntarily off-limits to hunting for the sole reason that shooting the roost often forces the crows to relocate, thus ending the hunting opportunities until another roost is found. With crow populations and associated problems – crop predation, mess, and noise being the three primary concerns – on the rise in some areas, however, roost shoots have become the norm. Though it may last only an evening or two, shooting a crow roost can be some of the fastest

Crow hunting is a popular off-season activity for the shotgunner; however, check your state's regulations as to any restrictions.

wingshooting short of Argentina doves that most gunners will experience.

In most cases, however, roosts are left undisturbed. Instead, flight lines – the air paths between the roost and a food source – or feeding areas are located. Blinds are situated near these areas, decoys are arranged, and calls are employed. Locating and determining a flight line is done through scouting. It's best to first locate a roost, and then over the course of several mornings and/or evenings, determine which routes the birds take to and from this roost. Often, crows, as with waterfowl, will use landmarks or topographical features to guide them. This can be a ridge, a river, or a break in a treeline. Or it can be as subtle as a single tree. Regardless, take note of such features as they can prove outstanding blind locations.

Feeding areas, too, can be hot spots. One of the most unusual feeding areas

I've ever hunted was near the Long Beach Peninsula in Washington State. A friend had permission to hunt a parcel where the landowner had contracted with the local crabbers, who then used the property as a waste station for their refuse, i.e. dead crabs, shells, old bait, and the like. Piles the size of panel vans of crab carcasses and shells dotted the property, and the stench was appalling; however, the crows loved it and looked upon the rotting crustaceans like Fat Albert looks at an all-you-can-eat buffet. Not normally prone to a weak stomach, I had to pack both nostrils with Vicks-soaked cotton balls – and still the smell was revolting. But we shot crows! Boy, howdy, did we shoot crows.

Normally, the feeding areas preferred by crows aren't nearly as disgusting as were these piles of crab. Pecan groves, harvested corn, or recently cut wheat or hay can all be magnets to the black

It's best to first locate a roost, and then over the course of several mornings and/or evenings, determine which routes the birds take to and from this roost.

The author and gunning partner, Adrian McClellan, hang a handful of crow decoys prior to a hunt in northern Iowa.

One of the best blinds I've ever hunted out of consisted of a two-person sized hole carved out of a huge tangle of Washington state blackberry bushes.

hoards, and smell considerably better. Here, as with flight lines, it's a matter of a little bit of driving and a little bit of looking. Once you've found a number of crows in what looks like a feeding mood, a quick talk with the landowner can usually result in permission being granted.

Next, blinds, and blinds are both the most elemental and the most complicated of factors in the crow equation. They're elemental in the fact that it's impossible to hide too well from a crow, and complex in that they must conceal everything completely while at the same time allowing for unobstructed viewing and shooting. Tall order, but it's possible.

Recently, some crow hunters have taken to using commercially made blinds such as those constructed by Avery Outdoors, Final Approach, Gooseview, or Strong Built – all of which, and more, can be found online at www.cabelas.com. Available in a variety of camouflage patterns and made so as to accept additional natural materials, these lightweight, portable blinds are perfect for the mobile crow hunter. But this isn't to say that natural blinds or a simple combination of burlap and native materials won't work just as well. One of the best blinds I've ever hunted out of consisted of a two-person sized hole carved out of a huge tangle of Washington state blackberry bushes. Located in a fenceline adjoining a well-used feedlot, the briar patch had long been accepted by the local crows as a natural part of the environment. And aside from a few scrapes and scratches courtesy of the brambles, gunning partner, Tony Miller, and I enjoyed several excellent – and well-hidden – shoots from their interior.

Camouflage clothing rounds out this section on blinds, and here, the mantra is simple – There is no such thing as an insignificant detail when it comes to hiding from a crow's razor-sharp eyes. That said, I'd highly recommend complete head-to-toe camouflage clothing, including head nets or face paints and gloves. Guns, likewise, should sport a camo pattern, or at the very least, possess dull or matte finish. It helps to periodically look around to make certain that shiny objects – shotshell hulls, thermos tops, candy wrappers, and the like – aren't exposed and betraying your presence. Trust me, crows overlook nothing, and neither should you.

Crow decoys and their placement are two areas often best left to personal preference. Hailing from northern Washington, Tony Miller has been hunting crows for close to three decades, and in that time, has come to learn a thing or two about using plastic fakes to fool these keen birds.

"As a general rule," said Miller, "I'll set my decoys to make it look like crows feeding. Like they've really found something great to eat. I'll combine the decoys on the ground with a few – 8 or 10 – posted as sentries. These I'll put in high, visible places, like on fence posts or even in trees."

"Don't have all your decoys facing one direction," he continued. "This creates the appearance that something's wrong in that direction. Scatter them out, but not too spread out. If you spread 'em too thin, you'll have a hard time getting birds to land or come within effective range. And leave a gap in your decoy spread, just like you would for ducks. You want to give them someplace to land."

Traditionally, Miller admits he's been a fan of big spreads – number-wise – for crows; however, for every rule, they say, there is that exception. "I use quite a few decoys," said Miller, "unless I'm hunting a spot that I've hunted before. Then, I'll not only try to change my blind location, but I'll change up the decoy spread, too. Maybe only use 18 decoys, and spread them out thin. I do that quite often, this big spread one day and little spread the next."

And Robo-Crow, the black feathered counterpart to the famous – and infamous – electronic spinning wing Robo-Duck? Not surprisingly, there is indeed a Robo-Crow (www.mojodecoys. com); however, according to Miller, the jury's still out on the use of this new-fangled device. "I don't feel like it (Robo-Crow) improved the hunt all that much," said Miller. "To me, your location seems to be a much bigger issue than your decoy spread, and particularly whether or not you use one of these electronic decoys. Maybe if you're trying to run the old 'owl and wounded crow' setup, these electronics might make a difference. Personally, though, I'd put more emphasis on scouting a location and choosing a blind site."

Calling is the final element in any crow hunt, successful or otherwise. Like most species of birds, crows have their own particular vernacular – and it only makes sense to know what you're saying before you say it. "Listen to some crow language," said Miller, who suggested hunters learn by purchasing a cassette or CD featuring this so-called crow talk. Or, better yet he says, is simply spending time outdoors and listening to how crows interact verbally with one another. Then, as with most game calling, it's a matter of mimicry.

Crow callers today have two choices in terms of calling gear – electronics, and the traditional mouth calls. While modern electronic callers do provide high quality, all at the touch of a button, they can't in many cases impart the personality – the inflection – into a calling sequence as can the gunner skilled with a mouth call.

"I like a combination of the two," said Miller, himself – Trust me on this – an extremely talented mouth caller. "But I do have good luck with a mouth call. With a mouth call, you can get awful tired. And with the electronics, there is the 'background noise' factor; that is, there's always some crow noise in the background. It makes it sound

Many crow hunters have taken to using electronic callers like the Hunter's Buddy model being used here.

One of the most pleasant things about hunting crows, other than the fact that the birds are literally everywhere, is that the shotguns used can be as minor league as a $50 hand-me-down single-shot or as major league as any $2,000 over/under.

like there's a lot of crows around, and that, combined with a big spread, can often be deadly."

As for a traditional crow calling sequence, it's pretty elemental. "You want to use a hail call … some sort of greeting call or announcement to begin with. An occasional caw-caw," said Miller. "Once the shooting starts though, go to a distress call. Get excited. Announce that there's a problem. And sometimes, you can pull some birds back for a second volley."

One of the most pleasant things about hunting crows, other than the fact that the birds are literally everywhere, is that the shotguns used can be as minor league as a $50 hand-me-down single-shot or as major league as any $2,000 over/under. On any given day, Tony Miller can typically be found shooting a favorite Benelli Super Black Eagle. Me? The nod goes to either a pet Remington 11-87 or a Winchester Super X2. The common denominator here is not that guns are 12-gauges nor that they're autoloaders, but rather, they are the guns that both Miller and I use extensively for waterfowling. Why waterfowl guns in a crow blind?

"I like shooting my Super Black Eagle at crows because, one, I like the gun, and two, it allows me to keep in practice or in tune with the particular shotgun that I'll use in the duck blind come October," said Miller. "There's never a lapse or a break in the time I'm using it." Myself, I agree with Miller's reasoning, and employ my duck guns for crow shoots 99 percent of the time. Practice, they say, can make one more proficient.

While the shotguns may be waterfowl guns, the ammunition used in most crow shoots isn't waterfowl specific. In many cases, gunners are still permitted to use lead shot during crow hunts, and in such situations, I'm prone to using

one to 1-1/4-ounce loads of #6 or #7.5 shot. Crows are remarkably fragile birds, and it doesn't take a huge shot charge of big pellets to consistently bring them down. If it's steel I'm using, which on public lands is often the case, I'll fill the X2 or 11-87 with Winchester steel #7s.

Ordinarily, here is the point at which I shock and astound some readers by extolling the virtues of eating crow; however, given the recent incidences of West Nile virus, and the fact that crows both are a primary target and carrier of the disease, we'll forgo the recipes for now. Let me just say that crow as a main dish is definitely not a stranger to a surprising number of folks. And we'll leave it at that.

Pigeons

Most boys – most kids, for that matter – are hell on something. In my formative years, most of which revolved around hunting or shooting as much as humanly possible, I was hell on pigeons.

In my world, then as it is now, there are two kinds of wild pigeons, or rock doves, if you'd like to call them that. There are city pigeons – those that you see in metropolitan areas across the country. The ones that waddle and coo and defile statues and monuments when they're not eating popcorn, breadcrumbs, or pecking at cigarette butts. And there are country pigeons, the ones that live under abandoned railroad trestles or in the haymows of dilapidated old barns out in the proverbial middle of nowhere. Myself, I'm drawn to the latter, as their daily fight for survival makes them a wary and thus challenging quarry; however, that's not to say that city pigeons, presented with enough hunting pressure, can't become as cagy as those living past the city limits signs – they can, and do.

I suppose that like crows and as you'll see with starlings, you can hunt pigeons either at the roost or at a feeding area. Roosts, though, pose a problem, often because the roosts will be within the city limits and thus, off limits to any type of hunting. Roosts outside the city limits, even if huntable, might be best voluntarily declared off limits so as not to pressure the birds out of the immediate area. This, then, leaves feeding areas, which includes waterholes and sources of grit.

As a boy, I had some of my best pigeon shoots over fresh-mown hay or, better yet, fresh cut winter wheat. In the wake of a cutting, birds would come from miles around to take advantage of the fallen seeds and seed heads. Here, the techniques were no different than in dove hunting. Scout, find a field, evaluate

the activity, obtain permission, hide yourself, and hunt. June, at least in the northeastern corner of Ohio where I grew up, was a good month for hunting over newly-cut fields, as was July. August usually meant a second cutting, and a renewal of bird activity in areas that had grown too tall and too nutritionally sparse as to be productive. August, too, meant an excellent opportunity to warm up prior to doves, teal, and early Canada geese. Fields that included a water source – a stock tank or pond, for instance – were even more attractive. These could be hunted by two shooters or groups, one on the field and the second at the water's edge.

Grit or gravel areas can be another hotspot. For reasons best known to the birds themselves, pigeons often will travel several miles to pick grit at a

> **As a boy, I had some of my best pigeon shoots over fresh-mown hay or, better yet, fresh cut winter wheat.**

Pigeons have been a long favorite among shotgunners looking to keep themselves sharp in the off-season.

Widely used in the United Kingdom by those gunning wood pigeons, pigeon decoys aren't near as well-known nor as commonly seen an item here in the U.S.; however, that's not to say they don't work – they do.

specific location, even though similar sources may be more convenient. For years, I gunned wild pigeons over a circular spot of bare ground at the edge of an annual soybean field. Brine (salt water) leaching up through the soil around an abandoned oil wellhead kept the ground devoid of vegetation, and the pigeons absolutely loved it! No cover meant predators couldn't surprise the grit-picking birds, and nearby ragweed and immature beans made for excellent eating. Many mornings I'd crouch in the beans near the circle, and drop two dozen or more birds before the city folk were ever in their desk chairs.

Over the years, my pigeon blinds ranged from the informal to the elaborate. Camouflaged clothing and a hide in the ragweed worked, as have a dozen square hay bales arranged in a box-like fashion along the edge of a cut field. In cases where there simply wasn't any cover available, I've taken to using one of the low-profile layout blinds now popular with goose hunters. A little bit of wheat or straw stubble, and the blind becomes near invisible. These blinds are also lightweight and thus very portable, making it easy to relocate anywhere within a field as the birds dictate. Regardless of the type of blind used, camouflage and concealment are key. A wild pigeon's eyesight and natural wariness should not be underestimated; that is, unless you prefer to keep shooting opportunities at a minimum.

Widely used in the United Kingdom by those gunning wood pigeons, pigeon decoys aren't near as well-known nor as commonly seen an item here in the U.S.; however, that's not to say they don't work – they do. Tremendously gregarious birds, pigeons in the air see birds on the ground as having something they don't – namely, food – and those in the air will often respond to decoys without hesitation.

Typically, I will use the first few birds of the morning as the day's decoys. A forked stick under the chin and a natural arrangement is all that's necessary. You can also make your own pigeon silhouette decoys with little more than some 1/4-inch plywood, a jig saw, and a variety of house paints. Blocks can also be carved out of Styrofoam or scrap pieces of pine. Perhaps surprisingly, commercially made pigeon decoys are available. Most of these come from makers in the U.K.; however, silhouette style decoys are available from Precision Reloading (www.precisionreloading.com) in Connecticut.

Historically on the menu of prince and pauper alike, and whether baked, stewed, roasted, grilled, slow-cooked, or in a pie – Yes, Virginia, there truly is a recipe for *Pigeon Pie* – pigeon can prove a tremendous culinary experience. Any recipe applicable to upland birds such as grouse or pheasant can certainly have pigeon substituted for the primary ingredient. And truth be known, it's actually quite difficult to make a mistake when it comes to preparing these wonderful birds. Don't overcook them, and don't mask the delicate flavor with a bunch of spices and sauces, and you'll be on your way to an award-winning dinner.

Starlings

When the topic of wingshooting, even an off-season type of wingshooting, is raised, few folks – if any – would automatically think of starlings; however, some of the hottest shooting I've ever experienced, doves included, has come courtesy of this black bothersome import. And one of the nicest things about gunning starlings? Unlike crows, there are no starling calls and no little black decoys. All you need are several boxes of light field loads and a feedlot or an old roosting barn during the month of February. And don't worry about a handwarmer. That gun barrel is going to be handwarmer enough.

I'm sure that something kind can be said about starlings; however, I can't for the life of me think of what it is. These non-natives were brought to the United States in the late 1800s for, of all things, their musical talent. And I will admit that an adult starling is capable of quite a wide range of song, not to mention mimicry to rival that of the most skilled myna bird or mockingbird. The Audubon Society shows starlings to have arrived in the States in 1890, where they were released into New York's Central Park. Fifty years later, the birds were introduced into California, and shortly after, into British Columbia. Fifty years later, starlings could be found in all 50 states and northern Mexico.

As has been the case with carp and other introduced species, the problems with starlings soon overshadowed the reason behind their initial release. True, the birds are quite musically inclined; however, their propensity for gathering in large numbers – 1,000-bird flocks are not uncommon – has created concern in several different arenas. One, they're extremely noisy, which in and of itself isn't life-threatening, but does eventually get on one's nerves. Secondly, these large gatherings of starlings can wreak havoc on agricultural crops, including corn, grains, berries, and other fruit crops. Too, these immense flocks of starlings can create serious problems when located near airports. In 1960, a British Harrier jet crashed after sucking a flock of starlings into one of its turbine intakes. Later that same year, 62 people were killed when an Eastern Airlines jet crashed. The cause? A flock of starlings in an engine. Incidentally, Canada geese head the list of bird species involved in bird-plane incidents; however, it's clear that starlings aren't far behind.

To continue. Third, a thousand feeding starlings will, eventually, result in a 1,000 birds worth of droppings. And unfortunately, the birds seem to care not if the target of these droppings is ground, farm machinery, rooftop, or silage intended for cattle feed. In the case

In some states, rabbits like this cottontail are hunted year-round, making them a fine – and delicious – off-season choice.

With few natural predators save some of the smaller, quicker raptors, starlings, which in southern climes will raise two or three broods of three to four young each annually, increase in number and range almost unchecked.

of the latter, the ingestion by cattle of dropping-soiled feed can result in illness and even loss. Finally, starlings compete quite viciously for natural tree cavities which, and at the risk of choosing sides, might be used for less destructive and problematic species such as bluebirds, screech owls, swallows and the like. With few natural predators save some of the smaller, quicker raptors, starlings, which in southern climes will raise two or three broods of three to four young each annually, increase in number and range almost unchecked.

To the uninitiated, hunting starlings might at first seem a bit unchallenging; however, nothing could be farther from the truth. Pressured by the gun, starlings can become quite crow-like in their wariness, flaring from uncamouflaged forms and, given enough pressure, even deserting roosts and feeding areas altogether. Throw in a little wind or some overhead cover or feedlot obstacles, and even the most accomplished shooters can grow frustrated. Good friend, Tony Miller, and I once gunned an old railroad line in southwestern Washington. The birds were trading back and forth between a silage feedlot and a roost site along the Columbia River. Seated on five gallon buckets filled with one-ounce loads of #7-1/2 and #8 shot, we shot at birds streaking across the 50-yard break in the timbered stretch that was either side of the rails. It was as quick and as challenging a shoot as I'd had in some time, and I'm not ashamed to say that I made more than my fair share of empty hulls – with few dropped birds to show for my efforts. Miller, a tremendous wingshooter, did a bit better, but still spent a goodly portion of his morning in Bang-Missed, Bang-Missed mode.

Starlings are often best hunted at one of two locations – feeding areas, or roost sites. One of the finest feeding areas I've ever hunted was along the shores of the Columbia River in Washington state. Large sand feedlots had been fenced along the water, and each evening the cattlemen would roll up in trucks to dump pile upon pile of silage – chopped corn, stalks and all – into big wooden hoppers and bins. And likewise each evenings, clouds of starlings, along with crows and pigeons, from both sides of the river would descend on the feedlots to take advantage of this free meal. Initially, gunning these black fighter jets was as simple as standing or sitting next to a convenient cottonwood or alder, and pass-shooting the flocks as they winged into the lots. After being harassed a time or two, however, the starlings began to associate bipedal gun-toting forms as bad news, and it became commonplace to see entire 100-bird flocks flare from anything resembling a shooting position. Camouflage and even impromptu blinds became the rule, and the shooting picked back up.

Feedlots can be hunted at any time during the course of the year; however, and understandably, the shooting gets hotter as the weather grows correspondingly colder, and the birds lose the insects, bugs, beetles, and grubs that make up the bulk of their warm-weather diet. Some of the best shoots I experienced while still in Washington came after the close of waterfowl season during the months of February and March, with many lasting until mid-April and the coming of turkey season.

Roosts are another fantastic location to set up a starling shoot, and can provide excellent gunning during the mid-summer months when the shooting around the feedlots begins to slow. As with crow roosts, starling roosts can be over-gunned or shot out. That said, and in an effort to preserve the shooting as long as possible, it's often best to scout and then gun a flightline – a path between the roost and a food or water source – rather than the roost proper. Reminiscent of pass shooting, this type of gunning can provide top-notch practice, particularly for waterfowlers.

Trees aren't the only roost sites favored by starlings. Years ago, I helped 'manage' an inordinately large flock of starlings, literally thousands of birds, that had chosen an in-use Morton style machine shed as their nightly hide. In the weeks that we gunned this particular site – and we shot the roost primarily as the landowner wanted to regain use of building! – it wasn't unusual for three of us to shoot 200 rounds apiece in the last couple hours before dark. Needless to say, we did a lot of reloading during the evening hours between shoots. These particular shoots took place in February, a time when the southwestern Ohio winters gathered the birds in huge numbers and forced them indoors; however, I've since spoken with my gunning colleagues who have told me that they've enjoyed similarly paced mid-summer trips to the same locale.

Starlings, like their larger black brethren, crows, don't require heavy loads, large shot, or shoulder bruising land cannons. A lightweight 20-gauge filled with 7/8 or one-ounce loads of the aforementioned #7-1/2 or #8 shot is more than adequate, though the 12 with one-ounce or 1-1/8-ounce loads is unquestionably more popular. Modified tubes will work well in most situations; however, I have seen pass-shooting instances where a full choke might have been a better choice, thus it never hurts to include a full tube in your blind bag or field pack.

And now here's one you might not have considered – starling on the table. From the pages of Eddie Meier's 1950 collection titled The Hungry Sportsman's

Fish and Game Cookbook, a recipe for "Casserole of Starling" involves placing starling breasts in a casserole dish and baking in a hot oven, temperature being your decision, for 10 minutes. These are then doused with mushrooms, red wine, onions, peeled grapes, and chicken bouillon, and allowed to roast further until tender, however long that might be. Believe it or not, there are also recipes for "Starling Breasts on Peanut Dressing" and "Roast Starlings," neither of which I've tried, but I'm game … I think.

> **Trees aren't the only roost sites favored by starlings.**

Though perhaps more popular with centerfire shooters, jackrabbits can nonetheless prove challenging for the scattergunner.

Turkey hunters are showing a trend toward heavy high-velocity loads for both spring and fall hunting.

High-Velocity Ammunition:
Myth, or Magic

By M.D. Johnson

There was a time back in The Day, when shotgunners didn't concern themselves with velocity. "You grabbed a box of high brass #5 shot," the old-timers will tell you, "and you headed into the field." It didn't matter what you were hunting. "Nope," they'll say, taking another pinch of snuff, "those #5s were the ticket. How fast were they going? Hell, I don't know. Fast enough, I guess." And then they'd laugh. Those old guys were always laughing.

Today, though, the feelings and opinions about shotgun ammunition, velocity, and its influence on performance aren't nearly as casual as they once were. True, we've become a more technologically-driven people, shotgunners included, but does this have anything to do with the increased interest being given high-velocity shotshells over the course of the past decade? More specifically, what brought about this new *High-Speed* revolution, and does velocity – 1,450 feet-per-second (fps) versus 1,225 fps – really make that much of a difference in the field or on the range?

High-velocity defined

It makes sense here to start with a definition; that is, what constitutes a high-velocity shotshell load?

"In a target load," says Phil Bourjaily, shotgunning editor for *Field & Stream*, "I would say anything over 1,250 fps. In a lead hunting load, that would go to 1,300 fps. And with steel and some of the other non-toxics, I'd make that 1,400 fps."

Let's take a minute and examine the differences. In the case of lead target loads, high-velocity is more a product of tradition than anything else. Rather, such target loads have traditionally been pushed at 1,100 to 1,200 fps. A break from this tradition – a target load now chronographed at 1,250 fps or higher – then qualifies as high-velocity. The same could be said about lead hunting loads, a.k.a. game and field loads. Again, tradition has these relatively light shot charges, the Old Man's high-brass #5s for instance, traveling at from 1,150 fps to 1,250 fps. The situation changes, however, when the topic turns to steel shot or any of the other non-toxic materials which are less dense than lead, a subject to be discussed in detail shortly.

Why velocity?

Often the first question asked regarding high-velocity shotshells is also the most elemental – Why the need for speed? In truth, there are several answers.

> *In the case of lead target loads, high-velocity is more a product of tradition than anything else.*

By law of physics, a #4 lead pellet traveling at 1,450 fps will deliver more on-target kinetic energy measured in foot/pounds than will a similarly sized pellet launched at 1,200 fps at an equal distance. For the hunter, such an increase in energy translates into improved on-target performance; that

High-velocity loads can be found in the uplands, wetlands, and on the trap and skeet range today.

is, game-killing effectiveness. This increase means better penetration of the individual pellets striking the target. More energy and great penetration, then, equal cleaner kills.

It sounds great, but when you take a close mathematical look at the numbers, there doesn't seem to be that much of a difference. Compare, for instance, a steel #2 pellet fired at 1,325 fps, and another traveling at 1,450 fps. At 40 yards, this 125-fps discrepancy has shrunk to but 40 fps. This translates into a 1/3-foot/pound advantage for the faster load as compared to the slower, or an increase of approximately seven percent in favor of the high-velocity shotshell.

Does it really make a difference, this mere 1/3-foot/pound increase? As dramatic a difference were it a 30-foot/pound advantage? Certainly not, but consider this. For every three such *high-speed* pellets that strike a target – a 40-yard mallard, perhaps – you've transferred an additional full foot/pound of energy onto that 3-pound target. This is energy that would not have existed with the slower ammunition. What's more, these faster pellets have the ability to penetrate farther into the target, thus increasing the chances that vital organs will be hit. Put it all together, and the scales do tip toward the side of the higher velocity shotshell. Significantly? Perhaps not, but every little bit can and does help.

Reduced leads are another reason behind this surge in velocity's popularity. This difference is perhaps more significant to trap and skeet shooters than it might be to the man in the field; however, a short flight time and lead is a short flight time and lead, whether you're standing at the 16-yard line or knee-deep in a duck marsh.

But as with energy, a comparison between high-velocity and standard

Trapshooters are recognizing the advantages of high-velocity ammunition, particularly on longer targets or in sporting clays applications.

More so than most, waterfowlers are reaping the benefits of high-velocity shotgun ammunition, such as this FASTEEL from Kent Cartridge.

The truth is, the difference in lead on a 90-degree crossing target at 40 yards between a standard-velocity round (1,375 fps) and a high-velocity load (1,450 fps) is approximately 6 inches, more or less.

ammunition in terms of shortened leads is not night and day; that is, if you're waiting to see leads cut by 2 to 3 feet, thanks to high-velocity shotshells … well, you have a bit more waiting to do. The truth is, the difference in lead on a 90-degree crossing target at 40 yards between a standard-velocity round (1,375 fps) and a high-velocity load (1,450 fps) is approximately 6 inches, more or less. Past 40 yards, this difference might present itself as substantial; however, at normal distances – 40 yards and under – most field shooters will find it unnecessary to change their leads at all, high-velocity or no.

High-velocity ammunition is almost a given for today's waterfowler.

That said; a high-velocity round's shorter flight time does, it's believed, contribute to a greater number of what might be referred to as *up-front* hits. These are pellets which strike a target – again, our mythical mallard – in the front portion and which, in doing so, stand more likely to penetrate a vital organ, i.e heart, lungs, brain, or spinal column. This is in contrast to pellet strikes farther back and in less lethal regions of the body.

These velocity-related advantages – increased energy and penetration, reduced leads, and the greater likelihood of up-front hits – aren't without their cost. First, there's the fact that the faster you push pellets, the faster those pellets slow down. Think of it as if the pellets were battery-operated cars. Each identical car has three settings – slow, medium, and fast – with the obvious difference being speed, along with battery drain or battery life. Each battery offers 10 power units. The slow setting uses 1 unit/hour; medium requires three units/hour; and fast, five units/hour. With no more explanation than this, it's easy to see that while the fast setting will allow the car to cover a given distance in a shorter period of time, it will also power down more quickly than will the other two. Again, and to the shooter working at normal ranges, this heightened power-down as a result of an increased initial velocity is probably insignificant; however, once distances begin to increase, the decreased lethality of the individual pellets, now the product of less velocity rather than more, begins to make itself apparent.

Then there's recoil. Mister Newton said it best with his "For every action, there is an equal and opposite reaction." Simply put, increasing the *oomph* at the muzzle increases the corresponding punch behind the buttplate; however,

is the jump in felt recoil as a result of using these high-velocity shotshells really all that noticeable? To the heavily garbed waterfowler who shoots but eight rounds during the course of a day's hunt, or to the grouse hunter who fires four shotshells while afield, the answer stands a good 99 percent chance of being no. Conversely, ask the trapshooter who goes through 200 of these 1,300 fps rounds in an afternoon, 50 of which are

The author approaches an Iowa red fox taken with a Winchester Super X2 and high-velocity 3-inch #2s.

Lighter or less dense than lead or any of the existing federally-approved non-toxic alternatives, steel pellets must be driven faster in order to provide and retain sufficient energy – or at least in this case, energy values which approximate that of the other alternatives.

the Italian *Baschieri* and *Pellagri Ultra-Velocity* shotshells that rush out of the muzzle at 1,400 fps, and he's going to say – Yes, I do notice it.

The final consideration, or rather price to pay, in this high-velocity equation is payload. Explained, it's simpler to push a lighter object to a set speed than it is to push a heavier object to the same speed. To address this, ammunition manufacturers have downsized shot charges in order to achieve increased velocity. The two simply go hand-in-hand. For instance, Winchester's Supreme line of turkey loads offer a 3-inch, 12-gauge round with 2 ounces of #5 at 1,125 fps, while the same hull in a high-velocity – 1,300 fps – format packs 1-3/4 ounces. True, that's but a difference of 42 pellets; however, when only six or eight of those #5s in the right place will do the job just fine, then this smaller payload becomes a significant variable.

Why not, some might ask, opt for a larger pellet instead of increased velocity? Say, upsizing from #2 steel to BB? Yes, the larger pellet with its greater mass and with velocities equal, will have more foot/pounds of energy; however, increasing pellet size in order to increase energy does the same thing to payload as does downsizing the shot charge to gain speed. In both cases, pellet count decreases. Myself? I'd much rather have 142 pellets (1-1/8 ounce) of #2 steel hustling along at 1,550 fps than 96 steel #BBs (1-3/8 ounce) moving at 1,350 fps. True, the #BBs have, at 40 yards, approximately 50 percent more foot/pounds of energy – roughly 7 foot/pounds versus 4 foot/pounds – than do the steel #2s; *however*, there are approximately 50 percent <u>more</u> pellets in the #2 load. That's almost 50 additional pellets, each possessing 4 foot/pounds of energy at 40 yards, which have the potential to impact the target. And I'll take multiple hits

with sufficient retained energy, such as was shown here, over single hits with greater foot/pounds, any day.

Steel and speed

Given this background, along with a comparison between the densities of lead and steel pellets – 10.9 grams per cubic centimeter for the former, 7.8 g/cc for the latter – it becomes understandable when one hears the comment that high-velocity shotshells were made for steel shot. It only makes sense. Lighter or less dense than lead or any of the existing federally-approved non-toxic alternatives, steel pellets must be driven faster in order to provide and retain sufficient energy – or at least in this case, energy values which approximate that of the other alternatives. Short of increasing these velocities, the only option available is upsizing the individual pellets and we've already addressed the shortcoming of bigger pellets and their correspondingly decreased pellet counts.

All this leaves us with two questions. First, how, if at all, does an increase in velocity influence patterns? What about high-velocity lead shotshells? Is a quick-stepping lead load really all that necessary?

The answer to Question One is nebulous; that is, velocity can influence patterns, but an increase in velocity doesn't necessary translate into altered patterns, better or worse. To explain. The non-toxics are tremendously hard. Steel, for example, is roughly 10 times as hard as lead. Tungsten-iron is more than 20 times harder than lead. The remaining non-toxics – bismuth, Hevi-Shot, and tungsten-matrix – are all either as hard or harder than their toxic predecessor. What all this means is a lack of pellet deformation. When a shotshell is fired, setback occurs; that is, the violent transition from no motion to speeds in excess of 1,500 fps forces the pellets, which make up a shot charge, together just as your head would be thrown back against the seat at the launch of a Top-Fuel dragster. This violence within the shotshell hull can cause the individual pellets to become deformed, and deformed pellets typically don't fly true. The result? A *blown* pattern. Such patterns commonly exhibit holes or gaps, often with multiple fringe hits or fliers, and are poor performers, both on the range and in the field. However, because these non-toxics are so incredibly hard, deformation is almost non-existent.

Question Two, likewise, is somewhat arbitrary. Minus buffering and modern, high-tech, protective shot cups, soft traditional lead pellets pushed at above standard velocities had a very good chance of emerging from the muzzle looking more like Frisbees than spheres – and it's a task to get 150 Frisbees to fly in the same general direction

while maintaining some semblance of symmetry. Today, however, specialized wads combined with hard-plated – nickel or copper is most common – lead shot have all but eliminated radical pellet deformation.

Good news, but it still doesn't answer the question about the need for speed with lead shotshells. In the case of quicker lead loads, there are probably two points of order. One, any increase in retained energy is a good thing, as long as it doesn't come at too high a price such as increased recoil or radically decreased payload/pellet count. And secondly, the fact that a jump in velocity can afford some forgiveness in terms of reaction time and lead is also a positive. Significantly so with lead? Perhaps not, but as a good friend of mine says, "All shotgun shooting is, to a large extent, psychological." If, then, speed is a variable in the equation that is confidence behind the buttplate, then more power to you.

> *Today, however, specialized wads combined with hard-plated – nickel or copper is most common – lead shot have all but eliminated radical pellet deformation.*

Famed call maker and decoy designer, Fred Zink, believes in the benefits of high-velocity ammunition for today's waterfowler.

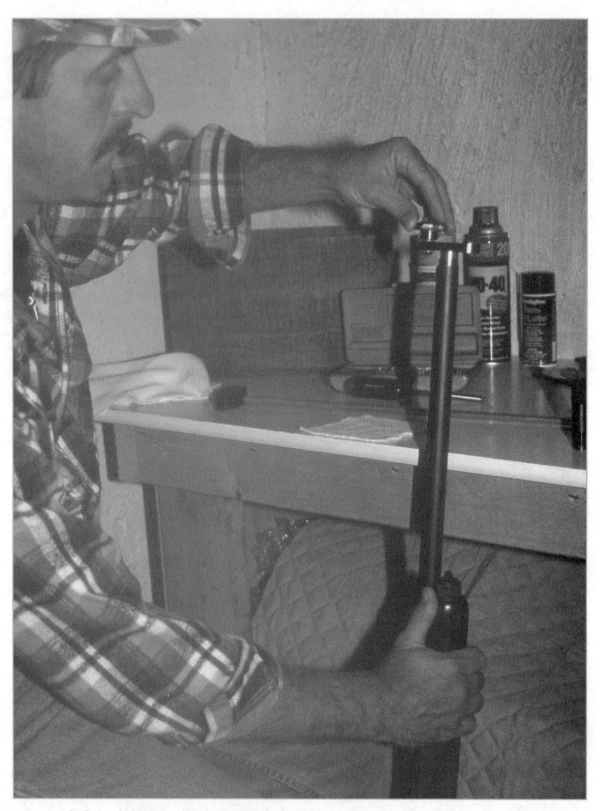

Don't overlook the chokes tubes. Brush the threads clean with a soft toothbrush and apply a very light coat of silicon or Teflon.

Shaking Down your Shotgun

By M.D. Johnson

My father had, and has to this day, a very simple theory when it comes to firearm maintenance. "If you take it into the field, it gets wiped down," he'd say at the end of the day's hunt. "If you shoot it, even once, it gets broken down and cleaned." How often, some would ask. And it was here that my father's Czechoslovakian heritage would shine. "If you take it into the field…" Never did I hear him finish the statement a second time.

Over the 28 years since my first fox squirrel, I've seen both ends of the gun-cleaning spectrum and everything in between. Some, like my father, take his cleaning ritual to what many would consider an extreme; however, today, he's still shooting the same Remington Model 1100 autoloader that he purchased in 1972, complete with, as he's very fond of saying, the original O-ring. At the other end of the line, there are those who consider shotgun maintenance to be an annual event, much like the outdoor writer – yes, I said the outdoor writer – who in all sincerity said that he cleaned his shotgun once a year. "Whether it needs it or not," he said. And if I remember correctly, that comment came just before his complaining about that so-and-so autoloader that just wouldn't cycle properly. Any wonder, what with 365 days worth of, as my father called it,

crud and corruption hiding in amongst the workings?

Fortunately for everyone who takes a shotgun into the field or onto the trap range, shotgun cleaning and maintenance before, during, and after the shooting event doesn't have to rank logistically with the launching of the space shuttle. In fact, there are only three things that hunters and shooters need to know in order to keep their favorite scattergun looking good and performing at its best – what to clean it with, how to clean it, and how to put it away. Knowing these three things, there's absolutely no reason why a 30-year-old shotgun like my father's shouldn't look as good as a three-year-old. Here, age really doesn't matter; it's all in how well the gun ages.

A selection of gun care products from Birchwood-Casey makes shotgun maintenance easy.

URBANDALE PUBLIC LIBRARY
3520 86TH STREET
URBANDALE, IA 50322-4056

While screwdrivers may only come into play occasionally during routine shotgun maintenance, they're indispensable nonetheless for performing the proverbial 1,001 other jobs that will inevitably come up during the process.

THE ULTIMATE GUN-CLEANING KIT

Putting together an effective cleaning kit is neither difficult nor expensive; in fact, just the opposite is true. And once compiled and organized, a good kit will, with minor periodic refurbishings, last for the life of both the gun and the shooter. Or in the case of some traditional, hand-me-down wooden cleaning rods, longer than either one.

Tools and other implements

As mentioned earlier, the tools that go into the ultimate gun cleaning kit aren't many, but they're important, both to the success of the task, as well as to the ease with which the job's completed. And as we all know, easy jobs are also the most likely to be started and finished with regularity.

For starters, the kit needs a good, quality set of screwdrivers. While screwdrivers may only come into play occasionally during routine shotgun maintenance, they're indispensable nonetheless for performing the proverbial 1,001 other jobs that will inevitably come up during the process. The set in my personal kit is designed by the folks at B-Square in Fort Worth, Texas, and comes complete with an excellent selection of flathead, Phillips, and hex head tips, all of which are magnetic – a plus when working with small screws and bolts – and which fit into a comfortable and very durable handle.

Next are the cleaning rods, patches, and brushes. When I was growing up, the same man who taught me that every time a shotgun was fired it also was disassembled and cleaned thoroughly would have worn a purple nightgown on the opening day of duck season rather than use anything but a wooden cleaning rod. Today, however, wooden shotgun cleaning rods are more often seen in the hunting memorabilia collections of traditional gunners than they are around the cleaning table. Most have been replaced by sturdy, breakdown versions made of light steel or aluminum, or in some cases, strong and very unbreakable synthetics such as Kevlar or graphite. Regardless of the style, a cleaning rod should (1) break down into easily-transported sections that can be either carried in the hunting vehicle or taken on an out-of-town hunting trip as well as used at home, (2) have a strong, secure handle that won't twist or

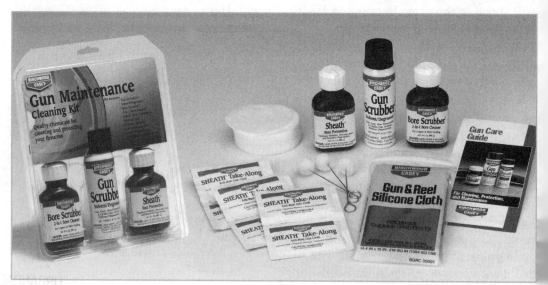

A complete shotgun maintenance system from Birchwood-Casey.

torque, (3) feature half-inch-minimum threads and sockets for strength and resistence to bending in use, and (4) have a selection of compatible needle tips and brass brushes. The needle tips are used with patches, usually soft cotton pieces of fabric torn from old tee-shirts, or, better yet, old thermal underwear, while the brass brushes are employed when heavy duty cleanings like the removal of powder or wadding build-up in the barrel, breech, or on the bolt face becomes necessary.

In my kit, I keep a selection of solvents and lubricants, each used depending on the time of year and the in-the-field conditions. For hunt-to-hunt cleanings and routine maintenance, WD-40 works wonders, both as a rust inhibitor and as a lubricant. During cold weather, however, when WD-40 occasionally has a tendency to gum up and impede cycling, I'll switch to what I'll call an "oxymoron oil," Remington's Rem Dri-Lube. This spray-on lubricant goes on dry, hence the name, and contains Teflon, which creates an invisible almost frictionless barrier between the metal workings of my autoloader and keeps the gun operating flawlessly even in below zero temperatures. And for that end-of-the-year-cleaning, I'll switch gears and use a penetrating catalyst, a group of synthetics into which the popular Liquid Wrench falls. These penetrating lubricants get into every nook and cranny, and literally flush any accumulated unburnt powder and other residues from the gun's interior. It may sound like overkill, but it all goes back to having the right tool for the job at hand.

Under accessories, I have several items, beginning with a small selection of brass drifts and punches. These are used to remove pins and studs, such as the pair of trigger group pins on my Remington 11-87. To accompany the

drifts and punches, I have a small hard-plastic hammer and a short section of one-half-inch soft pine board, both of which can and are used interchangeably for removal and reinstallation of pins and in any cases where a little extra persuasion might be called for. Three different toothbrushes – soft, medium, and extra hard bristle – get called on to remove debris from hard-to-reach places, as well as to extract the mud that inevitably gets into the checkering during each and every waterfowl hunt. My kit also contains a piece of fine grade steel wool, an excellent tool for removing the burnt powder and gas residues which form periodically around the O-ring collar of my 11-87, as well as a zip-lock bag filled with cotton swabs, themselves used for any one of a million different gun cleaning projects.

SHOTGUN CLEANING 101 – 201 – 301

The trick to successful shotgun cleaning, if there indeed is one, is to make the task as easy as possible. Doing so not only changes the task from a chore to a process, but by making the cleaning routine simpler and more convenient, you as

In my kit, I keep a selection of solvents and lubricants, each used depending on the time of year and the in-the-field conditions.

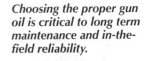

Choosing the proper gun oil is critical to long term maintenance and in-the-field reliability.

Lightweight portable gun "wipes" making in-the-field cleaning a snap.

a shooter are more likely to do the job – and do it right – on a much more regular and thorough basis. It's just human nature.

Essentially, shotgun cleaning can be broken down into three segments or time periods: pre-season cleaning, the seasonal cleaning that takes place throughout the spring or fall, and post-season or pre-storage cleaning; however, just like you didn't walk right out of grade school into college, there's more to shotgun cleaning than just, well, cleaning.

Know your firearm

The basic concept when working with anything mechanical is first learning how the machine works. And knowing how it works depends on knowing each of the parts and the role that each plays in the proper function of that machine. Shotguns are nothing more than machines, and are certainly no different in this respect from a computer or an automobile.

With this in mind, the first step is for you to get to know your shotgun, inside and out. If you're unfamiliar with how your shotgun works and what that little "do-hickey under that carrier thing" is and what it does, just break down – we won't tell anyone – and get the owner's manual. Using the manual as a guide, disassemble the gun only to the point as instructed in the literature for routine cleaning. Going any further, such as breaking down bolts or attempting to disassemble trigger groups is often

A quick "punch" with a cleaning rod and oily rag is all it takes to maintain the interior of any shotgun barrel.

not only unnecessary, but can be very frustrating if not embarrassing when you find yourself forced to walk into the gunsmith's shop carrying a stock and barrel in one hand and a paper sack filled with parts in the other. Once you've learned how your shotgun works and what the different parts are and do, it's easy then to recognize those parts that need more cleaning attention than do others. And in time, this knowledge will make the task easier, and that's what we're striving for.

Before, during, and after

While pre-season cleaning may at first seem unnecessary, there are several good reasons for the process. First, it allows the opportunity to check on the gun's condition during storage. This is particularly important in humid climates where moisture can invade even the strongest storage protection system, causing rust and generally bad things to occur. Secondly, a good cleaning just prior to the season opener can serve as a check-all for those unexplainable things such as loose or missing screws, beads, pins, plugs, rings, and other parts, the loss of which is typically attributed to the all-too-familiar storage gremlin, when in reality it is the result of poor or lacking maintenance. And finally, a pre-season check provides an irresistible excuse for taking the gun out to the trap or skeet range or sporting clays course, and shaking loose the off-season cobwebs from both gun and gunner.

It's my suggestion that gun cleaning during the hunting

Gun Scrubber, a Birchwood-Casey gun care product, is an excellent way to start the cleaning process.

With gas-operated autoloaders like this 11-87, it's important to give attention to the gas ports during the cleaning process.

Take down or disassemble your shotgun only as much as you need to give it a good, thorough cleaning.

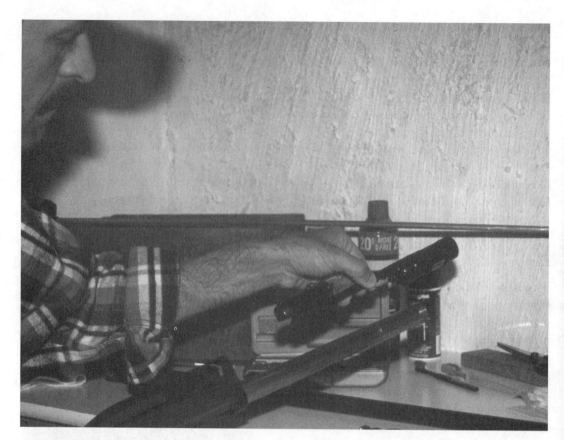

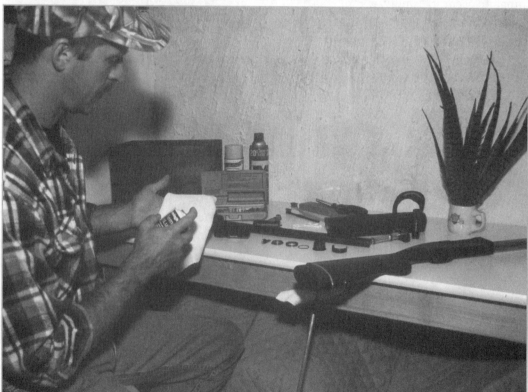

Don't overdo it on the gun oil, regardless of the type you're using. A little goes a long way.

season should be scheduled according to my father's credo of "taken out - wiped down; fired - broken down and cleaned." The reason most shotguns are neglected during the hunting season is simple. There's just too many things to do, what with hunting all day, meals, game cleaning, and work or, better yet, another hunting trip, the next day. Too often, the shotgun gets placed in the corner and left until the next time, and in some cases, that next time might be a week or longer into the future. Because of this tendency to procrastinate when it comes to gun cleaning, it's best to include the maintenance aspect into the whole of the hunting routine. Personally, my day only ends when the guns are cleaned and properly stored. If the shotgun du jour wasn't fired during the day, then it's a simple matter to go over the piece with a lightly lubricated cloth, after which the gun's stored in its case. If there was some shooting, then the shotgun's broken down, the barrel cleaned or "punched out," and all of the working parts disassembled, cleaned, and reassembled.

A toothbrush is an indispensable piece of cleaning equipment.

It's a tough habit to get into, but once established, the cleaning routine becomes just that – routine.

Throughout the season, different weather conditions will call for different types of cleaning. Warm, dry weather is easy, as typically all that's required is either a simple wipe-down or break-down and routine cleaning. In wet weather, however, the gun must first be towel-

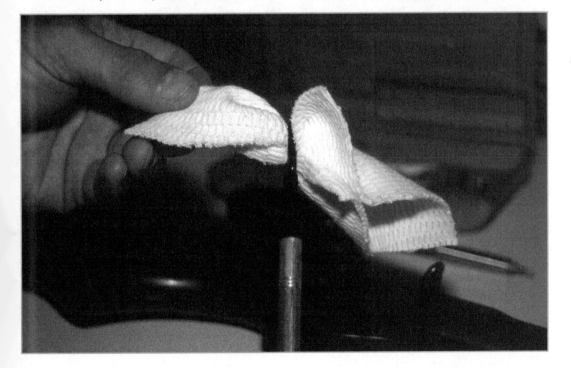

Whether it's wood or metal, make sure the cleaning rod you buy is of good quality. The same goes for the tips and other accessories.

A small, lightweight field cleaning kit is a good idea for the traveling shotgunner.

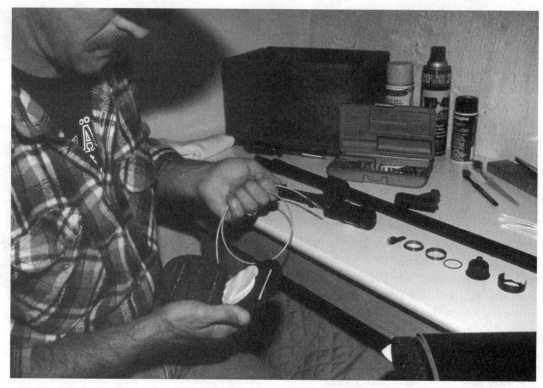

dried, and disassembled, fired or not, in order to ensure that all the water has been removed. Cold temperatures call for a slightly different technique, one which my father called sweating. When cold steel meets the warm temperatures in your home, condensation forms, just like the water droplets that form on the outside of a glass of iced tea in the summertime. Because of this, shotguns brought out of the cold should be left to sweat, or increase in temperature to match that of their surroundings. Once this happens, the gun can be wiped down, broken down, and cleaned.

The act of shotgun cleaning itself is in reality a simple matter. The secret, if there is one, is to perform the process the same way each time. When cleaning my Remington Model 11-87 autoloader, for instance, first the fore-end, the gas cylinder collar, and barrel are removed, followed by the O-ring and the gas pistons. Then the operating handle is pulled from the bolt, and the action bar

assembly with the bolt is pulled from the breech. Should weather or time of year dictate an in-depth cleaning, both trigger group pins are punched out, and the trigger group along with the link are removed. As each is removed, it's placed on a clean white towel. After each part is cleaned, the shotgun's reassembled. Monotonous? Perhaps, but this method allows not only a complete and thorough cleaning, but provides me with the opportunity to visually check each major operating part for signs of wear, a step that on more than one occasion has saved me from a hunt-ending breakdown or malfunction.

Year-end cleaning involves little more than a final in-depth going-over as the shotgun's prepared for long-term storage. With my 11-87, this means that the trigger group, trigger group pins, bolt, gas pistons, and gas cylinder collar all go into the dishwasher with a little bit of Calgon and a whole lot of the hottest water I can get out of our water heater.

Once finished, the parts are removed and given a final drying, with both the bolt and the trigger group getting the once-over with a hair dryer to make sure all the water has been forced from the smallest nooks and crannies. Now dry, each part is wiped with a clean, soft rag saturated with WD-40. The barrel is punched out and lubricated inside and out, and the gas ports reamed with a pipe cleaner to remove any powder residue. Before reassembly, the magazine tube and the breech – again, in and out – are wiped down and likewise lubricated. Once fully assembled, the entire shotgun is again wiped down, including the stock and fore-end. It's been my experience that a light coat of WD-40 on both stock and fore-end during the season and prior to storage helps prevent drying and cracking, and has had no ill effects on the color of the wood; however, some expensive woods might be discolored by such a process.

Shotguns prepared using the end-of-the-year method described above are ready to go into storage; however, many questions are raised about how and where such guns should be stored. After such a detailed cleaning, our firearms are slipped into a silicone-impregnated gun sock – I make my own by purchasing inexpensive camouflage gun covers, putting them in a zip-lock bag, and misting the bag full of WD-40. Shaking the bag every half-hour for two to three hours ensures complete coverage – and stored in a hard-sided, locking gun case, two guns per case. Into the case, I place a clean, folded rag that has been lightly sprayed with WD-40, as well as two or three packets of crystal silica gel. Both the rag and the gel absorb any moisture that may get into the case, while the gun sock provides a final layer of protection. The cases are then stored in a dehumidified room that can be temperature-controlled during periods of radical weather fluctuations or in cases of high humidity. Once every two months during the off-season, the guns are checked, and the cases marked with the date of the inspection.

Is it a lot of meaningless, Type-A work and worry? I don't think so, but if anyone needs a little more convincing as to the validity and importance of these routines, there's a 20-year-old 16 gauge Remington 1100 in the closet that looks as good today as it did in 1979 when my father bought it for me. And, yes, it's in a sock.

Before reassembly, the magazine tube and the breech – again, in and out – are wiped down and likewise lubricated.

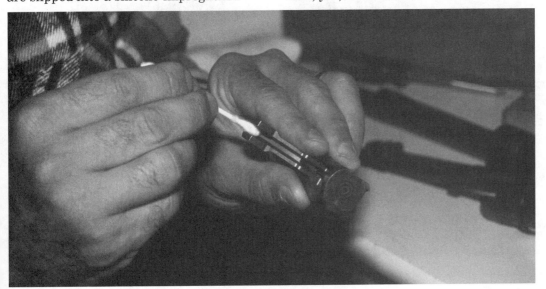

Like a toothbrush, a supply of cotton swabs should be included in your shotgun cleaning equipment.

Dove hunting often requires lots of shooting. Controlling recoil helps you ease the impact on your shoulder.

Taming the Recoil Tiger

By M.D. Johnson

I'll never forget the day the young man – a strong strapping construction worker, mind you – brought the pump gun to the house. Boy howdy, but he was proud of his new Mossberg 835. Chambered for the latest and greatest, the 3-1/2-inch 12-gauge shotshell, the fellow was certain that this was THE turkey gun. "Let's go out back and shoot it," he said. I didn't have to be asked twice.

Okay, so to make a long story short ... If I remember correctly, the first round out of the muzzle elicited something that to me sounded like, "Man, that was rough." The second, however, came with a grunt of mixed pain and surprise. Oh, and a bloody nose. "Youth wanna thoot this," the young man asked, the gun in one hand, and the other reaching for the hanky in his back pocket. I declined.

Let's face it. Unless you're related to the Marquis de Sade', recoil isn't fun. By definition, recoil relates to Mister Issac Newton's Third Law of Motion, which says for every action, there is an equal *and* opposite reaction. With a firearm, this translates into one simple fact – The same amount of energy, measured in foot/pounds, going out the muzzle is also simultaneously being directed at you, the shooter. Or rather, your shoulder. Welcome to Recoil!

Let's take a quick look at some numbers in order to put this concept of recoil and what can be done about it in perspective. At the muzzle, a one-ounce Winchester rifled shotgun slug with a muzzle velocity of 1,600 feet-per-second (FPS) will generate 2,700 foot/pounds of energy. That's more than a ton of energy which, because it's going forward, is required to also go backwards; that is, in your direction. However, true recoil energy, or the foot/pounds of energy felt at your shoulder when you fire this shotgun slug is only going to be roughly 32 foot/pounds. That's still quite the jolt, but without question much better than 2,700 pounds! Where did the energy go? In this most elemental example, it's the

Changing to a smaller gauge – a 20-gauge for a 12, for example – is an obvious and often effective recoil reducing strategy.

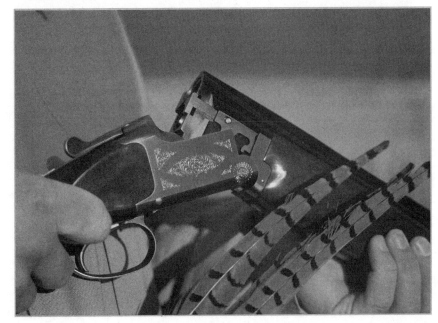

Subject yourself to such abuse on a regular basis, and over time, this constant recoil can result in serious injury, including back and neck problems, hearing loss, and nerve damage.

weight of the gun alone – here, a shotgun weighing approximately 8.5 pounds – as compared to the weight or mass of the shotshell itself that helps eliminate or absorb almost 85 percent of the energy produced upon firing the gun; however, we'll come back to that in a moment.

But before you get too excited about this 85-percent reduction, let's look at a couple other things. Yes, 32 foot/pounds *is* substantially less than 2,700; however, to the target shooter who may fire 100 rounds in the course of an afternoon, or the dove hunter who fires 50 shotshells to reach his limit, this repeated pounding is going to add up. Subject yourself to such abuse on a regular basis, and over time, this constant recoil can result in serious injury, including back and neck problems, hearing loss, and nerve damage. Finally, and while the 32 foot/pounds figure is at the high-end for most target shotgun shooters, it's relatively sedate when compared to the higher-payload, high-velocity rounds commonly used in the field by waterfowlers and turkey hunters. Throw a muzzleloader packed with 150 grains of Pyrodex or a

.30-06 pushing a 180-grain bullet into the mix, and this 32 foot/pounds is going to quickly fade into the distance.

Okay, the mathematics lesson is over and recoil a reality, what can be done about it? Actually, there are several things that hunters and shooters can do to decrease the punch they feel at their shoulders. Some, such as those involving physically modifying or altering the barrel, are a bit more drastic, and costly, than are some of the other options; however, whether simple or complicated, all are possible of taming the tiger that is recoil while dramatically increasing a very important factor on the end opposite the muzzle – the Enjoyment Factor.

Shoot an autoloader

As we talked about earlier, the recoil you feel at your shoulder is a direct result of the energy going out the barrel. Now, just imagine if you could bleed some of that energy off *before* it exited the muzzle? Or more precisely, use some of that energy to your benefit as opposed to your punishment? That's exactly what a gas-operated firearm does. A gas-operated semi-automatic shotgun such as Remington's Model 1100, a personal favorite of mine and a well-entrenched fixture among the nation's target and field shooters, actually uses a portion of the gas pressure generated upon firing to cycle the action; that is, to eject the spent shotshell and ready the next in the chamber. The fact that a portion of this pressure or energy is used to operate the action means less energy exiting the barrel. And this translates into a decrease in felt recoil.

A word of warning – not all gas-operated autoloaders are created equal in terms of recoil. A seven-pound 20-gauge semi-auto shooting high-velocity waterfowl loads will make you stand up

Few things "kick" like blackpowder shotguns; however, some simple strategies can help tame even the toughest shooters.

and take notice much more so than will a 9.5-pound 12-gauge filled with relatively slow (1,300 FPS) one-ounce field loads. Just because a shotgun is gas-operated *doesn't* always mean it's also low recoil. The physical weight of the gun plays a primary role, as does the type of ammunition being used.

Switch ammunition

While we're on the subject of ammunition, here's another variable that can be changed in order to lessen recoil. High-velocity shotshells, or those in excess of roughly 1,300 FPS, by virtue of the speed generated are going to produce more felt recoil than will a traditional trap or field load traveling at, say, 1,100 to 1,200 FPS. Heavier payloads too, be they larger shot charges or bigger bullets, will also have more punch due to the power or pressures needed for these rounds to perform efficiently

That said, it becomes easy to see that by simply changing the ammunition you shoot – slower shotshells or lighter loads and bullets – can and will help save your shoulder. TIP – Always match the shotshell, rifle cartridge, or

muzzleloading projectile to the game. There's no need to shoot a .416 Rigby at whitetails or 3.5-inch 12-gauge BBs at bunnies. Your body will thank you for doing neither.

Add a recoil pad

Aside from switching to a slower and/or lighter type of ammunition, one of the easiest and most effective methods for decreasing recoil is through the use of a good – *key word: good* – recoil pad. Though many of today's shotguns come from the factory with better than 10 years ago recoil pads, they still often leave much to be desired, particularly for those shooting large bore big-game cartridges or heavy waterfowl or turkey loads.

Two excellent after-market recoil pads, both suggested by a high-volume shotgunning friend, are the Kick-Eez (417-649-2100) and the Pachmayr Decelerator (800-225-9626). Unless you're skilled in the art, installation and final shaping of the Kick-Eez pads must be done by a trained gunsmith; however, the Decelerator is available in any one of several pre-fit forms designed

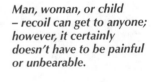

That said, it becomes easy to see that by simply changing the ammunition you shoot – slower shotshells or lighter loads and bullets – can and will help save your shoulder.

Man, woman, or child – recoil can get to anyone; however, it certainly doesn't have to be painful or unbearable.

A smaller gauge – 20 or 28, for example – where applicable, can prove the first step in reducing recoil.

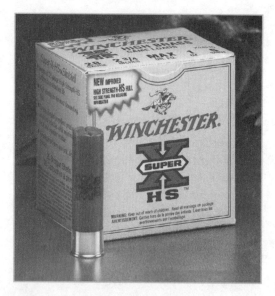

for many of today's more popular firearms, each of which can be installed with a screwdriver in a few minutes.

Modify the barrel

For most shooters, switching ammunition or installing a recoil pad will work wonders; however, if you're quite

Young Gordon Bourjaily, and hunting buddy, Ike, with a light recoiling 20-gauge Youth Model fitted with a quality pad.

serious about taking this recoil issue to the next level, then perhaps a physical change to the firearm itself is in line. Today, there are three primary categories when it comes to barrel modifications and recoil.

1. Lengthening the forcing cone – The forcing cone is the gradual taper inside a shotgun barrel from the chamber to the bore proper. Lengthening this cone allows for a gentler constriction of the shot charge over a greater distance, thus – theoretically – lessening the abrupt *jolt* felt when the charge squeezes into the narrower space.

2. Enlarging the bore – This refers to increasing the inside diameter of the shotgun bore itself, and as does lengthening the forcing cone, helps decrease that initial jolt.

3. Porting – Porting is a process by which a series of small holes are drilled into the final inch or two of the barrel at the muzzle. These holes allow a portion of the escaping gases to bleed off in a direction other than forward.

Unfortunately, and while Methods 1 and 2 do indeed help reduce felt recoil, their influence is subtle to the point of meaning little to the casual shooter. The 100-round per day trapshooter? Yes. The fellow who shoots 10 rounds all day from a goose pit? Probably not. As for porting, its primary function is to suppress muzzle jump, or the quick rise in the barrel upon firing, thus allowing the shooter to remain on target for a quick second or third shot. Where porting does make a difference in terms of recoil is to the cheek or face – a definite plus for those who enjoy their teeth right where the Good Lord put them.

Change your clothes

Finally, there's absolutely nothing wrong with putting a little extra padding between the buttplate and your shoulder. After all, we're not all built like Mister Schwarzenegger. Sighting in your .30-06 for your first elk hunt? A sandbag or shot-bag minus a portion of the pellets can help soak up quite a bit of the abuse handed out during your time on the range. For you mobile dove or early-season waterfowlers, there's the PAST recoil shield (877-509-9160), a thin suede-like pad that straps onto your chest not unlike a shoulder holster. I've worn a PAST for the past two seasons while patterning hard-hitting turkey shotguns, and walked away from even lengthy sessions unscathed.

Unless Mister Newton comes back and revises his Third Law of Motion, recoil is going to be something that shooters will have to deal with indefinitely.

Fortunately, there are ways of taming the tiger, and knocking those foot/pounds of energy down to a much more manageable level.

Proper clothing and pads can make an extended day at the patterning range much less painful, particularly for turkey hunters or slug shooters.

It's not just ladies and young folk who are susceptible to recoil. Newton's Law affects all shooters.

Adrian McClellan exchanges one tube for another during an in-depth patterning session prior to turkey season.

Choke Tubes:
Putting the *Squeeze* On

By M.D. Johnson

I can see it like it was yesterday. Hell, this morning. A too-short boy with a too-long gun was standing waist deep in a northeastern Ohio beaver swamp. Head down. Gun tracking. Later, as they retrieved the bird, the man remarked that given the variables of distance, inexperience, and the world's worst case of gun fit, he figured that hen mallard to be about the safest bird on the planet.

"It was all of 75 yards," the man mentioned to John Shafer, proprietor of Shafer's Tavern, all the while contemplating his traditional post-hunt Pabst Blue Ribbon. "Maybe 80. Would have never believed it, but I was standing right next to the boy."

That was 24 years ago. The boy? Well, that was me. And that too-long gun? A Mossberg Model 500 pump. Purchased at a sporting goods store in Salt Lake City, Utah, in 1966, the shotgun was my father's gift to himself in part, I believe, for surviving 13 months as Uncle Sam's guest in Southeast Asia.

But what made this particular shotgun so unique is not so much its history, though there is quite a bit of that, but instead a 3.5-inch black bulge on the muzzle. Reading simply "Poly-Choke" in gold-embossed cursive writing, the adjustable ported unit offered the shooter – me – one of six different levels of construction ranging

from slug to improved-modified to that ultimate game-getter, X-Full. Back then, there were no choke tubes. No choke tube wrenches. No little carrying cases with the snap-tight closures and compartmentalized foam-lined interiors. Everything, every choke change that was deemed necessary, was accomplished in less than three seconds and with few tools other than five fingers and a twist of the wrist. Did it work? Well, sure it worked. Certainly with such a device screwed down to X-Full, even a 75-yard

A selection of choke tubes from noted manufacturer, Briley Manufacturing, of Houston, Texas.

mallard wasn't safe. Or was that 80 yards?

Today, my father's Poly-Choke is all but a thing of the past. Gone the route of hang-on automobile air conditioner, the Poly-Choke and its high-roller brother, the Deluxe Poly-Choke, though still manufactured by the folks at Marble Arms in Gladstone, Michigan, are very seldom seen either in the field or on the trap range. This is not surprising given the recent generations that have placed as much emphasis on looks as they have on performance. The unsightly "dog turd at the end of the barrel" – boy, I hated that Poly-Choke – has been replaced by more aesthetically pleasing, streamlined internal choke tubes, tins of Tube Lube, and fancy ergonomically designed choke tube wrenches.

But regardless of whether the operation requires the flick of a wrist or the twist of a wrench, chokes are today as much a subject of discussion and controversy – and, yes, even a little mystery and intrigue – as they were in the days of legendary market hunter and duck shootist, Fred Kimble, some 100 years ago. Hopefully, the words that follow will help take a little grey out of the choke scene and make it just a little more black and white.

Chokes 101

In its simplest, most easily understood form, a shotgun's choke, be it an integrated choke – that is, a permanent part of the barrel – or an interchangeable choke tube, can be perhaps best compared to the nozzle on a garden hose. At its most open setting, water passing through the nozzle emerges in a wide spray. Twisting the nozzle head, or decreasing the size of the hole through which the water flows, results in the water exiting the nozzle not in a spray, but in a stream. Both spray and stream travel the same distance; however, where the water spray may measure two feet in diameter at a given distance from the nozzle, the water stream may at the

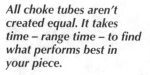

All choke tubes aren't created equal. It takes time – range time – to find what performs best in your piece.

same distance measure only six inches. This example, where water-shot pellets and nozzle-choke are one and the same, provides the basis for an explanation on chokes and their function.

That said, an obvious question arises concerning the importance of this action. Better yet, why would something like this be desirable? Again, the answer is quite simple. It all goes back to the fact that the shotgun is a short-range firearm designed to distribute a pattern or spread of pellets over a large, and hopefully game-encompassing, area. By squeezing or constricting this group of pellets before they ever left the barrel, shooters hoped to slow the inevitable spread of the shot. Doing so accomplished two things: first, it created denser patterns at greater distances, thus increasing the effective range of the piece. It's one thing, shooters thought, to have pellets with energy enough to break a clay target or cleanly harvest a mallard; however, if there were three feet of space between each of the pellets at 40 yards, the odds of a pellet-and-duck encounter were iffy at best. Chokes, then, were an effort to lessen this pellet-to-pellet distance. Secondly, these denser patterns often resulted in multiple hits on-target, which in turn increased the shotgun's efficiency as a harvester of winged fowl.

Today, as was the case in the mid-1800s when chokes and choke development were first given any serious consideration, the degree of choke that a particular shotgun or tube provides is determined by the percentage of the total number of shot pellets contained in a particular shot charge which fall within a 30-inch circle located 40 yards from the shooter. Traditionally, the chart has read as such – 35 to 45 percent, cylinder bore; 45 to 55 percent, improved cylinder; 55 to 65 percent, modified; and 65 to

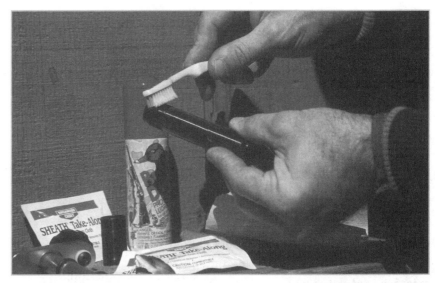

Choke tube maintenance is sorely overlooked by many shotgunners today. A quick brush and light oiling is all that's necessary.

75 percent, full choke. Here, obviously, cylinder bore is the least constricted; full, the most. In translation, a shotshell containing one ounce of #5 lead shot holds approximately 170 pellets. If 105, or 62 percent of the total number of pellets, were to print inside that 30-inch circle at 40 yards, this then would be considered a modified choke.

In addition to shot percentages, the degree of constriction or choke can, although less commonly so than the traditional improved, modified, and full classifications, also be designated as a measurement, where this measurement indicates the inside diameter (ID) of the shotgun muzzle at the choke. For example, a traditional 12-gauge barrel, choked cylinder or open bore, would measure approximately .730 inches. In contrast, a full choke will read .695 to .700 inches. By way of comparison, some of today's tightest or most constrictive turkey choke tubes will measure .655 inch – a reading that gives an entirely new meaning to the concept of full chokes!

The influence of ammunition

As much as it may like to, choke and choke alone cannot take full credit

> *By squeezing or constricting this group of pellets before they ever left the barrel, shooters hoped to slow the inevitable spread of the shot.*

Finding the proper combination of choke and shotshell is a matter of range time and patterning. It's a necessity.

for shotgun pattern performance. Ammunition, or rather the recent improvements in ammunition design and manufacture, plays a major role in just what happens 40 yards downrange each time the trigger is pulled. Copper plating shot, for instance, allows soft lead pellets to resist deformation during firing. And ballistically speaking, a round pellet flies much truer than do those with flattened edges, surfaces that can catch the wind, acting much like a

wing and causing the pellet or pellets to veer right or left of center. Wads, too, have assisted in preserving the original shape of the individual pellets within a shot charge, not only by preventing shot-to-barrel contact to a greater degree, but also by serving as a vastly improved cushion or shock absorber designed to keep the pellets' spherical form intact. Specially formulated powdered buffers, more efficient propellants and primers – these advancements in shotshell design, along with the help of a choke tube and the abilities or inabilities of the person behind the butt plate, are what determine the end result some 120 feet away.

Turkey tubes: Trial and error

Few shotgunners would argue that turkey hunting has done more for the design and development of the modern specialized choke tube – hunting tube, that is – than has any event, before

Perhaps some of the most specialized choke tubes available today are those designed for turkey hunters.

or since. Not satisfied with what the shotgun manufacturers touted as full chokes, turkey hunters – although many were as much inventor as they were hunter – began experimenting, most looking to determine the extent to which a shotshell charge could be constricted before that charge demonstrated any adverse effects such as blotchy or odd-shaped patterns.

Almost immediately, problems began to show themselves. In truth, the problem was two-fold, entailing both pellet deformation and, for lack of a better phrase, pellet alignment. The dilemma itself was simple. Upon reaching the start of the constriction or choke, the soft lead pellets were violently squeezed into a much smaller area. This compacting of pellets often resulted in pellet deformation, and as was mentioned earlier, pellets which are out-of-round display a tendency to fly erratically. The second part of the problem, pellet alignment, had to do with the fact that a portion of the pellets in the shot charge were still jostling for position in this recently-altered package even as they left the muzzle. This movement, combined with the aforementioned pellet deformation, often resulted in patterns that looked more like a random placement of fly specks on an old window than they did an effective harvester of wild turkeys.

Fortunately, the solution was as elemental as was the problem – constrict the shot charge more gradually and over a greater distance, <u>and</u> allow the individual pellets to realign themselves within the charge <u>before</u> exiting the muzzle. Armed with this new information, designers began to both lengthen and taper the choke's forcing cone – the point at which the choke actually begins to affect the shot charge – in an effort to reduce the severity of what had been a sudden and very dramatic change in the shot charge. Too, more thought was given to that section of the choke immediately following the constriction, and it was soon found that by extending this parallel or non-constricted portion of the choke, pellets were afforded the opportunity to realign themselves fully <u>before</u> the charge left the muzzle.

In time, turkey choke tube innovators and designers would achieve that which was never before thought possible

Here, shotgunning writer, Phil Bourjaily, analyzes one of several dozen patterns printed during an in-depth session prior to waterfowl season.

Perhaps some of the most specialized choke tubes available today are those designed for turkey hunters.

Like shotshells between manufacturers, chokes even of the same constriction can perform differently. It's a matter of time and trial.

– a 90 percent pattern at 40 yards. In black-and-white terms, this translates into 405 of 450 pellets (two ounces of #6 shot) falling within a 30-inch circle at 40 yards! To turkey hunters, these new tubes represented the Holy Grail of shotgunning; to turkeys, they meant trouble – pure and simple.

The final word on choke tubes

Not magical instruments, choke tubes, regardless of whether their inside diameters measure .730 inch or .655 inch, are only as good as is the individual pulling the trigger. To take that a step further, he who merely buys and installs one of these new special-purpose choke tubes and heads afield without spending time on the range is doing both himself and that incredible natural resource, the wild turkey, a great disservice. For those new to the world of specialty chokes, it's sometimes best to think of these devices as simply one ingredient in a much larger recipe, a list that includes among other things the best in modern ammunition, sights or optics, experience, patience, and practice.

Better yet, think of it more like a recipe for success.

For more information

Today's turkey hunters have at their disposal a long list of companies, many of whom make choke tube design and innovation a priority. Below are some of the major players in this country's choke tube story.

Mad Max and Lohman Long Shot choke tubes
c/o Outland Sports
800-922-9034
www.outland-sports.com

The Undertaker by Hunter's Specialties
319-395-0321; www.hunterspec.com

Briley
785-632-3169; www.briley.com

Comp-n-Choke, or Kick's Gobblin' Thunder
888-875-7906
www.comp-n-choke.com

Ballistic Specialties
800-276-2550; www.angleport.com

Hastings
785-632-3169; www.hastingsbarrels.com/replacechoke.html

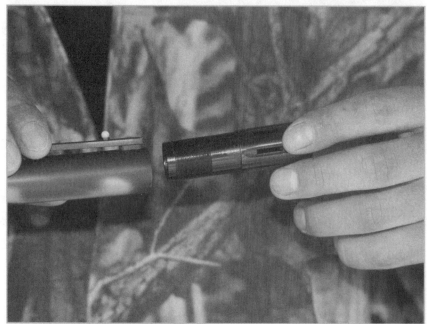

Includes a wide variety of sporting guns and guns suitable for various competitions.

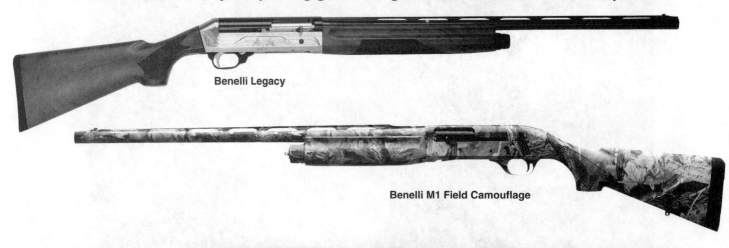

Benelli Legacy

Benelli M1 Field Camouflage

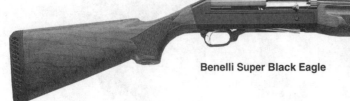

Benelli Super Black Eagle

BENELLI LEGACY SHOTGUN

Gauge: 12, 20, 2-3/4" and 3" chamber. **Barrel:** 24", 26", 28" (Full, Mod., Imp. Cyl., Imp. Mod., cylinder choke tubes). Mid-bead sight. **Weight:** 5.8 to 7.6 lbs. **Length:** 49-5/8" overall (28" barrel). **Stock:** Select European walnut with satin finish. **Features:** Uses the rotating bolt inertia recoil operating system with a two-piece steel/aluminum etched receiver (bright on lower, blue upper). Drop adjustment kit allows the stock to be custom fitted without modifying the stock. Introduced 1998. Imported from Italy by Benelli USA, Corp.
Price: **$1,400.00**

Benelli Sport II Shotgun

Similar to the Legacy model except has dual tone blue/silver receiver, two carbon fiber interchangeable ventilated ribs, adjustable butt pad, adjustable buttstock, and functions with ultra-light target loads. Walnut stock with satin finish. Introduced 1997. Imported from Italy by Benelli U.S.A.
Price: **$1,400.00**

BENELLI M1 FIELD SHOTGUN

Gauge: 12, 20 ga. **Barrel:** 21", 24", 26", 28". **Weight:** 7 lbs., 4 oz. **Stock:** High impact polymer; wood on 26", 28". **Sights:** Red bar. **Features:** Sporting version of the military & police gun. Uses the rotating Montefeltro bolt system. Ventilated rib; blue finish. Comes with set of five choke tubes. Imported from Italy by Benelli U.S.A.
Price: . . . (Synthetic) **$985.00**; (Wood) **$1,000.00**; (Timber HD) **$1,085.00**
Price: 24" rifled barrel . . . . . (Synthetic) **$1,060.00**; Timber HD **$1,165.00**
Price: Synthetic stock, left-hand version (24", 26", 28" brls.) . . . **$1,005.00**
Price: Timber HD camo left-hand, 21", 24" barrel **$1,105.00**
Price: MI Field Steadygrip **$1,175.00**

Benelli Montefeltro Shotgun

Similar to the M1 Super except has checkered walnut stock with satin finish. Uses the Montefeltro rotating bolt system with a simple inertia recoil design. Full, Imp. Mod., Mod., Imp. Cyl. choke tubes, 12 and 20 ga. Weighs 6.8-7.1 lbs. Finish is blue. Introduced 1987.
Price: 24", 26", 28" **$1,005.00**
Price: Left-hand, 26", 28" **$1,020.00**

BENELLI SUPER BLACK EAGLE SHOTGUN

Gauge: 12, 3-1/2" chamber. **Barrel:** 24", 26", 28" (Cyl. Imp. Cyl., Mod., Imp. Mod., Full choke tubes). **Weight:** 7 lbs., 5 oz. **Length:** 49-5/8" overall (28" barrel). **Stock:** European walnut with satin finish, or polymer. Adjustable for drop. **Sights:** Red bar front. **Features:** Uses Montefeltro inertia recoil bolt system. Fires all 12 gauge shells from 2-3/4" to 3-1/2" magnums, vent rib. Introduced 1991. Imported from Italy by Benelli U.S.A.
Price: With 26" and 28" barrel, wood stock **$1,300.00**
Price: Timber HD Camo 24", 26", 28" barrel. **$1,385.00**
Price: With 24", 26" and 28" barrel, polymer stock **$1,290.00**
Price: Left-hand, 24", 26", 28", polymer stock **$1,345.00**
Price: Left-hand, 24", 26", 28", camo stock **$1,435.00**
Price: Steadygrip Turkey Gun **$1,465.00**

Benelli Super Black Eagle Slug Gun

Similar to the Benelli Super Black Eagle except has 24" rifled barrel with 2-3/4" and 3" chamber, drilled and tapped for scope. Uses the inertia recoil bolt system. Matte-finish receiver. Weight is 7.5 lbs., overall length 45.5". Wood or polymer stocks available. Introduced 1992. Imported from Italy by Benelli U.S.A.
Price: With wood stock **$1,345.00**
Price: With polymer stock **$1,335.00**
Price: 24" barrel, Timber HD Camo **$1,460.00**

Benelli Executive Series Shotgun

Similar to the Legacy except has grayed steel lower receiver, hand-engraved and gold inlaid (Grade III), and has highest grade of walnut stock with drop adjustment kit. Barrel lengths 26" or 28"; 2-3/4" and 3" chamber. Special order only. Introduced 1995. Imported from Italy by Benelli U.S.A.
Price: Grade I (engraved game scenes) **$5,465.00**
Price: Grade II (game scenes with scroll engraving) **$6,135.00**
Price: Grade III (full coverage, gold inlays) **$7,065.00**

BERETTA AL391 TEKNYS

Gauge: 12, 20 gauge; 3" chamber, semi-auto. **Barrel:** 26", 28". **Weight:** 5.9 lbs. (20 ga.), 7.3 lbs. (12 ga.). **Length:** N/A. **Stock:** X-tra wood (special process wood enhancement). **Features:** Flat 1/4 rib, TruGlo Tru-Bead sight, recoil reducer, stock spacers, overbored bbls., flush choke tubes. Comes with fitted, lined case.
Price: **$1,194.00**
Price: Teknys Gold (green enamel inlays, oil-finished walnut . . . **$1,515.00**
Price: Teknys Gold Sporting (blue inlays, select walnut) **$1,653.00**

Beretta AL391 Urika Gold Sporting

Beretta AL391 Urika Sporting

Beretta A391 Xtrema 3.5

Browning Gold Deer Hunter

BERETTA AL391 URIKA AUTO SHOTGUNS

Gauge: 12, 20 gauge; 3" chamber. **Barrel:** 22", 24", 26", 28", 30"; five Mobilchoke choke tubes. **Weight:** 5.95 to 7.28 lbs. **Length:** Varies by model. **Stock:** Walnut, black or camo synthetic; shims, spacers and interchangeable recoil pads allow custom fit. **Features:** Self-compensating gas operation handles full range of loads; recoil reducer in receiver; enlarged trigger guard; reduced-weight receiver, barrel and forend; hard-chromed bore. Introduced 2000. Imported from Italy by Beretta USA.
Price: AL391 Urika (12 ga., 26", 28", 30" barrels) **$1,035.00**
Price: AL391 Urika (20 ga., 24", 26", 28" barrels) **$1,035.00**
Price: AL391 Urika Synthetic
(12 ga., 24", 26", 28", 30" barrels) **$1,035.00**
Price: AL391 Urika Camo. (12 ga., Realtree Hardwoods
or Max 4-HD) **$1,139.00**

Beretta AL391 Urika Gold and Gold Sporting Auto Shotguns

Similar to AL391 Urika except features deluxe wood, jeweled bolt and carrier, gold-inlaid receiver with black or silver finish. Introduced 2000. Imported from Italy by Beretta USA.
Price: AL391 Urika Gold Sporting
(12 or 20, black receiver, engraving) **$1,377.00**
Price: AL391 Urika Gold Sporting
(12 ga., silver receiver, engraving) **$1,377.00**

Beretta AL391 Urika Sporting Auto Shotguns

Similar to AL391 Urika except has competition sporting stock with rounded rubber recoil pad, wide ventilated rib with white front and mid-rib beads, satin-black receiver with silver markings. Available in 12 and 20 gauge. Introduced 2000. Imported from Italy by Beretta USA.
Price: AL391 Urika Sporting. **$1,101.00**

Beretta AL391 Urika Trap Auto Shotguns

Similar to AL391 Urika except in 12 ga. only, has wide ventilated rib with white front and mid-rib beads, Monte Carlo stock and special trap recoil pad. Gold Trap features highly figured walnut stock and forend, gold-filled Beretta logo and signature on receiver. Optima bore and Optima choke tubes. Introduced 2000. Imported from Italy by Beretta USA.
Price: AL391 Urika Trap **$1,101.00**

Beretta AL391 Urika Parallel Target RL and SL Auto Shotguns

Similar to AL391 Urika except has parallel-comb, Monte Carlo stock with tighter grip radius to reduce trigger reach and stepped ventilated rib. SL model has same features but with 13.5" length of pull stock. Introduced 2000. Imported from Italy by Beretta USA.
Price: AL391 Urika Parallel Target RL **$1,101.00**
Price: AL391 Urika Parallel Target SL **$1,101.00**

Beretta AL391 Urika Youth Shotgun

Similar to AL391 except has a 24" or 26" barrel with 13.5" stock for youth and smaller shooters. Introduced 2000. From Beretta USA.
Price: **$1,035.00**

BERETTA A391 XTREMA 3.5 AUTO SHOTGUNS

Gauge: 12 ga. 3-1/2" chamber. **Barrel:** 24", 26", 28". **Weight:** 7.8 lbs. **Stock:** Synthetic. **Features:** Semi-auto goes with two-lug rotating bolt and self-compensating gas valve, extended tang, cross bolt safety, self-cleaning, with case.
Price: Synthetic **$1,035.00**
Price: Realtree Hardwood HD Camo and Max 4-HD **$1,139.00**

BROWNING GOLD HUNTER AUTO SHOTGUN

Gauge: 12, 3" or 3-1/2" chamber; 20, 3" chamber. **Barrel:** 12 ga.-26", 28", 30", Invector Plus choke tubes; 20 ga.-26", 30", Invector choke tubes. **Weight:** 7 lbs., 9 oz. (12 ga.), 6 lbs., 12 oz. (20 ga.). **Length:** 46-1/4" overall (20 ga., 26" barrel). **Stock:** 14"x1-1/2"x2-1/3"; select walnut with gloss finish; palm swell grip. **Features:** Self-regulating, self-cleaning gas system shoots all loads; lightweight receiver with special non-glare deep black finish; large reversible safety button; large rounded trigger guard, gold trigger. The 20 gauge has slightly smaller dimensions; 12 gauge have back-bored barrels, Invector Plus tube system. Introduced 1994. Imported by Browning.
Price: 12 or 20 gauge, 3" chamber. **$894.00**
Price: 12 ga., 3-1/2" chamber. **$1,038.00**
Price: Extra barrels. . . . . **$336.00 to $415.00**

Includes a wide variety of sporting guns and guns suitable for various competitions.

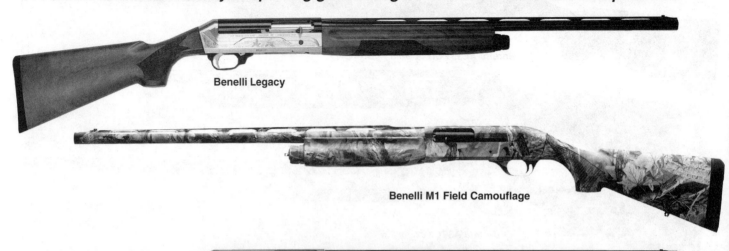

Benelli Legacy

Benelli M1 Field Camouflage

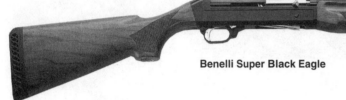

Benelli Super Black Eagle

BENELLI LEGACY SHOTGUN

Gauge: 12, 20, 2-3/4" and 3" chamber. **Barrel:** 24", 26", 28" (Full, Mod., Imp. Cyl., Imp. Mod., cylinder choke tubes). Mid-bead sight. **Weight:** 5.8 to 7.6 lbs. **Length:** 49-5/8" overall (28" barrel). **Stock:** Select European walnut with satin finish. **Features:** Uses the rotating bolt inertia recoil operating system with a two-piece steel/aluminum etched receiver (bright on lower, blue upper). Drop adjustment kit allows the stock to be custom fitted without modifying the stock. Introduced 1998. Imported from Italy by Benelli USA, Corp.
Price: **$1,400.00**

Benelli Sport II Shotgun

Similar to the Legacy model except has dual tone blue/silver receiver, two carbon fiber interchangeable ventilated ribs, adjustable butt pad, adjustable buttstock, and functions with ultra-light target loads. Walnut stock with satin finish. Introduced 1997. Imported from Italy by Benelli U.S.A.
Price: **$1,400.00**

BENELLI M1 FIELD SHOTGUN

Gauge: 12, 20 ga. **Barrel:** 21", 24", 26", 28". **Weight:** 7 lbs., 4 oz. **Stock:** High impact polymer; wood on 26", 28". **Sights:** Red bar. **Features:** Sporting version of the military & police gun. Uses the rotating Montefeltro bolt system. Ventilated rib; blue finish. Comes with set of five choke tubes. Imported from Italy by Benelli U.S.A.
Price: . . . (Synthetic) **$985.00**; (Wood) **$1,000.00**; (Timber HD) **$1,085.00**
Price: 24" rifled barrel . . . . . (Synthetic) **$1,060.00**; Timber HD **$1,165.00**
Price: Synthetic stock, left-hand version (24", 26", 28" brls.) . . . **$1,005.00**
Price: Timber HD camo left-hand, 21", 24" barrel. **$1,105.00**
Price: MI Field Steadygrip **$1,175.00**

Benelli Montefeltro Shotgun

Similar to the M1 Super except has checkered walnut stock with satin finish. Uses the Montefeltro rotating bolt system with a simple inertia recoil design. Full, Imp. Mod., Mod., Imp. Cyl. choke tubes, 12 and 20 ga. Weighs 6.8-7.1 lbs. Finish is blue. Introduced 1987.
Price: 24", 26", 28" **$1,005.00**
Price: Left-hand, 26", 28" **$1,020.00**

BENELLI SUPER BLACK EAGLE SHOTGUN

Gauge: 12, 3-1/2" chamber. **Barrel:** 24", 26", 28" (Cyl. Imp. Cyl., Mod., Imp. Mod., Full choke tubes). **Weight:** 7 lbs., 5 oz. **Length:** 49-5/8" overall (28" barrel). **Stock:** European walnut with satin finish, or polymer. Adjustable for drop. **Sights:** Red bar front. **Features:** Uses Montefeltro inertia recoil bolt system. Fires all 12 gauge shells from 2-3/4" to 3-1/2" magnums, vent rib. Introduced 1991. Imported from Italy by Benelli U.S.A.
Price: With 26" and 28" barrel, wood stock. **$1,300.00**
Price: Timber HD Camo 24", 26", 28" barrel. **$1,385.00**
Price: With 24", 26" and 28" barrel, polymer stock **$1,290.00**
Price: Left-hand, 24", 26", 28", polymer stock **$1,345.00**
Price: Left-hand, 24", 26", 28", camo stock **$1,435.00**
Price: Steadygrip Turkey Gun **$1,465.00**

Benelli Super Black Eagle Slug Gun

Similar to the Benelli Super Black Eagle except has 24" rifled barrel with 2-3/4" and 3" chamber, drilled and tapped for scope. Uses the inertia recoil bolt system. Matte-finish receiver. Weight is 7.5 lbs., overall length 45.5". Wood or polymer stocks available. Introduced 1992. Imported from Italy by Benelli U.S.A.
Price: With wood stock **$1,345.00**
Price: With polymer stock **$1,335.00**
Price: 24" barrel, Timber HD Camo **$1,460.00**

Benelli Executive Series Shotgun

Similar to the Legacy except has grayed steel lower receiver, hand-engraved and gold inlaid (Grade III), and has highest grade of walnut stock with drop adjustment kit. Barrel lengths 26" or 28"; 2-3/4" and 3" chamber. Special order only. Introduced 1995. Imported from Italy by Benelli U.S.A.
Price: Grade I (engraved game scenes) **$5,465.00**
Price: Grade II (game scenes with scroll engraving) **$6,135.00**
Price: Grade III (full coverage, gold inlays) **$7,065.00**

BERETTA AL391 TEKNYS

Gauge: 12, 20 gauge; 3" chamber, semi-auto. **Barrel:** 26", 28". **Weight:** 5.9 lbs. (20 ga.), 7.3 lbs. (12 ga.). **Length:** N/A. **Stock:** X-tra wood (special process wood enhancement). **Features:** Flat 1/4 rib, TruGlo Tru-Bead sight, recoil reducer, stock spacers, overbored bbls., flush choke tubes. Comes with fitted, lined case.
Price: **$1,194.00**
Price: Teknys Gold (green enamel inlays, oil-finished walnut . . . **$1,515.00**
Price: Teknys Gold Sporting (blue inlays, select walnut) **$1,653.00**

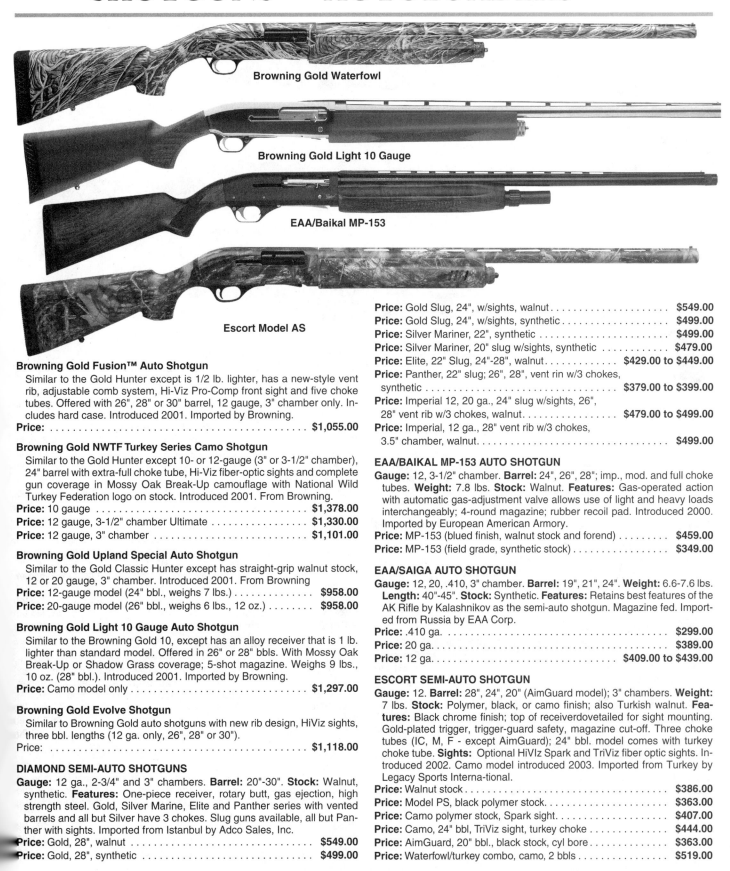

Browning Gold Waterfowl

Browning Gold Light 10 Gauge

EAA/Baikal MP-153

Escort Model AS

Browning Gold Fusion™ Auto Shotgun

Similar to the Gold Hunter except is 1/2 lb. lighter, has a new-style vent rib, adjustable comb system, Hi-Viz Pro-Comp front sight and five choke tubes. Offered with 26", 28" or 30" barrel, 12 gauge, 3" chamber only. Includes hard case. Introduced 2001. Imported by Browning.

Price: **$1,055.00**

Browning Gold NWTF Turkey Series Camo Shotgun

Similar to the Gold Hunter except 10- or 12-gauge (3" or 3-1/2" chamber), 24" barrel with extra-full choke tube, Hi-Viz fiber-optic sights and complete gun coverage in Mossy Oak Break-Up camouflage with National Wild Turkey Federation logo on stock. Introduced 2001. From Browning.

Price: 10 gauge **$1,378.00**
Price: 12 gauge, 3-1/2" chamber Ultimate **$1,330.00**
Price: 12 gauge, 3" chamber **$1,101.00**

Browning Gold Upland Special Auto Shotgun

Similar to the Gold Classic Hunter except has straight-grip walnut stock, 12 or 20 gauge, 3" chamber. Introduced 2001. From Browning

Price: 12-gauge model (24" bbl., weighs 7 lbs.) **$958.00**
Price: 20-gauge model (26" bbl., weighs 6 lbs., 12 oz.) **$958.00**

Browning Gold Light 10 Gauge Auto Shotgun

Similar to the Browning Gold 10, except has an alloy receiver that is 1 lb. lighter than standard model. Offered in 26" or 28" bbls. With Mossy Oak Break-Up or Shadow Grass coverage; 5-shot magazine. Weighs 9 lbs., 10 oz. (28" bbl.). Introduced 2001. Imported by Browning.

Price: Camo model only **$1,297.00**

Browning Gold Evolve Shotgun

Similar to Browning Gold auto shotguns with new rib design, HiViz sights, three bbl. lengths (12 ga. only, 26", 28" or 30").

Price: **$1,118.00**

DIAMOND SEMI-AUTO SHOTGUNS

Gauge: 12 ga., 2-3/4" and 3" chambers. **Barrel:** 20"-30". **Stock:** Walnut, synthetic. **Features:** One-piece receiver, rotary butt, gas ejection, high strength steel. Gold, Silver Marine, Elite and Panther series with vented barrels and all but Silver have 3 chokes. Slug guns available, all but Panther with sights. Imported from Istanbul by Adco Sales, Inc.

Price: Gold, 28", walnut **$549.00**
Price: Gold, 28", synthetic **$499.00**
Price: Gold Slug, 24", w/sights, walnut **$549.00**
Price: Gold Slug, 24", w/sights, synthetic **$499.00**
Price: Silver Mariner, 22", synthetic **$499.00**
Price: Silver Mariner, 20" slug w/sights, synthetic **$479.00**
Price: Elite, 22" Slug, 24"-28", walnut .... **$429.00 to $449.00**
Price: Panther, 22" slug; 26", 28", vent rin w/3 chokes, synthetic .... **$379.00 to $399.00**
Price: Imperial 12, 20 ga., 24" slug w/sights, 26", 28" vent rib w/3 chokes, walnut .... **$479.00 to $499.00**
Price: Imperial, 12 ga., 28" vent rib w/3 chokes, 3.5" chamber, walnut **$499.00**

EAA/BAIKAL MP-153 AUTO SHOTGUN

Gauge: 12, 3-1/2" chamber. **Barrel:** 24", 26", 28"; imp., mod. and full choke tubes. **Weight:** 7.8 lbs. **Stock:** Walnut. **Features:** Gas-operated action with automatic gas-adjustment valve allows use of light and heavy loads interchangeably; 4-round magazine; rubber recoil pad. Introduced 2000. Imported by European American Armory.

Price: MP-153 (blued finish, walnut stock and forend) **$459.00**
Price: MP-153 (field grade, synthetic stock) **$349.00**

EAA/SAIGA AUTO SHOTGUN

Gauge: 12, 20, .410, 3" chamber. **Barrel:** 19", 21", 24". **Weight:** 6.6-7.6 lbs. **Length:** 40"-45". **Stock:** Synthetic. **Features:** Retains best features of the AK Rifle by Kalashnikov as the semi-auto shotgun. Magazine fed. Imported from Russia by EAA Corp.

Price: .410 ga. **$299.00**
Price: 20 ga. **$389.00**
Price: 12 ga. .... **$409.00 to $439.00**

ESCORT SEMI-AUTO SHOTGUN

Gauge: 12. **Barrel:** 28", 24", 20" (AimGuard model); 3" chambers. **Weight:** 7 lbs. **Stock:** Polymer, black, or camo finish; also Turkish walnut. **Features:** Black chrome finish; top of receiver dovetailed for sight mounting. Gold-plated trigger, trigger-guard safety, magazine cut-off. Three choke tubes (IC, M, F - except AimGuard); 24" bbl. model comes with turkey choke tube. **Sights:** Optional HiViz Spark and TriViz fiber optic sights. Introduced 2002. Camo model introduced 2003. Imported from Turkey by Legacy Sports Interna-tional.

Price: Walnut stock **$386.00**
Price: Model PS, black polymer stock **$363.00**
Price: Camo polymer stock, Spark sight **$407.00**
Price: Camo, 24" bbl, TriViz sight, turkey choke **$444.00**
Price: AimGuard, 20" bbl., black stock, cyl bore **$363.00**
Price: Waterfowl/turkey combo, camo, 2 bbls **$519.00**

Includes a wide variety of sporting guns and guns suitable for various competitions.

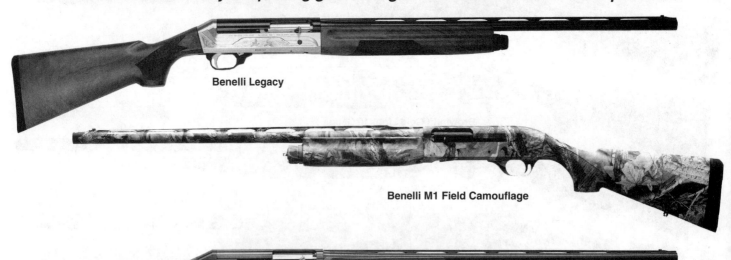

Benelli Legacy

Benelli M1 Field Camouflage

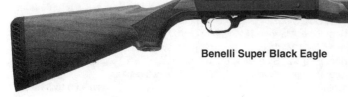

Benelli Super Black Eagle

BENELLI LEGACY SHOTGUN

Gauge: 12, 20, 2-3/4" and 3" chamber. **Barrel:** 24", 26", 28" (Full, Mod., Imp. Cyl., Imp. Mod., cylinder choke tubes). Mid-bead sight. **Weight:** 5.8 to 7.6 lbs. **Length:** 49-5/8" overall (28" barrel). **Stock:** Select European walnut with satin finish. **Features:** Uses the rotating bolt inertia recoil operating system with a two-piece steel/aluminum etched receiver (bright on lower, blue upper). Drop adjustment kit allows the stock to be custom fitted without modifying the stock. Introduced 1998. Imported from Italy by Benelli USA, Corp.
Price: **$1,400.00**

Benelli Sport II Shotgun

Similar to the Legacy model except has dual tone blue/silver receiver, two carbon fiber interchangeable ventilated ribs, adjustable butt pad, adjustable buttstock, and functions with ultra-light target loads. Walnut stock with satin finish. Introduced 1997. Imported from Italy by Benelli U.S.A.
Price: **$1,400.00**

BENELLI M1 FIELD SHOTGUN

Gauge: 12, 20 ga. **Barrel:** 21", 24", 26", 28". **Weight:** 7 lbs., 4 oz. **Stock:** High impact polymer; wood on 26", 28". **Sights:** Red bar. **Features:** Sporting version of the military & police gun. Uses the rotating Montefeltro bolt system. Ventilated rib; blue finish. Comes with set of five choke tubes. Imported from Italy by Benelli U.S.A.
Price: . . . (Synthetic) **$985.00**; (Wood) **$1,000.00**; (Timber HD) **$1,085.00**
Price: 24" rifled barrel . . . . . (Synthetic) **$1,060.00**; Timber HD **$1,165.00**
Price: Synthetic stock, left-hand version (24", 26", 28" brls.) . . . **$1,005.00**
Price: Timber HD camo left-hand, 21", 24" barrel. **$1,105.00**
Price: MI Field Steadygrip **$1,175.00**

Benelli Montefeltro Shotgun

Similar to the M1 Super except has checkered walnut stock with satin finish. Uses the Montefeltro rotating bolt system with a simple inertia recoil design. Full, Imp. Mod, Mod., Imp. Cyl. choke tubes, 12 and 20 ga. Weighs 6.8-7.1 lbs. Finish is blue. Introduced 1987.
Price: 24", 26", 28" **$1,005.00**
Price: Left-hand, 26", 28" **$1,020.00**

BENELLI SUPER BLACK EAGLE SHOTGUN

Gauge: 12, 3-1/2" chamber. **Barrel:** 24", 26", 28" (Cyl. Imp. Cyl., Mod., Imp. Mod., Full choke tubes). **Weight:** 7 lbs., 5 oz. **Length:** 49-5/8" overall (28" barrel). **Stock:** European walnut with satin finish, or polymer. Adjustable for drop. **Sights:** Red bar front. **Features:** Uses Montefeltro inertia recoil bolt system. Fires all 12 gauge shells from 2-3/4" to 3-1/2" magnums, vent rib. Introduced 1991. Imported from Italy by Benelli U.S.A.
Price: With 26" and 28" barrel, wood stock. **$1,300.00**
Price: Timber HD Camo 24", 26", 28" barrel. **$1,385.00**
Price: With 24", 26" and 28" barrel, polymer stock **$1,290.00**
Price: Left-hand, 24", 26", 28", polymer stock **$1,345.00**
Price: Left-hand, 24", 26", 28", camo stock **$1,435.00**
Price: Steadygrip Turkey Gun **$1,465.00**

Benelli Super Black Eagle Slug Gun

Similar to the Benelli Super Black Eagle except has 24" rifled barrel with 2-3/4" and 3" chamber, drilled and tapped for scope. Uses the inertia recoil bolt system. Matte-finish receiver. Weight is 7.5 lbs., overall length 45.5". Wood or polymer stocks available. Introduced 1992. Imported from Italy by Benelli U.S.A.
Price: With wood stock **$1,345.00**
Price: With polymer stock **$1,335.00**
Price: 24" barrel, Timber HD Camo **$1,460.00**

Benelli Executive Series Shotgun

Similar to the Legacy except has grayed steel lower receiver, hand-engraved and gold inlaid (Grade III), and has highest grade of walnut stock with drop adjustment kit. Barrel lengths 26" or 28"; 2-3/4" and 3" chamber. Special order only. Introduced 1995. Imported from Italy by Benelli U.S.A.
Price: Grade I (engraved game scenes). **$5,465.00**
Price: Grade II (game scenes with scroll engraving) **$6,135.00**
Price: Grade III (full coverage, gold inlays) **$7,065.00**

BERETTA AL391 TEKNYS

Gauge: 12, 20 gauge; 3" chamber, semi-auto. **Barrel:** 26", 28". **Weight:** 5.9 lbs. (20 ga.), 7.3 lbs. (12 ga.). **Length:** N/A. **Stock:** X-tra wood (special process wood enhancement). **Features:** Flat 1/4 rib, TruGlo Tru-Bead sight, recoil reducer, stock spacers, overbored bbls., flush choke tubes. Comes with fitted, lined case.
Price: **$1,194.00**
Price: Teknys Gold (green enamel inlays, oil-finished walnut . . . **$1,515.00**
Price: Teknys Gold Sporting (blue inlays, select walnut) **$1,653.00**

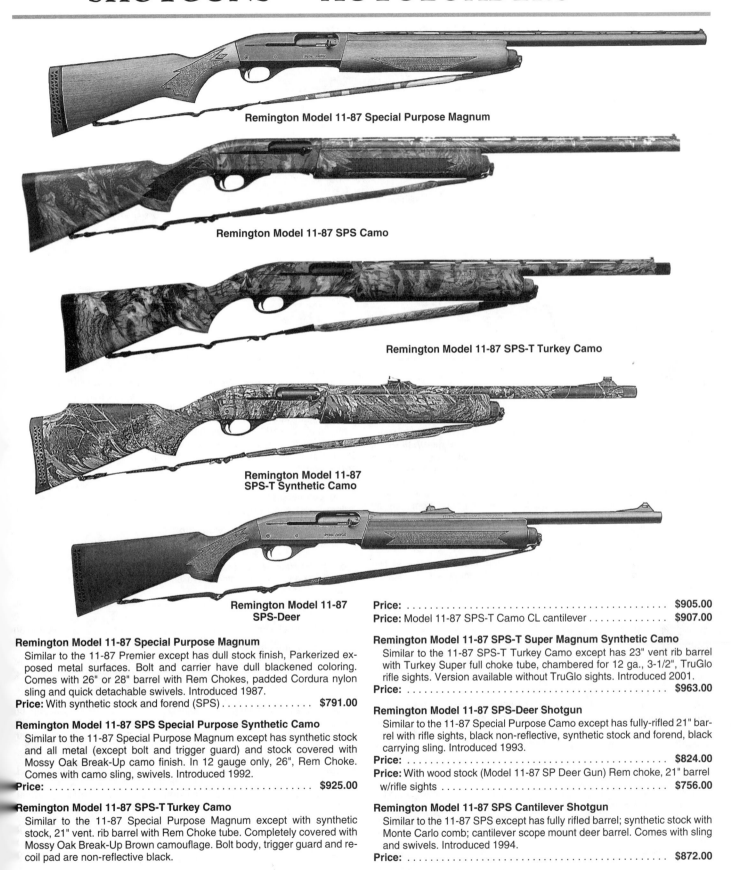

Remington Model 11-87 Special Purpose Magnum

Remington Model 11-87 SPS Camo

Remington Model 11-87 SPS-T Turkey Camo

Remington Model 11-87 SPS-T Synthetic Camo

Remington Model 11-87 SPS-Deer

Remington Model 11-87 Special Purpose Magnum
Similar to the 11-87 Premier except has dull stock finish, Parkerized exposed metal surfaces. Bolt and carrier have dull blackened coloring. Comes with 26" or 28" barrel with Rem Chokes, padded Cordura nylon sling and quick detachable swivels. Introduced 1987.
Price: With synthetic stock and forend (SPS) **$791.00**

Remington Model 11-87 SPS Special Purpose Synthetic Camo
Similar to the 11-87 Special Purpose Magnum except has synthetic stock and all metal (except bolt and trigger guard) and stock covered with Mossy Oak Break-Up camo finish. In 12 gauge only, 26", Rem Choke. Comes with camo sling, swivels. Introduced 1992.
Price: **$925.00**

Remington Model 11-87 SPS-T Turkey Camo
Similar to the 11-87 Special Purpose Magnum except with synthetic stock, 21" vent. rib barrel with Rem Choke tube. Completely covered with Mossy Oak Break-Up Brown camouflage. Bolt body, trigger guard and recoil pad are non-reflective black.

Price: **$905.00**
Price: Model 11-87 SPS-T Camo CL cantilever **$907.00**

Remington Model 11-87 SPS-T Super Magnum Synthetic Camo
Similar to the 11-87 SPS-T Turkey Camo except has 23" vent rib barrel with Turkey Super full choke tube, chambered for 12 ga., 3-1/2", TruGlo rifle sights. Version available without TruGlo sights. Introduced 2001.
Price: **$963.00**

Remington Model 11-87 SPS-Deer Shotgun
Similar to the 11-87 Special Purpose Camo except has fully-rifled 21" barrel with rifle sights, black non-reflective, synthetic stock and forend, black carrying sling. Introduced 1993.
Price: **$824.00**
Price: With wood stock (Model 11-87 SP Deer Gun) Rem choke, 21" barrel w/rifle sights **$756.00**

Remington Model 11-87 SPS Cantilever Shotgun
Similar to the 11-87 SPS except has fully rifled barrel; synthetic stock with Monte Carlo comb; cantilever scope mount deer barrel. Comes with sling and swivels. Introduced 1994.
Price: **$872.00**

Includes a wide variety of sporting guns and guns suitable for various competitions.

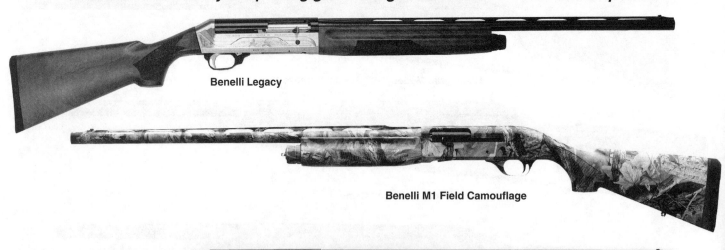

Benelli Legacy

Benelli M1 Field Camouflage

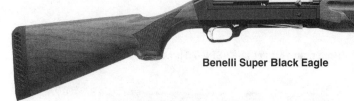

Benelli Super Black Eagle

BENELLI LEGACY SHOTGUN

Gauge: 12, 20, 2-3/4" and 3" chamber. **Barrel:** 24", 26", 28" (Full, Mod., Imp. Cyl., Imp. Mod., cylinder choke tubes). Mid-bead sight. **Weight:** 5.8 to 7.6 lbs. **Length:** 49-5/8" overall (28" barrel). **Stock:** Select European walnut with satin finish. **Features:** Uses the rotating bolt inertia recoil operating system with a two-piece steel/aluminum etched receiver (bright on lower, blue upper). Drop adjustment kit allows the stock to be custom fitted without modifying the stock. Introduced 1998. Imported from Italy by Benelli USA, Corp.

Price: **$1,400.00**

Benelli Sport II Shotgun

Similar to the Legacy model except has dual tone blue/silver receiver, two carbon fiber interchangeable ventilated ribs, adjustable butt pad, adjustable buttstock, and functions with ultra-light target loads. Walnut stock with satin finish. Introduced 1997. Imported from Italy by Benelli U.S.A.

Price: **$1,400.00**

BENELLI M1 FIELD SHOTGUN

Gauge: 12, 20 ga. **Barrel:** 21", 24", 26", 28". **Weight:** 7 lbs., 4 oz. **Stock:** High impact polymer; wood on 26", 28". **Sights:** Red bar. **Features:** Sporting version of the military & police gun. Uses the rotating Montefeltro bolt system. Ventilated rib; blue finish. Comes with set of five choke tubes. Imported from Italy by Benelli U.S.A.

Price: . . . (Synthetic) **$985.00**; (Wood) **$1,000.00**; (Timber HD) **$1,085.00**
Price: 24" rifled barrel . . . . . (Synthetic) **$1,060.00**; Timber HD **$1,165.00**
Price: Synthetic stock, left-hand version (24", 26", 28" brls.) . . . **$1,005.00**
Price: Timber HD camo left-hand, 21", 24" barrel. **$1,105.00**
Price: MI Field Steadygrip **$1,175.00**

Benelli Montefeltro Shotgun

Similar to the M1 Super except has checkered walnut stock with satin finish. Uses the Montefeltro rotating bolt system with a simple inertia recoil design. Full, Imp. Mod., Mod., Imp. Cyl. choke tubes, 12 and 20 ga. Weighs 6.8-7.1 lbs. Finish is blue. Introduced 1987.

Price: 24", 26", 28" **$1,005.00**
Price: Left-hand, 26", 28" **$1,020.00**

BENELLI SUPER BLACK EAGLE SHOTGUN

Gauge: 12, 3-1/2" chamber. **Barrel:** 24", 26", 28" (Cyl. Imp. Cyl., Mod., Imp. Mod., Full choke tubes). **Weight:** 7 lbs., 5 oz. **Length:** 49-5/8" overall (28" barrel). **Stock:** European walnut with satin finish, or polymer. Adjustable for drop. **Sights:** Red bar front. **Features:** Uses Montefeltro inertia recoil bolt system. Fires all 12 gauge shells from 2-3/4" to 3-1/2" magnums, vent rib. Introduced 1991. Imported from Italy by Benelli U.S.A.

Price: With 26" and 28" barrel, wood stock. **$1,300.00**
Price: Timber HD Camo 24", 26", 28" barrel. **$1,385.00**
Price: With 24", 26" and 28" barrel, polymer stock **$1,290.00**
Price: Left-hand, 24", 26", 28", polymer stock **$1,345.00**
Price: Left-hand, 24", 26", 28", camo stock **$1,435.00**
Price: Steadygrip Turkey Gun **$1,465.00**

Benelli Super Black Eagle Slug Gun

Similar to the Benelli Super Black Eagle except has 24" rifled barrel with 2-3/4" and 3" chamber, drilled and tapped for scope. Uses the inertia recoil bolt system. Matte-finish receiver. Weight is 7.5 lbs., overall length 45.5". Wood or polymer stocks available. Introduced 1992. Imported from Italy by Benelli U.S.A.

Price: With wood stock **$1,345.00**
Price: With polymer stock **$1,335.00**
Price: 24" barrel, Timber HD Camo **$1,460.00**

Benelli Executive Series Shotgun

Similar to the Legacy except has grayed steel lower receiver, hand-engraved and gold inlaid (Grade III), and has highest grade of walnut stock with drop adjustment kit. Barrel lengths 26" or 28"; 2-3/4" and 3" chamber. Special order only. Introduced 1995. Imported from Italy by Benelli U.S.A.

Price: Grade I (engraved game scenes) **$5,465.00**
Price: Grade II (game scenes with scroll engraving) **$6,135.00**
Price: Grade III (full coverage, gold inlays) **$7,065.00**

BERETTA AL391 TEKNYS

Gauge: 12, 20 gauge; 3" chamber, semi-auto. **Barrel:** 26", 28". **Weight:** 5.9 lbs. (20 ga.), 7.3 lbs. (12 ga.). **Length:** N/A. **Stock:** X-tra wood (special process wood enhancement). **Features:** Flat 1/4 rib, TruGlo Tru-Bead sight, recoil reducer, stock spacers, overbored bbls., flush choke tubes. Comes with fitted, lined case.

Price: **$1,194.00**
Price: Teknys Gold (green enamel inlays, oil-finished walnut . . . **$1,515.00**
Price: Teknys Gold Sporting (blue inlays, select walnut) **$1,653.00**

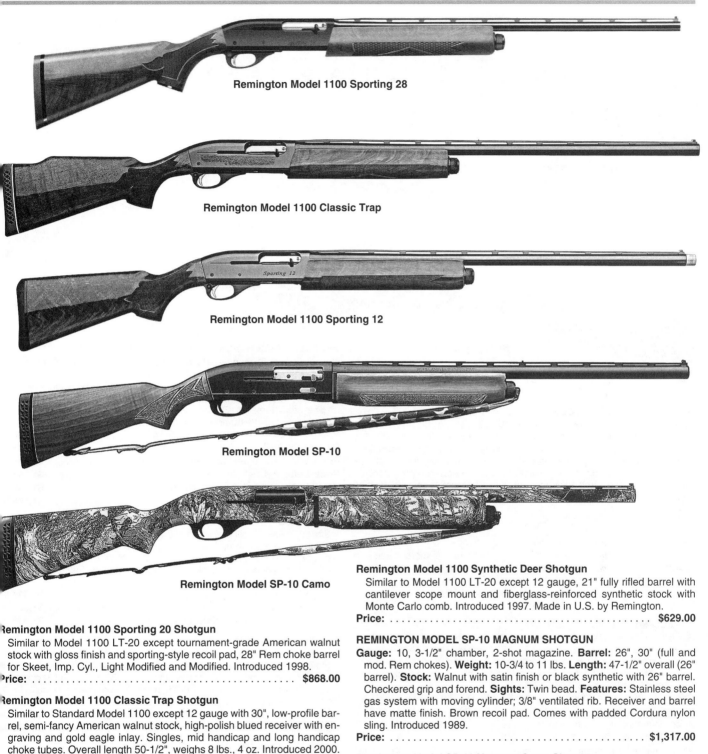

Remington Model 1100 Sporting 28

Remington Model 1100 Classic Trap

Remington Model 1100 Sporting 12

Remington Model SP-10

Remington Model SP-10 Camo

Remington Model 1100 Sporting 20 Shotgun
Similar to Model 1100 LT-20 except tournament-grade American walnut stock with gloss finish and sporting-style recoil pad, 28" Rem choke barrel for Skeet, Imp. Cyl., Light Modified and Modified. Introduced 1998.
Price: **$868.00**

Remington Model 1100 Classic Trap Shotgun
Similar to Standard Model 1100 except 12 gauge with 30", low-profile barrel, semi-fancy American walnut stock, high-polish blued receiver with engraving and gold eagle inlay. Singles, mid handicap and long handicap choke tubes. Overall length 50-1/2", weighs 8 lbs., 4 oz. Introduced 2000. From Remington Arms Co.
Price: **$895.00**

Remington Model 1100 Sporting 12 Shotgun
Similar to Model 1100 Sporting 20 Shotgun except in 12 gauge, 28" ventilated barrel with semi-fancy American walnut stock, gold-plated trigger. Overall length 49", weighs 8 lbs. Introduced 2000. From Remington Arms Co.
Price: **$901.00**

Remington Model 1100 Synthetic Deer Shotgun
Similar to Model 1100 LT-20 except 12 gauge, 21" fully rifled barrel with cantilever scope mount and fiberglass-reinforced synthetic stock with Monte Carlo comb. Introduced 1997. Made in U.S. by Remington.
Price: **$629.00**

REMINGTON MODEL SP-10 MAGNUM SHOTGUN
Gauge: 10, 3-1/2" chamber, 2-shot magazine. **Barrel:** 26", 30" (full and mod. Rem chokes). **Weight:** 10-3/4 to 11 lbs. **Length:** 47-1/2" overall (26" barrel). **Stock:** Walnut with satin finish or black synthetic with 26" barrel. Checkered grip and forend. **Sights:** Twin bead. **Features:** Stainless steel gas system with moving cylinder; 3/8" ventilated rib. Receiver and barrel have matte finish. Brown recoil pad. Comes with padded Cordura nylon sling. Introduced 1989.
Price: **$1,317.00**

Remington Model SP-10 Magnum Camo Shotgun
Similar to SP-10 Magnum except buttstock, forend, receiver, barrel and magazine cap are covered with Mossy Oak Break-Up camo finish; bolt body and trigger guard have matte black finish. Rem choke tube, 26" vent. rib barrel with mid-rib bead and Bradley-style front sight, swivel studs and quick-detachable swivels, non-slip Cordura carrying sling in same camo pattern. Introduced 1993.
Price: **$1,453.00**

Includes a wide variety of sporting guns and guns suitable for various competitions.

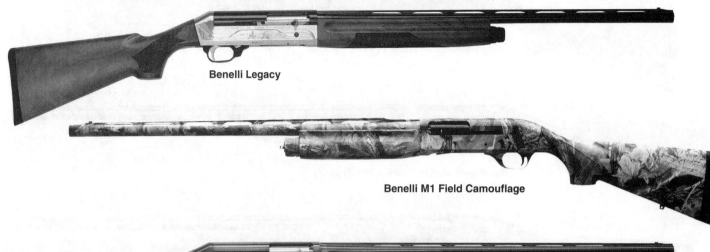

Benelli Legacy

Benelli M1 Field Camouflage

Benelli Super Black Eagle

BENELLI LEGACY SHOTGUN

Gauge: 12, 20, 2-3/4" and 3" chamber. **Barrel:** 24", 26", 28" (Full, Mod., Imp. Cyl., Imp. Mod., cylinder choke tubes). Mid-bead sight. **Weight:** 5.8 to 7.6 lbs. **Length:** 49-5/8" overall (28" barrel). **Stock:** Select European walnut with satin finish. **Features:** Uses the rotating bolt inertia recoil operating system with a two-piece steel/aluminum etched receiver (bright on lower, blue upper). Drop adjustment kit allows the stock to be custom fitted without modifying the stock. Introduced 1998. Imported from Italy by Benelli USA, Corp.

Price: **$1,400.00**

Benelli Sport II Shotgun

Similar to the Legacy model except has dual tone blue/silver receiver, two carbon fiber interchangeable ventilated ribs, adjustable butt pad, adjustable buttstock, and functions with ultra-light target loads. Walnut stock with satin finish. Introduced 1997. Imported from Italy by Benelli U.S.A.

Price: **$1,400.00**

BENELLI M1 FIELD SHOTGUN

Gauge: 12, 20 ga. **Barrel:** 21", 24", 26", 28". **Weight:** 7 lbs., 4 oz. **Stock:** High impact polymer; wood on 26", 28". **Sights:** Red bar. **Features:** Sporting version of the military & police gun. Uses the rotating Montefeltro bolt system. Ventilated rib; blue finish. Comes with set of five choke tubes. Imported from Italy by Benelli U.S.A.

Price: . . . (Synthetic) **$985.00**; (Wood) **$1,000.00**; (Timber HD) **$1,085.00**
Price: 24" rifled barrel . . . . . (Synthetic) **$1,060.00**; Timber HD **$1,165.00**
Price: Synthetic stock, left-hand version (24", 26", 28" brls.) . . . **$1,005.00**
Price: Timber HD camo left-hand, 21", 24" barrel. **$1,105.00**
Price: MI Field Steadygrip **$1,175.00**

Benelli Montefeltro Shotgun

Similar to the M1 Super except has checkered walnut stock with satin finish. Uses the Montefeltro rotating bolt system with a simple inertia recoil design. Full, Imp. Mod., Mod., Imp. Cyl. choke tubes, 12 and 20 ga. Weighs 6.8-7.1 lbs. Finish is blue. Introduced 1987.

Price: 24", 26", 28" **$1,005.00**
Price: Left-hand, 26", 28" **$1,020.00**

BENELLI SUPER BLACK EAGLE SHOTGUN

Gauge: 12, 3-1/2" chamber. **Barrel:** 24", 26", 28" (Cyl. Imp. Cyl., Mod., Imp Mod., Full choke tubes). **Weight:** 7 lbs., 5 oz. **Length:** 49-5/8" overall (28 barrel). **Stock:** European walnut with satin finish, or polymer. Adjustable for drop. **Sights:** Red bar front. **Features:** Uses Montefeltro inertia reco bolt system. Fires all 12 gauge shells from 2-3/4" to 3-1/2" magnums, ver rib. Introduced 1991. Imported from Italy by Benelli U.S.A.

Price: With 26" and 28" barrel, wood stock. **$1,300.00**
Price: Timber HD Camo 24", 26", 28" barrel. **$1,385.00**
Price: With 24", 26" and 28" barrel, polymer stock **$1,290.00**
Price: Left-hand, 24", 26", 28", polymer stock **$1,345.00**
Price: Left-hand, 24", 26", 28", camo stock **$1,435.00**
Price: Steadygrip Turkey Gun **$1,465.00**

Benelli Super Black Eagle Slug Gun

Similar to the Benelli Super Black Eagle except has 24" rifled barrel with 2-3/4" and 3" chamber, drilled and tapped for scope. Uses the inertia re coil bolt system. Matte-finish receiver. Weight is 7.5 lbs., overall length 45.5". Wood or polymer stocks available. Introduced 1992. Imported from Italy by Benelli U.S.A.

Price: With wood stock **$1,345.00**
Price: With polymer stock **$1,335.00**
Price: 24" barrel, Timber HD Camo **$1,460.00**

Benelli Executive Series Shotgun

Similar to the Legacy except has grayed steel lower receiver, hand-en graved and gold inlaid (Grade III), and has highest grade of walnut stoc with drop adjustment kit. Barrel lengths 26" or 28"; 2-3/4" and 3" chamber Special order only. Introduced 1995. Imported from Italy by Benelli U.S.A

Price: Grade I (engraved game scenes) **$5,465.00**
Price: Grade II (game scenes with scroll engraving) **$6,135.00**
Price: Grade III (full coverage, gold inlays) **$7,065.00**

BERETTA AL391 TEKNYS

Gauge: 12, 20 gauge; 3" chamber, semi-auto. **Barrel:** 26", 28". **Weight:** 5.9 lbs. (20 ga.), 7.3 lbs. (12 ga.). **Length:** N/A. **Stock:** X-tra wood (specia process wood enhancement). **Features:** Flat 1/4 rib, TruGlo Tru-Bead sight, recoil reducer, stock spacers, overbored bbls., flush choke tubes Comes with fitted, lined case.

Price: **$1,194.00**
Price: Teknys Gold (green enamel inlays, oil-finished walnut . . . **$1,515.00**
Price: Teknys Gold Sporting (blue inlays, select walnut) **$1,653.00**

Weatherby SAS Field

Weatherby SAS Slug

Winchester X2 NWTF Turkey

Winchester Super X2 Sporting Clays

Winchester Super X2 Field

WEATHERBY SAS (SEMI-AUTOMATIC SHOTGUNS)
6 Models: SAS Field, SAS Sporting Clays, SAS Shadow Grass, SAS Break-Up, SAS Synthetic and a Slug Gun.
Gauge: 12 ga. **Barrel:** Vent ribbed, 24"-30". **Stock:** SAS Field and Sporting Clays, walnut. SAS Shadow Grass, Break-Up, Synthetic, composite. **Sights:** SAS Sporting Clays, frass front and mid-point back. SAS Shadow Grass and Break-Up, HiViz front and brass mid. Synthetic has brass front. **Features:** Easy to shoot, load, clean, lightweight, lessened recoil, IMC system includes 3 chrome moly screw-in choke tubes. Slug gun has 22" rifled barrel with matte blue finish and cantilever base for scope mounting.
Price: . . . . $699.00 to 849.00

WINCHESTER SUPER X2 AUTO SHOTGUN
Gauge: 12, 3", 3-1/2" chamber. **Barrel:** Belgian, 24", 26", 28"; Invector Plus choke tubes. **Weight:** 7-1/4 to 7-1/2 lbs. **Stock:** 14-1/4"x1-3/4"x2". Walnut or black synthetic. **Features:** Gas-operated action shoots all loads without adjustment; vent. rib barrels; 4-shot magazine. Introduced 1999. Assembled in Portugal by U.S. Repeating Arms Co.

Price: Field, walnut or synthetic stock, 3" $874.00
Price: Magnum, 3-1/2", synthetic stock, 26" or 28" bbl. $988.00
Price: Camo Waterfowl, 3-1/2", Mossy Oak Shadow Grass $1,139.00
Price: NWTF Turkey, 3-1/2", Mossy Oak Break-Up camo. $1,165.00
Price: Universal Hunter Model $1,139.00

WINCHESTER SUPER X2 SPORTING CLAYS AUTO SHOTGUN
Similar to the Super X2 except has two gas pistons (one for target loads, one for heavy 3" loads), adjustable comb system and high-post rib. Back-bored barrel with Invector Plus choke tubes. Offered in 28" and 30" barrels. Introduced 2001. From U.S. Repeating Arms Co.
Price: Super X2 Sporting Clays $959.00
Price: Signature red stock $976.00

Winchester Super X2 Field 3" Auto Shotgun
Similar to the Super X2 except has a 3" chamber, walnut stock and forearm and high-profile rib. Back-bored barrel and Invector Plus choke tubes. Introduced 2001. From U.S. Repeating Arms Co.
Price: Super X2 Field 3", 26" or 28" bbl. $874.00

Includes a wide variety of sporting guns and guns suitable for competitive shooting.

Armscor M-30F Field

Benelli Nova Pump

Benelli Nova Pump Slug

Browning BPS 10 gauge

Browning BPS 10 gauge Mossy Oak® Shadow Grass

ARMSCOR M-30F FIELD PUMP SHOTGUN

Gauge: 12, 3" chamber. **Barrel:** 28" fixed Mod., or with Mod. and Full choke tubes. **Weight:** 7.6 lbs. **Stock:** Walnut-finished hardwood. **Features:** Dou-ble action slide bars; blued steel receiver; damascened bolt. Intro-duced 1996. Imported from the Philippines by K.B.I., Inc.

Price: With fixed choke **$239.00**
Price: With choke tubes **$269.00**

BENELLI NOVA PUMP SHOTGUN

Gauge: 12, 20. **Barrel:** 24", 26", 28". **Stock:** Synthetic, X-tra Brown 12 ga., Timber HD 20 ga. **Sights:** Red bar. **Features:** 2-3/4", 3" chamber (3-2/1" 12 ga. only). Montefeltro rotating bolt design with dual action bars, maga-zine cut-off, synthetic trigger assembly, 4-shot magazine. Introduced 1999. Imported from Italy by Benelli USA.

Price: Synthetic **$335.00**
Price: Timber HD **$400.00**
Price: Youth model **$415.00**

Benelli Nova Pump Slug Gun

Similar to the Nova except has 18.5" barrel with adjustable rifle-type or ghost ring sights; weighs 7.2 lbs.; black synthetic stock. Introduced 1999. Imported from Italy by Benelli USA.

Price: With rifle sights **$355.00**
Price: With ghost-ring sights **$395.00**

Benelli Nova Pump Rifled Slug Gun

Similar to Nova Pump Slug Gun except has 24" barrel and rifled bore; open rifle sights; synthetic stock; weighs 8.1 pounds.

Price: . . . . (Synthetic) **$500.00**; Timber HD **$575.00**

BROWNING BPS PUMP SHOTGUN

Gauge: 10, 12, 3-1/2" chamber; 12 or 20, 3" chamber (2-3/4" in target guns), 28, 2-3/4" chamber, 5-shot magazine, .410, 3" chamber. **Barrel:** 10 ga.- 24" Buck Special, 28", 30", 32" Invector; 12, 20 ga.-22", 24", 26", 28", 30", 32" (Imp. Cyl., mod. or full). .410-26" barrel. (Imp. Cyl., mod. and full choke tubes.) Also available with Invector choke tubes, 12 or 20 ga.; Up-land Special has 22" barrel with Invector tubes. BPS 3" and 3-1/2" have back-bored barrel. **Weight:** 7 lbs., 8 oz. (28" barrel). **Length:** 48-3/4" over-all (28" barrel). **Stock:** 14-1/4"x1-1/2"x2-1/2". Select walnut, semi-beaver-tail forend, full pistol grip stock. **Features:** All 12 gauge 3" guns except Buck Special and game guns have back-bored barrels with Invector Plus choke tubes. Bottom feeding and ejection, receiver top safety, high post vent. rib. Double action bars eliminate binding. Vent. rib barrels only. All 12 and 20 gauge guns with 3" chamber available with fully engraved re-ceiver flats at no extra cost. Each gauge has its own unique game scene. Introduced 1977. Imported from Japan by Browning.

Price: 12 ga., 3-1/2" Magnum Stalker (black syn. stock). **$562.00**
Price: 12, 20 ga., Hunter, Invector Plus **$494.00**
Price: 12 ga. Deer Hunter (22" rifled bbl., cantilever mount). **$606.00**
Price: 28 ga., Hunter, Invector **$528.00**
Price: .410, Hunter, Invector **$528.00**

Browning BPS 10 Gauge Shotguns

Chambered for the 10 gauge, 3-1/2" load. Offered in 24", 26" and 28" bar-rels. Offered with walnut, black composite (Stalker models) or camou-flage stock and forend. Introduced 1999. Imported by Browning.

Price: Stalker (composite). **$562.00**
Price: Mossy Oak® Shadow Grass or Break-Up Camo **$668.00**

Browning BPS 10 Gauge Camo Pump Shotgun

Similar to the BPS 10 gauge Hunter except completely covered with Mossy Oak Shadow Grass camouflage. Available with 24", 26", 28" bar-rel. Introduced 1999. Imported by Browning.

Price: **$668.00**

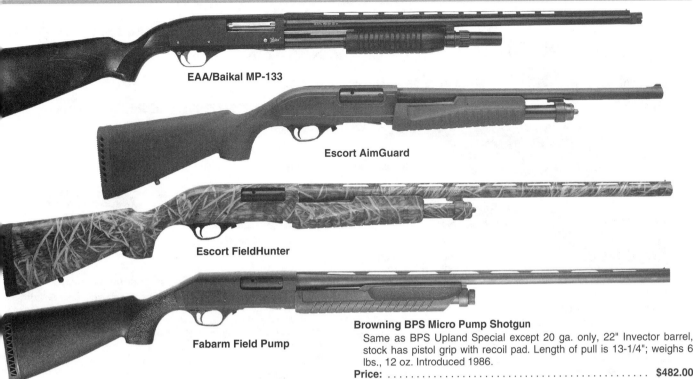

EAA/Baikal MP-133

Escort AimGuard

Escort FieldHunter

Fabarm Field Pump

Browning BPS Waterfowl Camo Pump Shotgun

Similar to the BPS Hunter except completely covered with Mossy Oak Shadow Grass camouflage. Available in 12 gauge, with 24", 26" or 28" barrel, 3" chamber. Introduced 1999. Imported by Browning.
Price: **$652.00**

Browning BPS Game Gun Deer Hunter

Similar to the standard BPS except has newly designed receiver/magazine tube/barrel mounting system to eliminate play, heavy 20.5" barrel with rifle-type sights with adjustable rear, solid receiver scope mount, "rifle" stock dimensions for scope or open sights, sling swivel studs. Gloss or matte finished wood with checkering, polished blue metal. Introduced 1992.
Price: **$568.00**

Browning BPS Game Gun Turkey Special

Similar to the standard BPS except has satin-finished walnut stock and dull-finished barrel and receiver. Receiver is drilled and tapped for scope mounting. Rifle-style stock dimensions and swivel studs. Has Extra-Full Turkey choke tube. Introduced 1992.
Price: **$500.00**

Browning BPS Stalker Pump Shotgun

Same gun as the standard BPS except all exposed metal parts have a matte blued finish and the stock has a durable black finish with a black recoil pad. Available in 10 ga. (3-1/2") and 12 ga. with 3" or 3-1/2" chamber, 22", 28", 30" barrel with Invector choke system. Introduced 1987.
Price: 12 ga., 3" chamber, Invector Plus.................... **$448.00**
Price: 10, 12 ga., 3-1/2" chamber......................... **$537.00**

Browning BPS NWTF Turkey Series Pump Shotgun

Similar to the BPS Stalker except has full coverage Mossy Oak® Break-Up camo finish on synthetic stock, forearm and exposed metal parts. Offered in 10 and 12 gauge, 3" or 3-1/2" chamber; 24" bbl. has extra-full choke tube and Hi-Viz fiber optic sights. Introduced 2001. From Browning.
Price: 10 ga., 3-1/2" chamber........................... **$637.00**
Price: 12 ga., 3-1/2" chamber........................... **$637.00**
Price: 12 ga., 3" chamber.............................. **$549.00**

Browning BPS Micro Pump Shotgun

Same as BPS Upland Special except 20 ga. only, 22" Invector barrel, stock has pistol grip with recoil pad. Length of pull is 13-1/4"; weighs 6 lbs., 12 oz. Introduced 1986.
Price: **$482.00**

DIAMOND 12 GA. PUMP SHOTGUN

Gauge: 12, 2-3/4" and 3" chambers. **Barrel:** 18"-30". **Weight:** 7 lbs. **Stock:** Walnut, synthetic. **Features:** Aluminum one-piece receiver sculpted for lighter weight. Double locking on fixed bolt. Gold, Elite and Panther series with vented barrels and 3 chokes. All series slug guns available (Gold and Elite with sights). Imported from Istanbul by ADCO Sales.
Price: Gold, 28" vent rib w/3 chokes, walnut **$359.00**
Price: Gold, 28", synthetic **$329.00**
Price: Gold Slug, 24" w/sights, walnut or synthetic .. **$329.00 to $359.00**
Price: Silver Mariner 18.5" Slug, synthetic **$399.00**
Price: Silver Mariner 22" vent rib w/3 chokes **$419.00**
Price: Elite, 22" slug w/sights; 24", 28" ventib w/3 chokes,
   walnut .... **$329.00 to $349.00**
Price: Panther, 28", 30" vent rib w/3 chokes, synthetic......... **$279.00**
Price: Panther,18.5", 22" Slug, synthetic .... **$209.00 to $265.00**
Price: Imperial 12 ga., 28" vent rib w/3 chokes, 3.5" chamber,
   walnut **$399.00**

EAA/BAIKAL MP-133 PUMP SHOTGUN

Gauge: 12, 3-1/2" chamber. **Barrel:** 18-1/2", 20", 24", 26", 28"; imp., mod. and full choke tubes. **Weight:** NA. **Stock:** Walnut; checkered grip and grooved forearm. **Features:** Hammer-forged, chrome-lined barrel with ventilated rib; machined steel parts; dual action bars; trigger-block safety; 4-shot magazine tube; handles 2-3/4" through 3-1/2" shells. Introduced 2000. Imported by European American Armory.
Price: MP-133 (blued finish, walnut stock and forend) **$359.00**

ESCORT PUMP SHOTGUN

Gauge: 12, 3" chamber. **Barrel:** 20", fixed (AimGuard model); 24" and 28" (Field Hunter models), choke tubes (M, IC, F); turkey choke with 24" bbl. **Weight:** 6.4 to 7 lbs. **Stock:** Polymer, black chrome or camo finish. **Features:** Alloy receiver w/ dovetail for sight mounting. Two stock adjusting spacers included. Introduced 2003. From Legacy Sports International.
Price: Field Hunter, black stock **$224.00**
Price: Field Hunter, camo stock **$271.00**
Price: Camo, 24" bbl. **$444.00**
Price: AimGuard, 20" bbl., black stock **$199.00**

Ithaca Model 37 Waterfowl

Ithaca Model 37 Deerslayer II

Mossberg Model 835
Mossy Oak Camo

FABARM FIELD PUMP SHOTGUN

Gauge: 12, 3" chamber. **Barrel:** 28" (24" rifled slug barrel available). **Weight:** 76.6 lbs. **Length:** 48.25" overall. **Stock:** Polymer. **Features:** Similar to Fabarm FP6 Pump Shotgun. Alloy receiver; twin action bars; available in black or Mossy Oak Break-Up™ camo finish. Includes cyl., mod. and full choke tubes. Introduced 2001. Imported from Italy by Heckler & Koch Inc.

Price: Matte black finish **$399.00**
Price: Mossy Oak Break-Up™ finish **$469.00**

ITHACA MODEL 37 DELUXE PUMP SHOTGUN

Gauge: 12, 16, 20, 3" chamber. **Barrel:** 26", 28", 30" (12 gauge), 26", 28" (16 and 20 gauge), choke tubes. **Weight:** 7 lbs. **Stock:** Walnut with cut-checkered grip and forend. **Features:** Steel receiver; bottom ejection; brushed blue finish, vent rib barrels. Reintroduced 1996. Made in U.S. by Ithaca Gun Co.

Price: **$633.00**
Price: With straight English-style stock **$803.00**
Price: Model 37 New Classic (ringtail forend, sunburst recoil pad, hand-finished walnut stock, 26" or 28" barrel) **$803.00**

ITHACA MODEL 37 WATERFOWL

Similar to Model 37 Deluxe except in 12 gauge only with 24", 26", or 30" barrel, special extended steel shot choke tube system. Complete coverage of Advantage Wetlands or Hardwoods camouflage. Introduced 1999. Made in U.S. by Ithaca Gun Co. Storm models have synthetic stock.

Price: . . . . **$499.00 to $549.00**

ITHACA MODEL 37 DEERSLAYER II PUMP SHOTGUN

Gauge: 12, 16, 20; 3" chamber. **Barrel:** 24", 26", fully rifled. **Weight:** 11 lbs. **Stock:** Cut-checkered American walnut with Monte Carlo comb. **Sights:** Rifle-type. **Features:** Integral barrel and receiver. Bottom ejection. Brushed blue finish. Reintroduced 1997. Made in U.S. by Ithaca Gun Co. Storm models have synthetic stock.

Price: **$633.00**
Price: Smooth Bore Deluxe **$582.00**
Price: Rifled Deluxe **$582.00**
Price: Storm **$399.00**

ITHACA MODEL 37 DEERSLAYER III PUMP SHOTGUN

Gauge: 12, 20, 2-3/4" and 3" chambers. **Barrel:** 26" free floated. **Weight:** 9 lbs. **Stock:** Monte Carlo laminate. **Sights:** Rifled. **Features:** Barrel length gives increased velocity. Trigger and sear set hand filed and stoned for creep free operation. Weaver-style scope base. Swivel studs. Matte blue.
Price: . . . . **Custom order only**

ITHACA MODEL 37 RUFFED GROUSE SPECIAL EDITION

Gauge: 20 ga. **Barrel:** 22", 24", interchangeable choke tubes. **Weight:** 5.25 lbs. **Stock:** American black walnut. **Features:** Laser engraved stock with line art drawing. Bottom eject. Vent rib and English style. Right- or left-hand thru simple safety change. Aluminum receiver. Made in U.S.A. by Ithaca Gun Co.
Price: **$840.00**

ITHACA TURKEYSLAYER STORM

Gauge: 12 or 20 ga., 3" chamber. **Barrel:** 24" ported. **Stock:** Composite. **Sights:** TruGlo front and rear. **Features:** Itha-Choke full turkey choke tube. Matte metal, Realtree Hardwoods pattern, swivel studs.
Price: Storm **$459.00**

ITHACA MODEL 37 ULTRALIGHT DELUXE

Gauge: 16 ga. 2-3/4" chamber. **Barrel:** 24", 26", 28". **Weight:** 5.25 lbs. **Stock:** Standard deluxe. **Sights:** Raybar. **Features:** Vent rib, drilled and tapped, interchangeable barrel. F, M, IC choke tubes.
Price: Deluxe **$649.00**
Price: Classic/English **$824.00**
Price: Classic/Pistol **$824.00**

MARLIN PARDNER PUMP

Gauge: 12 ga., 3". **Barrel:** 28" vent rib, screw-in modified choke tube. **Weight:** 7 1/2 pounds. **Length:** 48 1/2". **Stock:** American walnut, grooved forend, ventilated recoil pad. **Sights:** Bead front. **Features:** Machined steel receiver, double action bars, five-shot magazine.
Price: **$200.00**

MOSSBERG MODEL 835 ULTI-MAG PUMP

Gauge: 12, 3-1/2" chamber. **Barrel:** Ported 24" rifled bore, 24", 28", Accu-Mag choke tubes for steel or lead shot. **Weight:** 7-3/4 lbs. **Length:** 48-1/2" overall. **Stock:** 14"x1-1/2"x2-1/2". Dual Comb. Cut-checkered hardwood or camo synthetic; both have recoil pad. **Sights:** White bead front, brass mid-bead; Fiber Optic. **Features:** Shoots 2-3/4", 3" or 3-1/2" shells. Back-bored and ported barrel to reduce recoil, improve patterns. Ambidextrous thumb safety, twin extractors, dual slide bars. Mossberg Cablelock included. Introduced 1988.
Price: 28" vent. rib, hardwood stock **$394.00**
Price: Combos, 24" rifled or smooth bore, rifle sights, 24" vent. rib Accu-Mag Ulti-Full choke tube, Mossy Oak camo finish **$556.00**
Price: RealTree Camo Turkey, 24" vent. rib, Accu-Mag Extra-Full tube, synthetic stock **$460.00**
Price: Mossy Oak Camo, 28" vent. rib, Accu-Mag tubes, synthetic stock **$460.00**
Price: OFM Camo, 28" vent. rib, Accu-Mag Mod. tube, synthetic stock **$438.00**

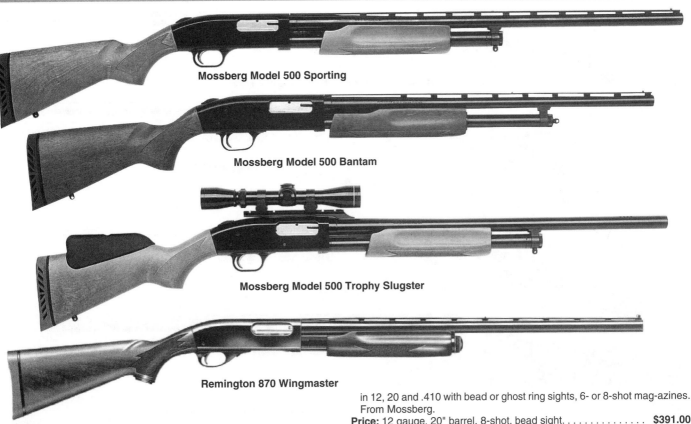

Mossberg Model 500 Sporting

Mossberg Model 500 Bantam

Mossberg Model 500 Trophy Slugster

Remington 870 Wingmaster

Mossberg Model 835 Synthetic Stock

Similar to the Model 835, except with 28" ported barrel with Accu-Mag Mod. choke tube, Parkerized finish, black synthetic stock and forend. Introduced 1998. Made in U.S. by Mossberg.

Price: **$394.00**

MOSSBERG MODEL 500 SPORTING PUMP

Gauge: 12, 20, .410, 3" chamber. **Barrel:** 18-1/2" to 28" with fixed or Accu-Choke, plain or vent. rib. **Weight:** 6-1/4 lbs. (.410), 7-1/4 lbs. (12). **Length:** 48" overall (28" barrel). **Stock:** 14"x1-1/2"x2-1/2". Walnut-stained hardwood. Cut-checkered grip and forend. **Sights:** White bead front, brass mid-bead; Fiber Optic. **Features:** Ambidextrous thumb safety, twin extractors, disconnecting safety, dual action bars. Quiet Carry forend. Many barrels are ported. Mossberg Cablelock included. From Mossberg.

Price: From about **$316.00**
Price: Sporting Combos (field barrel and Slugster barrel), from . . **$381.00**

Mossberg Model 500 Bantam Pump

Same as the Model 500 Sporting Pump except 12 (new for 2001) or 20 gauge, 22" vent. rib Accu-Choke barrel with choke tube set; has 1" shorter stock, reduced length from pistol grip to trigger, reduced forend reach. Introduced 1992.

Price: **$316.00**
Price: With Realtree Hardwoods camouflage finish (20 ga. only). **$364.00**

Mossberg Model 500 Camo Pump

Same as the Model 500 Sporting Pump except 12 gauge only and entire gun is covered with Mossy Oak Advantage camouflage finish. Receiver drilled and tapped for scope mounting. Comes with quick detachable swivel studs, swivels, camouflage sling, Mossberg Cablelock.

Price: From about **$364.00**

MOSSBERG MODEL 500 PERSUADER/CRUISER SHOTGUN

Similar to Mossberg Model 500 except has 18-1/2" or 20" barrel with cylinder bore choke, synthetic stock and blue or Parkerized finish. Available in 12, 20 and .410 with bead or ghost ring sights, 6- or 8-shot mag-azines. From Mossberg.

Price: 12 gauge, 20" barrel, 8-shot, bead sight. **$391.00**
Price: 20 gauge or .410, 18-1/2" barrel, 6-shot, bead sight **$353.00**
Price: 12 gauge, parkerized finish, 6-shot, 18-1/2" barrel,
  ghost ring sights **$468.00**
Price: Home Security 410 (.410, 18-1/2" barrel
  with spreader choke) **$335.00**

Mossberg Model 590 Special Purpose Shotgun

Similar to Model 500 except has parkerized or Marinecote finish, 9-shot magazine and black synthetic stock (some models feature Speed Feed. Available in 12 gauge only with 20", cylinder bore barrel. Weighs 7-1/4 lbs. From Mossberg.

Price: Bead sight, heat shield over barrel **$417.00**
Price: Ghost ring sight, Speed Feed stock. **$586.00**

MOSSBERG MODEL 500 SLUGSTER

Gauge: 12, 20, 3" chamber. **Barrel:** 24", ported rifled bore. Integral scope mount. **Weight:** 7-1/4 lbs. **Length:** 44" overall. **Stock:** 14" pull, 1-3/8" drop at heel. Walnut; Dual Comb design for proper eye positioning with or without scoped barrels. Recoil pad and swivel studs. **Features:** Ambidextrous thumb safety, twin extractors, dual slide bars. Comes with scope mount. Mossberg Cablelock included. Introduced 1988.

Price: Rifled bore, integral scope mount, 12 or 20 ga. **$361.00**
Price: Fiber Optic, rifle sights **$361.00**
Price: Rifled bore, rifle sights **$338.00**
Price: 20 ga., Standard or Bantam, from **$338.00**

REMINGTON MODEL 870 WINGMASTER

Gauge: 12ga., 16 ga., 3" chamber. **Barrel:** 26", 28", 30" (Rem chokes). **Weight:** 7-1/4 lbs.. **Length:** 46", 48". **Stock:** Walnut, hardwood, synthetic. **Sights:** Single bead (Twin bead Wingmaster). **Features:** Balistically balanced performance, milder recoil. Light contour barrel. Double action bars, cross-bolt safety, blue finish.

Price: Wingmaster, walnut, blued, 26", 28", 30" **$584.00**
Price: 870 Wingmaster Super Magnum, 3-1/2" chamber, 28" . . . **$665.00**

Remington Model 870 50th Anniversary Classic Trap

Remington Model 870 Marine Magnum

Remington Model 870 Wingmaster LW

Remington Model 870 Express Super Magnum

Remington Model 870 50th Anniversary Classic Trap Shotgun

Similar to Model 870 Wingmaster except has 30" ventilated rib, light contour barrel, singles, mid and long handicap choke tubes, semi-fancy American walnut stock, high-polish blued receiver with engraving. Chamber 2-1/2". From Remington Arms Co.

Price: **$792.00**

Remington Model 870 Marine Magnum

Similar to 870 Wingmaster except all metal plated with electroless nickel, black synthetic stock and forend. Has 18" plain barrel (cyl.), bead front sight, 7-shot magazine. Introduced 1992.

Price: **$573.00**

Remington Model 870 Wingmaster LW

Similar to Model 870 Wingmaster except in 20, 28 gauges and .410-bore only, 25" vent rib barrel with Rem choke tubes, high-gloss wood finish. 26" & 28" barrels-20 ga.

Price: 20 gauge **$584.00**
Price: .410-bore **$612.00**
Price: 28 gauge **$665.00**

Remington Model 870 Express

Similar to 870 Wingmaster except walnut-toned hardwood stock with solid, black recoil pad and pressed checkering on grip and forend. Outside metal surfaces have black oxide finish. Comes with 26" or 28" vent. rib barrel with mod. Rem choke tube.

Price: 12 ga., 20 ga., 16 ga. (28") **$332.00**
Price: Express Combo, 12 ga., 26" vent rib with mod. Rem choke and 20" fully rifled barrel with rifle sights, or Rem. choke.... **$443.00 to $476.00**
Price: Express L-H (left-hand), 12 ga., 28" vent rib with mod. Rem choke tube.................................... **$359.00**
Price: Express Synthetic, 12-ga, 26" or 28" **$332.00**
Price: Express Combo (20 ga.) with extra Deer rifled barrel, fully rifled or Rem. choke .... **$443.00 to $476.00**

Price: Express Small bore 28 ga., 25" **$359.00**
Price: Express Small bore .410, 25"...................... **$359.00**

Remington Model 870 Express Super Magnum

Similar to 870 Express except 28" vent. rib barrel with 3-1/2" chamber, vented recoil pad. Introduced 1998.

Price: **$376.00**
Price: Super Magnum Synthetic, 26"..................... **$376.00**
Price: Super Magnum Turkey Camo (full-coverage RealTree Advantage camo), 23" **$500.00**
Price: Super Magnum Combo (26" with Mod. Rem Choke and 20" fully rifled deer barrel with 3" chamber and rifle sights; wood stock) . **$523.00**
Price: Super Magnum Synthetic Turkey, 23" (black) **$389.00**

Remington Model 870 Wingmaster Super Magnum Shotgun

Similar to Model 870 Express Super Magnum except high-polish blued finish, 28" ventilated barrel with imp. cyl., modified and full choke tubes, checkered high-gloss walnut stock. Overall length 48", weighs 7-1/2 lbs. Introduced 2000.

Price: 3-1/2" chamber **$665.00**

Remington Model 870 Express Youth Gun

Same as Model 870 Express except 13" length of pull, 21" barrel with mod. Rem choke tube. Weighs 6.25 lbs. Hardwood stock with low-luster finish. Introduced 1991.

Price: 20 ga. Express Youth (1" shorter stock), from **$332.00**
Price: 20 ga. Youth Deer 20" FR/RS **$365.00**
Price: 16 ga. Youth Synthetic **$332.00**

Remington Model 870 Express Rifle-Sighted Deer Gun

Same as Model 870 Express except 20" barrel with fixed imp. cyl. choke, open iron sights, Monte Carlo stock. Introduced 1991.

Price: **$332.00**
Price: With fully rifled barrel **$365.00**
Price: Express Synthetic Deer (black synthetic stock, black matte metal) **$372.00**

Remington Model 870 Express Deer Gun

Remington Model 870 Express Turkey

Remington Model 870 SPS Super Slug Deer Gun

Remington Model 870 SPS-T Camo

Remington Model 870 Express Turkey
Same as Model 870 Express except 3" chamber, 21" vent rib turkey barrel and extra-full Rem. choke turkey tube; 12 ga. only. Introduced 1991.
Price: **$345.00**
Price: Express Turkey Camo stock has Skyline Excel camo, matte black metal **$399.00**
Price: Express Youth Turkey camo (as above with 1" shorter length of pull), 20 ga., Skyline Excel camo **$399.00**

Remington Model 870 Express Synthetic 18"
Similar to 870 Express with 18" barrel except synthetic stock and forend; 7-shot. Introduced 1994.
Price: **$319.00**

Remington Model 870 SPS Super Slug Deer Gun
Similar to the Model 870 Express Synthetic except has 23" rifled, modified contour barrel with cantilever scope mount. Comes with black synthetic stock and forend with swivel studs, black Cordura nylon sling. Introduced 1999. Fully rifled centilever barrel.
Price: **$580.00**

Remington Model 870 SPS-T Synthetic Camo Shotgun
Chambered for 12 ga., 3" shells, has Mossy Oak Break-Up® synthetic stock and metal treatment, TruGlo fiber optic sights. Introduced 2001.
Price: 20" RS, Rem. choke **$595.00**
Price: Youth version **$595.00**
Price: Super Magnum Camo, 23", CL Rem. Choke **$609.00**
Price: Super Magnum Camo 23", VT Rem. Choke **$591.00**

Price: 20 ga., Truglo sights, Rem. Choke, Mossy Oak Break-Up Camo **$595.00**

REMINGTON MODEL 870 SPS SUPER MAGNUM CAMO
Synthetic stock and all metal (except bolt and trigger guard) and stock covered with Mossy Oak Break-Up camo finish. In 12 gauge 3-1/2", 26", 28" vent rib, Rem choke. Comes with camo sling, swivels.
Price: **$591.00**

SARSILMAZ PUMP SHOTGUN
Gauge: 12, 3" chamber. **Barrel:** 26" or 28". Stocks: Oil-finished hardwood. **Features:** Includes extra pistol-grip stock. Introduced 2000. Imported from Turkey by Armsport Inc.
Price: With pistol-grip stock **$299.95**
Price: With metal stock **$349.95**

TRISTAR MODEL 1887
Gauge: 12. **Barrel:** 22". **Weight:** 8.75 lbs. **Length:** 40-1/2". Stocks: Walnut. **Features:** Imp. cylinder choke, 5 shell, oil finish. Introduced 2002. Made in Australia. Available through AcuSport Corp.
Price: With pistol-grip stock **$299.95**

WINCHESTER MODEL 1300 WALNUT FIELD PUMP
Gauge: 12, 20, 3" chamber, 5-shot capacity. **Barrel:** 26", 28", vent. rib, with Full, Mod., Imp. Cyl. Winchoke tubes. **Weight:** 6-3/8 lbs. **Length:** 42-5/8" overall. **Stock:** American walnut, with deep cut checkering on pistol grip, traditional ribbed forend; high luster finish. **Sights:** Metal bead front. **Features:** Twin action slide bars; front-locking rotary bolt; roll-engraved receiver; blued, highly polished metal; cross-bolt safety with red indicator. Introduced 1984. From U.S. Repeating Arms Co., Inc.
Price: **$439.00**

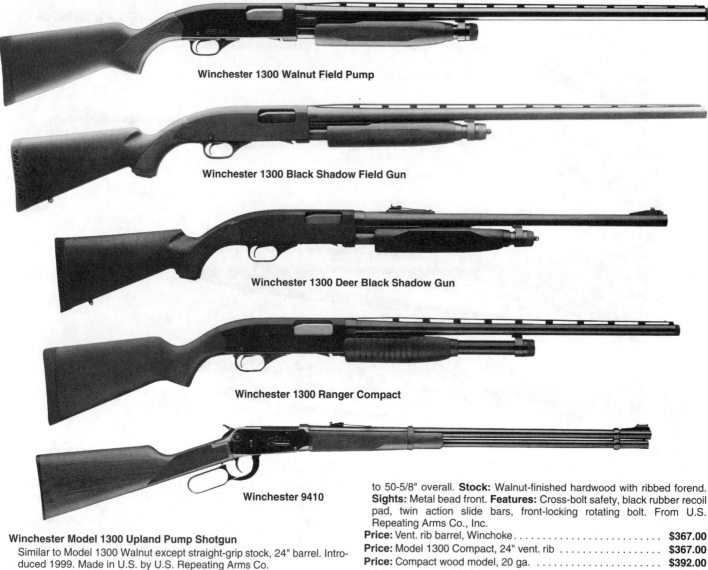

Winchester 1300 Walnut Field Pump

Winchester 1300 Black Shadow Field Gun

Winchester 1300 Deer Black Shadow Gun

Winchester 1300 Ranger Compact

Winchester 9410

Winchester Model 1300 Upland Pump Shotgun
Similar to Model 1300 Walnut except straight-grip stock, 24" barrel. Introduced 1999. Made in U.S. by U.S. Repeating Arms Co.
Price: **$439.00**

Winchester Model 1300 Black Shadow Field Shotgun
Similar to Model 1300 Walnut except black composite stock and forend, matte black finish. Has vent rib 26" or 28" barrel, 3" chamber, mod. WinChoke tube. Introduced 1995. From U.S. Repeating Arms Co., Inc.
Price: 12 or 20 gauge **$353.00**

Winchester Model 1300 Deer Black Shadow Shotgun
Similar to Model 1300 Black Shadow Turkey Gun except ramp-type front sight, fully adjustable rear, drilled and tapped for scope mounting. Black composite stock and forend, matte black metal. Smoothbore 22" barrel with one imp. cyl. WinChoke tube; 12 gauge only, 3" chamber. Weighs 6-3/4 lbs. Introduced 1994. From U.S. Repeating Arms Co., Inc.
Price: With rifled barrel. **$377.00**
Price: With cantilever scope mount. **$422.00**
Price: Combo (22" rifled and 28" smoothbore bbls.). **$455.00**
Price: Wood stock (20 ga., 22" rifled barrel) **$377.00**

WINCHESTER MODEL 1300 RANGER PUMP SHOTGUN
Gauge: 12, 20, 3" chamber, 5-shot magazine. **Barrel:** 28" vent. rib with Full, Mod., Imp. Cyl. Winchoke tubes. **Weight:** 7 to 7-1/4 lbs. **Length:** 48-5/8"

to 50-5/8" overall. **Stock:** Walnut-finished hardwood with ribbed forend. **Sights:** Metal bead front. **Features:** Cross-bolt safety, black rubber recoil pad, twin action slide bars, front-locking rotating bolt. From U.S. Repeating Arms Co., Inc.
Price: Vent. rib barrel, Winchoke. **$367.00**
Price: Model 1300 Compact, 24" vent. rib **$367.00**
Price: Compact wood model, 20 ga. **$392.00**

Winchester Model 1300 Turkey, Universal Hunter Shotgun
Rotary bolt action. Durable Mossy oak break-up finish on 26" VR barrel extra full turkey improved cylinder, modified and full WinChoke tubes included. 3", 12 gauge chamber.
Price: Universal Hunter **$515.00**
Price: Buck and Tom **$554.00**
Price: Short Turkey 512.00

WINCHESTER MODEL 9410 LEVER-ACTION SHOTGUN
Gauge: .410, 2-1/2" chamber. **Barrel:** 24" cyl. bore, also Invector choke system. **Weight:** 6-3/4 lbs. **Length:** 42-1/8" overall. **Stock:** Checkered walnut straight-grip; checkered walnut forearm. **Sights:** Adjustable "V" rear, TruGlo® front. **Features:** Model 94 rifle action (smoothbore) chambered for .410 shotgun. Angle Controlled Eject extractor/ejector; choke tubes; 9-shot tubular magazine; 13-1/2" length of pull. Introduced 2001. From U.S. Repeating Arms Co.
Price: 9410 fixed choke **$579.00**
Price: 9410 Packer w/chokes **$600.00**
Price: 9410 w/Invector, traditional model **$645.00**
Price: 9410 w/Invector, Packer model. **$667.00**
Price: 9410 w/Invector, semi-fancy traditional **$789.00**

Includes a variety of game guns and guns for competitive shooting.

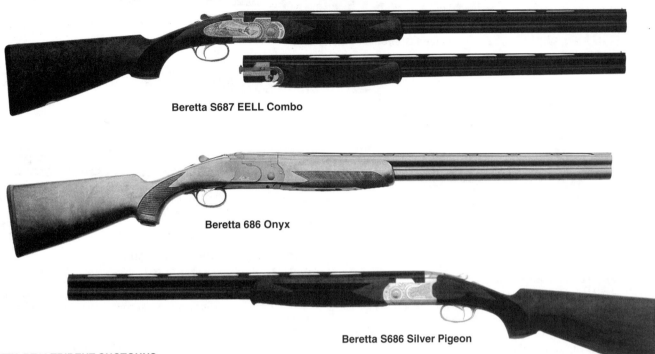

Beretta S687 EELL Combo

Beretta 686 Onyx

Beretta S686 Silver Pigeon

BERETTA DT10 TRIDENT SHOTGUNS

Gauge: 12, 2-3/4", 3" chambers. **Barrel:** 28", 30", 32", 34"; competition-style vent rib; fixed or Optima Choke tubes. **Weight:** 7.9 to 9 lbs. **Stock:** High-grade walnut stock with oil finish; hand-checkered grip and forend, adjustable stocks available. **Features:** Detachable, adjustable trigger group, raised and thickened receiver, forend iron has replaceable nut to guarantee wood-to-metal fit, Optima Bore to improve shot pattern and reduce felt recoil. Introduced 2000. Imported from Italy by Beretta USA.

Price: DT10 Trident Trap (selective, lockable single trigger,
adjustable stock). **$6,686.00**
Price: DT10 Trident Top Single **$6,686.00**
Price: DT10 Trident X Trap Combo
(single and o/u barrels) . . . . **$9,005.00-$9,557.00**
Price: DT10 Trident Skeet (skeet stock with rounded recoil
pad, tapered rib) **$6,866.00**
Price: DT10 Trident Sporting (sporting clays stock with
rounded recoil pad) **$6,383.00**
Price: DT10L Sporting **$7,797.00**

BERETTA SERIES 682 GOLD E SKEET, TRAP, SPORTING OVER/UNDERS

Gauge: 12, 2-3/4" chambers. **Barrel:** Skeet-28"; trap-30" and 32", imp. mod. & full and Mobilchoke; trap mono shotguns-32" and 34" Mobilchoke; trap top single guns-32" and 34" full and Mobilchoke; trap combo sets-from 30" O/U, to 32" O/U, 34" top single. **Stock:** Close-grained walnut, hand checkered. **Sights:** White Bradley bead front sight and center bead. **Features:** Receiver has Greystone gunmetal gray finish with gold accents. Trap Monte Carlo stock has deluxe trap recoil pad. Various grades available; contact Beretta USA for details. Imported from Italy by Beretta USA.

Price: 682 Gold E Trap with adjustable stock **$3,933.00**
Price: 682 Gold E Trap Top Combo . . . . **$3,485..00**
Price: 682 Gold E Sporting **$3,937.00**
Price: 682 Gold E Skeet, adjustable stock **$3,905.00**
Price: 682 Gold E Double Trap . . . . **NA**
Price: 687 EELL Diamond Pigeon Sporting **$6,207.00**

BERETTA 686 ONYX O/U SHOTGUN

Gauge: 12, 3" chambers. **Barrel:** 28", 30" (Mobilchoke tubes). **Weight:** 7.7 lbs. **Stock:** Checkered American walnut. **Features:** Intended for the beginning Sporting Clays shooter. Has wide, vented 12.5mm target rib, radiused recoil pad. Polished black finish on receiver and barrels. Introduced 1993. Imported from Italy by Beretta U.S.A.

Price: White Onyx. **$1,718.00**
Price: Onyx Pro **$1,856.00**
Price: Onyx Pro 3.5 . . . . **$1,929.00**

BERETTA 686 SILVER PIGEON O/U SHOTGUN

Gauge: 12, 20, 28, 3" chambers (2-3/4" 28 ga.). **Barrel:** 26", 28". **Weight:** 6.8 lbs. **Stock:** Checkered walnut. **Features:** Interchangeable barrels (20 and 28 ga.), single selective gold-plated trigger, boxlock action, auto safety, schnabel forend.

Price: Silver Pigeon S. **$1,994.00**
Price: Silver Pigeon S Combo **$2,757.00**

BERETTA ULTRALIGHT OVER/UNDER

Gauge: 12, 2-3/4" chambers. **Barrel:** 26", 28", Mobilchoke choke tubes. **Weight:** About 5 lbs., 13 oz. **Stock:** Select American walnut with checkered grip and forend. **Features:** Low-profile aluminum alloy receiver with titanium breech face insert. Electroless nickel receiver with game scene engraving. Single selective trigger; automatic safety. Introduced 1992. Imported from Italy by Beretta U.S.A.

Price: **$1,931.00**
Price: Silver Pigeon II **$2,270.00**
Price: Silver Pigeon II Combo. **$3.098.00**
Price: Silver Pigeon III **$2,408.00**
Price: Silver Pigeon IV **$2,684.00**
Price: Silver Pigeon V. **$3,171.00**

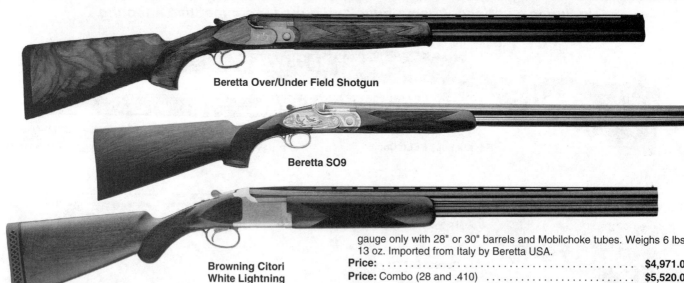

Beretta Over/Under Field Shotgun

Beretta SO9

Browning Citori White Lightning

Beretta Ultralight Deluxe Over/Under Shotgun

Similar to the Ultralight except has matte electroless nickel finish receiver with gold game scene engraving; matte oil-finished, select walnut stock and forend. Imported from Italy by Beretta U.S.A.

Price: **$2,323.00**

BERETTA OVER/UNDER FIELD SHOTGUNS

Gauge: 12, 20, 28, and .410 bore, 2-3/4", 3" and 3-1/2" chambers. **Barrel:** 26" and 28" (Mobilchoke tubes). **Stock:** Close-grained walnut. **Features:** Highly-figured, American walnut stocks and forends, and a unique, weather-resistant finish on barrels. Silver designates standard 686, 687 models with silver receivers; 686 Silver Pigeon has enhanced engraving pattern, schnabel forend; 686 Silver Essential has matte chrome finish; Gold indicates higher grade 686EL, 687EL models with full sideplates; Diamond is for 687EELL models with highest grade wood, engraving. Case provided with Gold and Diamond grades. Imported from Italy by Beretta U.S.A.

Price: S686 Silver Pigeon two-bbl. set **$2,587.00**
Price: S686 Silver Pigeon **$1,817.00**
Price: S687 Silver Pigeon II Sporting **$2,196.00**
Price: Combo 29" and 30" **$3,151.00**
Price: S687EL Gold Pigeon (gold inlays, sideplates) **$4,099.00**
Price: S687EL Gold Pigeon, .410, 26"; 28 ga., 28" **$4,273.00**
Price: S687 EL Gold Pigeon II (deep relief engraving) **$4,513.00**
Price: S687 EL Gold Pigeon II Sporting (D.R. engraving) **$4,554.00**

BERETTA MODEL SO5, SO6, SO9 SHOTGUNS

Gauge: 12, 2-3/4" chambers. **Barrel:** To customer specs. **Stock:** To customer specs. **Features:** SO5-Trap, Skeet and Sporting Clays models SO5; SO6- SO6 and SO6 EELL are field models. SO6 has a case-hardened or silver receiver with contour hand engraving. SO6 EELL has hand-engraved receiver in a fine floral or "fine English" pattern or game scene, with bas-relief chisel work and gold inlays. SO6 and SO6 EELL are available with sidelocks removable by hand. Imported from Italy by Beretta U.S.A.

Price: SO5 Trap, Skeet, Sporting **$13,000.00**
Price: SO6 Trap, Skeet, Sporting **$17,500.00**
Price: SO6 EELL Field, custom specs **$28,000.00**
Price: SO9 (12, 20, 28, .410, 26", 28", 30", any choke) **$31,000.00**

Beretta S687EL Gold Pigeon Sporting O/U

Similar to S687 Silver Pigeon Sporting except sideplates with gold inlay game scene, vent side and top ribs, bright orange front sight. Stock and forend are high grade walnut with fine-line checkering. Available in 12

gauge only with 28" or 30" barrels and Mobilchoke tubes. Weighs 6 lbs., 13 oz. Imported from Italy by Beretta USA.

Price: **$4,971.00**
Price: Combo (28 and .410) **$5,520.00**

BRNO ZH 300 OVER/UNDER SHOTGUN

Gauge: 12, 2-3/4" chambers. **Barrel:** 26", 27-1/2", 29" (Skeet, Imp. Cyl., Mod., Full). **Weight:** 7 lbs. **Length:** 44.4" overall. **Stock:** European walnut. **Features:** Double triggers; automatic safety; polished blue finish engraved receiver. Announced 1998. Imported from the Czech Republic by Euro-Imports.

Price: ZH 301, field **$594.00**
Price: ZH 302, skeet **$608.00**
Price: ZH 303, 12 ga. trap **$608.00**
Price: ZH 321, 16 ga. **$595.00**

BRNO 501.2 OVER/UNDER SHOTGUN

Gauge: 12, 2-3/4" chambers. **Barrel:** 27.5" (Full & Mod.). **Weight:** 7 lbs. **Length:** 44" overall. **Stock:** European walnut. **Features:** Boxlock action with double triggers, ejectors; automatic safety; hand-cut checkering. Announced 1998. Imported from The Czech Republic by Euro-Imports.

Price: **$850.00**

BROWNING CITORI O/U SHOTGUNS

Gauge: 12, 20, 28 and .410. **Barrel:** 26", 28" in 28 and .410. Offered with In-ector choke tubes. All 12 and 20 gauge models have back-bored barrels and Invector Plus choke system. **Weight:** 6 lbs., 8 oz. (26" .410) to 7 lbs., 13 oz. (30" 12 ga.). **Length:** 43" overall (26" bbl.). **Stock:** Dense walnut, hand checkered, full pistol grip, beavertail forend. Field-type recoil pad on 12 ga. field guns and trap and Skeet models. **Sights:** Medium raised beads, German nickel silver. **Features:** Barrel selector integral with safe-ty, automatic ejectors, three-piece takedown. Imported from Japan by Browning. Contact Browning for complete list of models and prices.

Price: Grade I, Hunter, Invector, 12 and 20 . . . . **$1,486.00**
Price: Grade I, Lightning, 28 and .410, Invector **$1,594.00**
Price: Grade III, Lightning, 28 and .410, Invector **$2,570.00**
Price: Grade VI, 28 and .410 Lightning, Invector **$3,780.00**
Price: Grade I, Lightning, Invector Plus, 12, 20 . . . . **$1,534.00**
Price: Grade I, Hunting, 28", 30" only, 3-1/2", Invector Plus **$1,489.00**
Price: Grade III, Lightning, Invector, 12, 20 . . . . **$2,300.00**
Price: Grade VI, Lightning, Invector, 12, 20 . . . . **$3,510.00**
Price: Gran Lightning, 26", 28", Invector, 12, 20 . . . . **$2,184.00**
Price: Gran Lightning, 28, .410 . . . . **$2,302.00**
Price: Micro Lightning, 20 ga., 24" bbl., 6 lbs., 4 oz. **$1,591.00**
Price: White Lightning (silver nitride receiver w/engraving, 12 or 20 ga., 26", 28") **$1,583.00**
Price: White Lightning, 28 or .410 gauge **$1,654.00**
Price: Citori Satin Hunter (12 ga., satin-finished wood, matte-finished barrels and receiver) 3-1/2" chambers **$1,535.00**

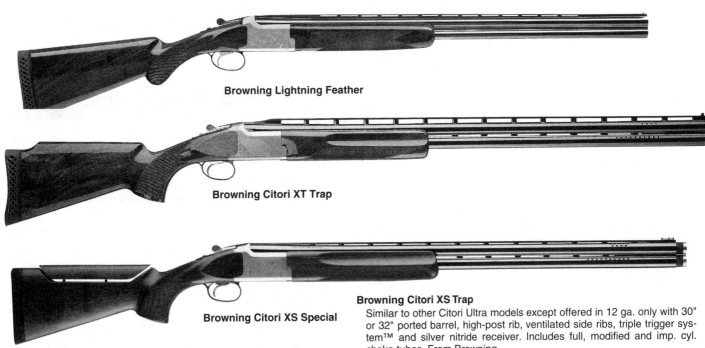

Browning Lightning Feather

Browning Citori XT Trap

Browning Citori XS Special

BROWNING LIGHTNING FEATHER CITORI OVER/UNDER

Similar to the standard Citori except available in 12, 20, 28 or .410 with, 26" or 28" barrels choked Imp. Cyl., Mod. and Full. Has pistol grip stock, rounded forend. Lightning Feather 12 weighs 7 lbs., 15 oz. (26" barrels); Lightning Feather 20 weighs 6 lbs., 10 oz. (26" barrels). Introduced 2004.

Price: Lightning, 28 or .410 . . . . **$1,659.00**
Price: Lightning 12 or 20 . . . . **$1,597.00**
Price: White Lightning, 28 or .410 . . . . **$1,738.00**
Price: White Lightning, 12 or 20 . . . . **$1,664.00**
Price: Citori 525 Field, 28 or .410 . . . . **$1,914.00**
Price: Citori 525 Field, 12 or 20 . . . . **$1,885.00**
Price: Citori Superlight Feather, 12 or 20 . . . . **$1,882.00**
Price: Citori Lightning Feather, 12 or 20 . . . . **$1,815.00**
Price: Citori Lightning Feather Combo (20 & 28) **$2,949.00**

Browning Citori XT Trap Over/Under

Similar to the Citori Special Trap except has engraved silver nitride receiver with gold highlights, vented side barrel rib. Available In 12 gauge with 30" or 32" barrels, Invector-Plus choke tubes. Introduced 1999. Imported by Browning.

Price: **$1,834.00**
Price: With adjustable-comb stock **$2,054.00**

Browning Citori Lightning Feather O/U

Similar to the 12 gauge Citori Grade I except has 2-3/4" chambers, rounded pistol grip, lightning-style forend, and lightweight alloy receiver. Weighs 6 lbs. 15 oz. with 26" barrels (12 ga.); 6 lbs., 2 oz. (20 ga., 26" bbl.), sil-vered, engraved receiver. Introduced 1999. Imported by Browning.

Price: 12 or 20 ga., 26" or 28" barrels **$1,693.00**
Price: Lightning Feather Combo
(20 and 28 ga. bbls., 27" each) **$2,751.00**

Browning Citori XS Skeet

Similar to other Citori Ultra models except features a semi-beavertail forearm with deep finger grooves, ported barrels and triple system. Adjustable comb is optional. Introduced 2000.

Price: 12 ga., 28" or 30" barrel **$2,363.00**
Price: 20 ga., 28" or 30" barrel **$2,363.00**

Browning Citori XS Trap

Similar to other Citori Ultra models except offered in 12 ga. only with 30" or 32" ported barrel, high-post rib, ventilated side ribs, triple trigger system™ and silver nitride receiver. Includes full, modified and imp. cyl. choke tubes. From Browning.

Price: 30" or 32" barrel **$2,209.00**
Price: Adjustable-comb Model **$2,475.00**

Browning Citori XS Special

Similar to other Citori XS models except offered in 12 gauge ony, silver nitride receiver with new Special engraving, adjustable comb, low profile rib, right-hand palm swell, Triple Trigger™ system, HiViz® Pro-Comb sight with mid bead, Invector-Plus™ choke system with five Midas chokes. From Browning.

Price: **$2,727.00**

Browning Citori XS Sporting

Similar to other Citori XS models except offered in 12 and 20 gauge. silver nitride receiver, schnabel forearm, ventilated side rib. Imported by Browning.

Price: 12 or 20 ga. **$2,400.00**

Browning Citori Feather Shotgun

Similar to the standard Citori. Available in Lightning and Superlight models only. Introduced 2000.

Price: 28" or 30" barrel . . . . **$2,266.00 To $2,338.00**

Browning Citori High Grade Shotguns

Similar to standard Citori except has engraved hunting scenes and gold inlays, High-grade, Hand-oiled walnut stock and forearm. Introduced 2000. From Browning.

Price: Citori VI Lightning blue or gray (gold inlays of ducks and pheasants) From **$3,797.00**
Price: Citori Grade III Superlight (bird scene engraving on grayed receiver, gold inlays) **$2,464.00**
Price: Citori 525 Golden Clays (engraving of game bird-clay bird transition, gold accents), 12 or 20 ga. **$4,236.00**

Browning Citori XS Sporting Clays

Similar to the Citori Grade I except has silver nitride receiver with gold accents, stock dimensions of 14-3/4"x1-1/2"x2-1/4" with satin finish, right-hand palm swell, schnabel forend. Comes with modified, imp. cyl. and skeet invector-plus choke tubes. Back-bored barrels; vented side ribs. Introduced 1999. Imported by Browning.

Price: 12, 20 ga. **$2,400.00**

Browning 525 Sporting Clays

Charles Daly Superior Trap

Charles Daly Field Hunter

Browning Lightning Sporting Clays

Similar to the Citori Lightning with rounded pistol grip and classic forend. Has high post tapered rib or lower hunting-style rib with 30" back-bored Invector Plus barrels, ported or non-ported, 3" chambers. Gloss stock finish, radiused recoil pad. Has "Lightning Sporting Clays Edition" engraved and gold filled on receiver. Introduced 1989.

Price: Low-rib, ported $1,691.00
Price: High-rib, ported. $1,770.00

BROWNING 525 SPORTING CLAYS

Gauge: 12, 20, 2-3/4" chambers. **Barrel:** 12 ga.-28", 30", 32" (Invector Plus tubes), back-bored; 20 ga.-28", 30" (Invector Plus tubes). **Weight:** 7 lbs., 13 oz. (12 ga., 28"). **Stock:** 14-13/16" (1/8")x1-7/16"x2-3/16" (12 ga.). Select walnut with gloss finish, cut checkering, schnabel forend. **Features:** Grayed receiver with engraving, blued barrels. Barrels are ported on 12 gauge guns. Has low 10mm wide vent rib. Comes with three interchangeable trigger shoes to adjust length of pull. Introduced in U.S. 1993. Imported by Browning.

Price: Grade I, 12, 20 ga., Invector Plus. $2,645.00
Price: Golden Clays, 12, 20 ga., Invector Plus $4,236.00

CHARLES DALY SUPERIOR TRAP AE MC

Gauge: 12, 2-3/4" chambers. **Barrel:** 30" choke tubes. **Weight:** About 7 lbs. **Stock:** Checkered walnut; pistol grip, semi-beavertail forend. **Features:** Silver engraved receiver, chrome moly steel barrels; gold single selective trigger; automatic safety, automatic ejectors; red bead front sight, metal bead center; recoil pad. Introduced 1997. Imported from Italy by K.B.I., Inc.

Price: $1,339.00

CHARLES DALY FIELD HUNTER OVER/UNDER SHOTGUN

Gauge: 12, 20, 28 and .410 bore (3" chambers, 28 ga. has 2-3/4"). **Barrel:** 28" Mod & Full, 26" Imp. Cyl. & Mod (.410 is Full & Full). **Weight:** About 7 lbs. **Length:** NA. **Stock:** Checkered walnut pistol grip and forend. **Features:** Blued engraved receiver, chrome moly steel barrels; gold single selective trigger; automatic safety; extractors; gold bead front sight. Introduced 1997. Imported from Italy by K.B.I., Inc.

Price: 12 or 20 ga. $799.00
Price: 28 ga. $879.00
Price: .410 bore $919.00

Charles Daly Field Hunter AE Shotgun

Similar to the Field Hunter except 28 gauge only; 26" (Imp. Cyl. & Mod., 28 gauge), 26" (Full & Full, .410); automatic; ejectors. Introduced 1997. Imported from Italy by K.B.I., Inc.

Price: 28 . . . . $999.00

Charles Daly Superior Hunter AE Shotgun

Similar to the Field Hunter AE except has silvered, engraved receiver. Introduced 1997. Imported from Italy by F.B.I., Inc.

Price: 28 ga. $1,129.00
Price: .410 bore $1,129.00

Charles Daly Field Hunter AE-MC

Similar to the Field Hunter except in 12 or 20 only, 26" or 28" barrels with five multichoke tubes; automatic ejectors. Introduced 1997. Imported from Italy by K.B.I., Inc.

Price: 12 or 20 . . . . $979.95

Charles Daly Superior Sporting O/U

Similar to the Field Hunter AE-MC except 28" or 30" barrels; silvered, engraved receiver; five choke tubes; ported barrels; red bead front sight. Introduced 1997. Imported from Italy by K.B.I., Inc.

Price: $1,259.95

CHARLES DALY DIAMOND REGENT GTX DL HUNTER O/U

Gauge: 12, 20, .410, 3" chambers, 28, 2-3/4" chambers. **Barrel:** 26", 28", 30" (choke tubes), 26" (Imp. Cyl. & Mod. in 28, 26" (Full & Full) in .410. **Weight:** About 7 lbs. **Stock:** Extra select fancy European walnut with 24" hand checkering, hand rubbed oil finish. **Features:** Boss-type action with internal side lumps. Deep cut hand-engraved scrollwork and game scene set in full sideplates. GTX detachable single selective trigger system with coil springs; chrome moly steel barrels; automatic safety; automatic ejectors, white bead front sight, metal bead center sight. Introduced 1997. Imported from Italy by K.B.I., Inc.

Price: 12 or 20 . . . . **Special order only**
Price: 28 . . . . **Special order only**
Price: .410 . . . . **Special order only**
Price: Diamond Regent GTX EDL Hunter (as above with engraved scroll and birds, 10 gold inlays), 12 or 20 . . . . **Special order only**
Price: As above, 28. . . . . **Special order only**
Price: As above, .410 . . . . **Special order only**

CHARLES DALY EMPIRE EDL HUNTER O/U

Gauge: 12, 20, .410, 3" chambers, 28 ga., 2-3/4". **Barrel:** 26", 28" (12, 20, choke tubes), 26" (Imp. Cyl. & Mod., 28 ga.), 26" (Full & Full, .410). **Weight:** About 7 lbs. **Stocks:** Checkered walnut pistol grip buttstock, semi-beaver-tail forend; recoil pad. **Features:** Silvered, engraved receiver; chrome moly barrels; gold single selective trigger; automatic safety; automatic ejectors, red bead front sight, metal bead middle sight. Introduced 1997. Imported from Italy by K.B.I., Inc.

Price: Empire EDL (dummy sideplates) 12 or 20 . . . . $1,559.95
Price: Empire EDL, 28 . . . . $1,559.95
Price: Empire EDL, .410. . . . . $1,599.95

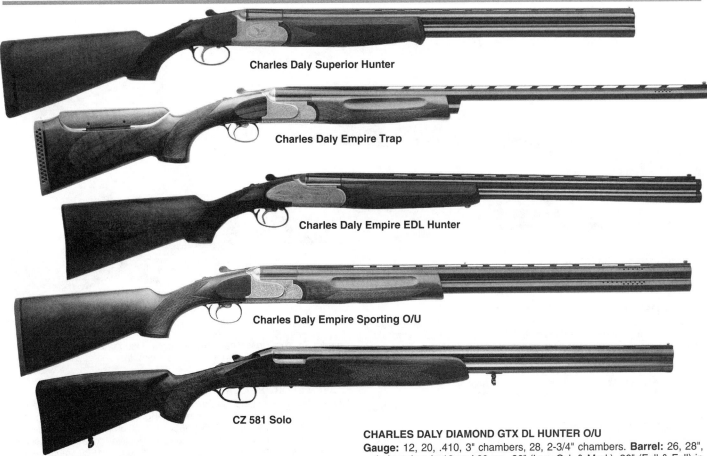

Charles Daly Superior Hunter

Charles Daly Empire Trap

Charles Daly Empire EDL Hunter

Charles Daly Empire Sporting O/U

CZ 581 Solo

Charles Daly Empire Sporting O/U

Similar to the Empire EDL Hunter except 12 or 20 gauge only, 28", 30" barrels with choke tubes; ported barrels; special stock dimensions. Introduced 1997. Imported from Italy by K.B.I., Inc.

Price: **$1,499.95**

CHARLES DALY EMPIRE TRAP AE MC

Gauge: 12, 2-3/4" chambers. **Barrel:** 30" choke tubes. **Weight:** About 7 lbs. **Stock:** Checkered walnut; pistol grip, semi-beavertail forend. **Features:** Silvered, engraved, reinforced receiver; chrome moly steel barrels; gold single selective trigger; automatic safety, automatic ejector; red bead front sight, metal bead center; recoil pad. Imported from Italy by K.B.I., Inc.

Price: **$1,539.95**

CHARLES DALY DIAMOND GTX SPORTING O/U SHOTGUN

Gauge: 12, 20, 3" chambers. **Barrel:** 28", 30" with choke tubes. **Weight:** About 8.5 lbs. **Stock:** Checkered deluxe walnut; Sporting clays dimensions. Pistol grip; semi-beavertail forend; hand rubbed oil finish. **Features:** Chromed, hand-engraved receiver; chrome moly steel barrels; GTX de-tachable single selective trigger system with coil springs, automatic safety; automatic ejectors; red bead front sight; ported barrels. Introduced 1997. Imported from Italy by K.B.I., Inc.

Price: . . . . **Price on request**

CHARLES DALY DIAMOND GTX TRAP AE-MC O/U SHOTGUN

Gauge: 12, 2-3/4" chambers. **Barrel:** 30" (Full & Full). **Weight:** About 8.5 lbs. **Stock:** Checkered deluxe walnut; pistol grip; trap dimensions; semi-beaver-tail forend; hand-rubbed oil finish. **Features:** Silvered, hand-engraved receiver; chrome moly steel barrels; GTX detachable single selec-tive trigger system with coil springs, automatic safety, automatic-ejectors, red bead front sight, metal bead middle; recoil pad. Imported from Italy by K.B.I., Inc.

Price: . . . . **Price on request**

CHARLES DALY DIAMOND GTX DL HUNTER O/U

Gauge: 12, 20, .410, 3" chambers, 28, 2-3/4" chambers. **Barrel:** 26, 28", choke tubes in 12 and 20 ga., 26" (Imp. Cyl. & Mod.), 26" (Full & Full) in .410-bore. **Weight:** About 8.5 lbs. **Stock:** Select fancy European walnut stock, with 24 lpi hand checkering; hand-rubbed oil finish. **Features:** Boss-type action with internal side lugs, hand-engraved scrollwork and game scene. GTX detachable single selective trigger system with coil springs; chrome moly steel barrels, automatic safety, automatic ejectors, red bead front sight, recoil pad. Introduced 1997. Imported from Italy by K.B.I., Inc.

Price: . . . . **Special order only**

CZ 581 SOLO OVER/UNDER SHOTGUN

Gauge: 12, 2-3/4" chambers. **Barrel:** 27.6" (Mod. & Full). **Weight:** 7.37 lbs. **Length:** 44.5" overall. **Stock:** Circassian walnut. **Features:** Automatic ejectors; double triggers; Kersten-style double lump locking system. Imported from the Czech Republic by CZ-USA.

Price: **$799.00**

EAA BAIKAL IZH27 OVER/UNDER SHOTGUN

Gauge: 12 (3" chambers), 16 (2-3/4" chambers), 20 (3" chambers), 28 (2-3/4" chambers), .410 (3"). **Barrel:** 26-1/2", 28-1/2" (imp., mod. and full choke tubes for 12 and 20 gauges; improved cylinder and modified for 16 and 28 gauges; improved modified and full for .410; 16 also offered in mod. and full). **Weight:** NA. **Stock:** Walnut, checkered forearm and grip. Imported by European American Armory.

Price: IZH-27 (12, 16 and 20 gauge) **$509.00**
Price: IZH-27 (28 gauge and .410) **$569.00**

EAA Baikal IZH27 Sporting O/U

Basic IZH-27 with barrel porting, wide vent rib with double sight beads, engraved nickel receiver, checkered walnut stock and forend with palm swell and semi beavertail, 3 screw chokes, SS trigger, selectable ejectors, auto tang safety

Price: 12 ga., 29" bbl. **$589.00**

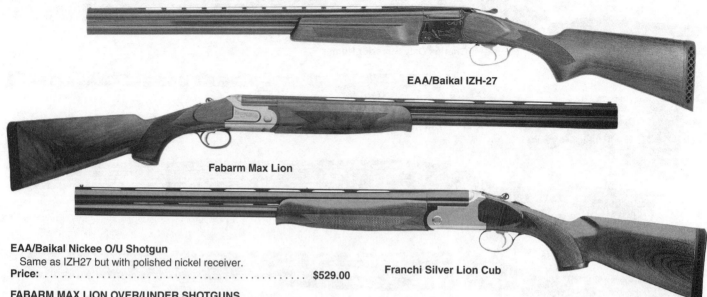

EAA/Baikal IZH-27

Fabarm Max Lion

Franchi Silver Lion Cub

EAA/Baikal Nickee O/U Shotgun
Same as IZH27 but with polished nickel receiver.
Price: **$529.00**

FABARM MAX LION OVER/UNDER SHOTGUNS
Gauge: 12, 3" chambers, 20, 3" chambers. **Barrel:** 26", 28", 30" (12 ga.); 26", 28" (20 ga.), choke tubes. **Weight:** 7.4 lbs. **Length:** 47.5" overall (26" barrel). **Stock:** European walnut; leather-covered recoil pad. **Features:** TriBore barrel, boxlock action with single selective trigger, manual safety, automatic ejectors; chrome-lined barrels; adjustable trigger. Silvered, engraved receiver. Comes with locking, fitted luggage case. Introduced 1998. Imported from Italy by Heckler & Koch, Inc.
Price: 12 or 20 . . . . **$1,799.00**

FABARM ULTRA CAMO MAG LION O/U SHOTGUN
Gauge: 12, 3-1/2" chambers. **Barrel:** 28" (cyl., imp. cyl., mod., imp. mod., full, SS-mod., SS-full choke tubes). **Weight:** 7.9 lbs. **Length:** 50" overall. **Stock:** Camo-colored walnut. **Features:** TriBore barrel, Wetlands Camo finished metal surfaces, single selective trigger, non-auto ejectors; leather-covered recoil pad. Locking hard plastic case. Introduced 1998. Imported from Italy by Heckler & Koch, Inc.
Price: **$1,229.00**

FABARM MAX LION PARADOX
Gauge: 12, 20, 3" chambers. **Barrel:** 24". **Weight:** 7.6 lbs. **Length:** 44.5" overall. **Stock:** Walnut with special enhancing finish. **Features:** TriBore upper barrel, both wood and receiver are enhanced with special finishes, color-case hardened type finish.
Price: 12 or 20 . . . . **$1,129.00**

FABARM SILVER LION OVER/UNDER SHOTGUNS
Gauge: 12, 3" chambers, 20, 3" chambers. **Barrel:** 26", 28", 30" (12 ga.); 26", 28" (20 ga.), choke tubes. **Weight:** 7.2 lbs. **Length:** 47.5" overall (26" barrels). **Stock:** Walnut; leather-covered recoil pad. **Features:** TriBore barrel, boxlock action with single selective trigger; silvered receiver with engraving; automatic ejectors. Comes with locking hard plastic case. Introduced 1998. Imported from Italy by Heckler & Koch, Inc.
Price: 12 or 20 . . . . **$1,229.00**

Fabarm Silver Lion Cub Model O/U
Similar to the Silver Lion except has 12.5" length of pull, is in 20 gauge only (3-1/2" chambers), and comes with 24" TriBore barrel system. Weight is 6 lbs. Introduced 1999. Imported from Italy by Heckler & Koch, Inc.
Price: **$1,229.00**

FABARM CAMO TURKEY MAG O/U SHOTGUN
Gauge: 12, 3-1/2" chambers. **Barrel:** 20" TriBore (Ultra-Full ported tubes). **Weight:** 7.5 lbs. **Length:** 46" overall. **Stock:** 14.5"x1.5"x2.29". Walnut. **Sights:** Front bar, Picatinny rail scope base. **Features:** Completely cov-

ered with Xtra Brown camouflage finish. Unported barrels. Introduced 1999. Imported from Italy by Heckler & Koch, Inc.
Price: **$1,199.00**

FABARM SPORTING CLAYS COMPETITION EXTRA O/U
Gauge: 12, 20, 3" chambers. **Barrel:** 12 ga. has 30", 20 ga. has 28"; ported TriBore barrel system with five tubes. **Weight:** 7 to 7.8 lbs. **Length:** 49.6" overall (20 ga.). **Stock:** 14.50"x1.38"x2.17" (20 ga.); deluxe walnut; leather-covered recoil pad. **Features:** Single selective trigger, auto ejectors; 10mm channeled rib; carbon fiber finish. Introduced 1999. Imported from Italy by Heckler & Koch, Inc.
Price: **$1,749.00**

FRANCHI ALCIONE FIELD OVER/UNDER SHOTGUN
Gauge: 12, 20, 3" chambers. **Barrel:** 26", 28"; IC, M, F tubes. **Weight:** 7.5 lbs. **Length:** 43" overall with 26" barrels. **Stock:** European walnut. **Features:** Boxlock action with ejectors, barrel selector mounted on trigger; silvered, engraved receiver, vent center rib, automatic safety, interchangeable 20 ga. bbls., left-hand available. Imported from Italy by Benelli USA. Hard case included.
Price: **$1,275.00**
Price: (20 gauge barrel set) **$460.00**

Franchi Alcione SX O/U Shotgun
Similar to Alcione Field model with high grade walnut stock and forend. Gold engraved removeable sideplates, interchangeable barrels.
Price: $1,800.00
Price: (12 gauge barrel set) . . . . **$450.00 to $500.00**
Price: (20 gauge barrel set) **$450.00**

Franchi Alcione Sport SL O/U Shotgun
Similar to Alcione except 2-3/4" chambers, elongated forcing cones and porting for Sporting Clays shooting. 10mm vent rib, tightly curved pistol grip, manual safety, removeable sideplates. Imported from Italy by Benelli USA.
Price: **$1,650.00**

FRANCHI ALCIONE TITANIUM OVER/UNDER SHOTGUN
Gauge: 12, 20, 3" chambers. **Barrel:** 26", 28"; IC, M, F tubes. **Weight:** 6.8 lbs. **Length:** 43", 45". **Stock:** Select walnut. **Sights:** Front/mid. **Features:** Receiver (titanium inserts) made of aluminum alloy. 7mm vent rib. Fast locking triggers. Left-hand available.
Price: **$1,425.00**

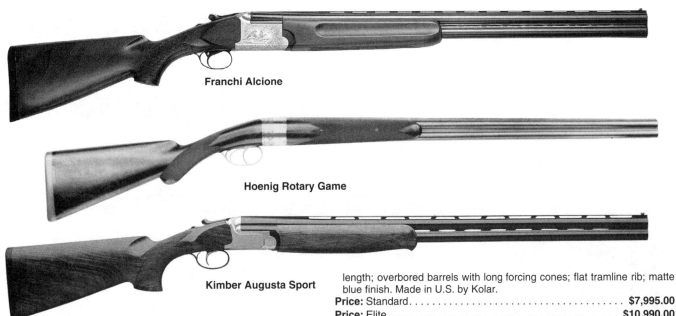

Franchi Alcione

Hoenig Rotary Game

Kimber Augusta Sport

FRANCHI 912 SHOTGUN
Gauge: 12 ga., 2-3/4", 3", 3-1/2"" chambers. **Barrel:** 24"-30". **Weight:** Appx. 7.6 lbs. **Length:** 46"-52". **Stock:** Walnut, synthetic, Timber HD. **Sights:** White bead front. **Features:** Based on 612 design, magazine cut-off, stepped vent rib, dual-recoil-reduction system.
Price: Satin walnut **$1,000.00**
Price: Synthetic **$940.00**
Price: Timber HD Camo **$1,050.00**

FRANCHI VELOCE OVER/UNDER SHOTGUN
Gauge: 20, 28. **Barrel:** 26", 28"; IC, M, F tubes. **Weight:** 5.5-5.8 lbs. **Length:** 43"-45". **Stock:** High grade walnut. **Features:** Aluminum receiver with steel reinforcement scaled to 20 gauge for light weight. Pistol grip stock with slip recoil pad. Imported by Benelli USA. Hard case included.
Price: **$1,425.00**
Price: 28 ga. **$1,500.00**

FRANCHI VELOCE ENGLISH OVER/UNDER SHOTGUN
Similar to Veloce standard model with straight grip English-style stock. Available with 26" barrels in 20 and 28 gauge. Hard case included.
Price: **$1,425.00**
Price: 28 ga. **$1,500.00**

HOENIG ROTARY ROUND ACTION GAME GUN
Gauge: 20, 28. **Barrel:** 26", 28", solid tapered rib. **Weight:** 6 lbs. and 6 1/4 lbs.**Stock:** English walnut to customer specifications. **Features:** Round action opens by rotating barrels, pulling forward. Inertia extraction system, rotary wing safety blocks strikers. Simple takedown without removing forend. Introduced 1997. Made in U.S.A. by George Hoenig.
Price: **$19,980.00**

Kimber Augusta Shotgun
Premium over/under, Boss type action. 12 ga. only. Tri-alloy barrel with choke tubes. Backbored 736. Long forcing cones. HiViz sight with center bead on vent ribl. Available with many features. Custom dimensions available. Imported from Italy by Kimber Mfg., Inc.
Price: **$6,000.00**

KOLAR SPORTING CLAYS O/U SHOTGUN
Gauge: 12, 2-3/4" chambers. **Barrel:** 30", 32", 34"; extended choke tubes. **Stock:** 14-5/8"x2-1/2"x1-7/8"x1-3/8". French walnut. Four stock versions available. **Features:** Single selective trigger, detachable, adjustable for length; overbored barrels with long forcing cones; flat tramline rib; matte blue finish. Made in U.S. by Kolar.
Price: Standard **$7,995.00**
Price: Elite **$10,990.00**
Price: Elite Gold **$12,990.00**
Price: Legend **$13,990.00**
Price: Select **$15,990.00**
Price: Custom . . . . **Price on request**

Kolar AAA Competition TRAP O/U Shotgun
Similar to the Sporting Clays gun except has 32" O/U /34" Unsingle or 30" O/U /34" Unsingle barrels as an over/under, unsingle, or combination set. Stock dimensions are 14-1/2"x2-1/2"x1-1/2"; American or French walnut; step parallel rib standard. Contact maker for full listings. Made in U.S. by Kolar.
Price: Over/under, choke tubes, Standard **$8,220.00**
Price: Unsingle, choke tubes, Standard **$8.600.00**
Price: Combo (30"/34", 32"/34"), Standard. **$10,995.00**

Kolar AAA Competition SKEET O/U Shotgun
Similar to the Sporting Clays gun except has 28" or 30" barrels with Kolarite AAA sub gauge tubes; stock of American or French walnut with matte finish; flat tramline rib; under barrel adjustable for point of impact. Many options available. Contact maker for complete listing. Made in U.S. by Kolar.
Price: Standard, choke tubes **$8,645.00**
Price: Standard, choke tubes, two-barrel set **$10,995.00**

KRIEGHOFF K-80 SPORTING CLAYS O/U
Gauge: 12. **Barrel:** 28", 30" or 32" with choke tubes. **Weight:** About 8 lbs. **Stock:** #3 Sporting stock designed for gun-down shooting. **Features:** Standard receiver with satin nickel finish and classic scroll engraving. Selective mechanical trigger adjustable for position. Choice of tapered flat or 8mm parallel flat barrel rib. Free-floating barrels. Aluminum case. Imported from Germany by Krieghoff International, Inc.
Price: Standard grade with five choke tubes, from **$8,150.00**

KRIEGHOFF K-80 SKEET SHOTGUN
Gauge: 12, 2-3/4" chambers. **Barrel:** 28", 30", (Skeet & Skeet), optional choke tubes). **Weight:** About 7-3/4 lbs. **Stock:** American Skeet or straight Skeet stocks, with palm-swell grips. Walnut. **Features:** Satin gray receiver finish. Selective mechanical trigger adjustable for position. Choice of ventilated 8mm parallel flat rib or ventilated 8-12mm tapered flat rib. Introduced 1980. Imported from Germany by Krieghoff International, Inc.
Price: Standard, Skeet chokes **$6,900.00**
Price: Skeet Special (28" or 30", tapered flat rib,
Skeet & Skeet choke tubes) **$7,575.00**

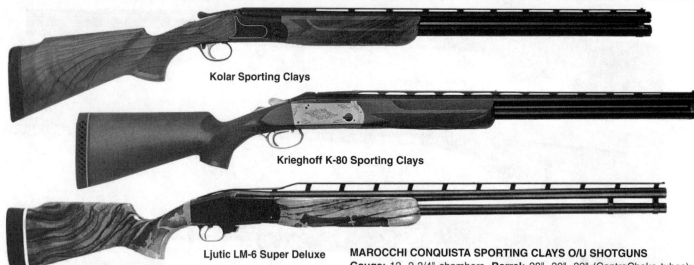

Kolar Sporting Clays

Krieghoff K-80 Sporting Clays

Ljutic LM-6 Super Deluxe

KRIEGHOFF K-80 O/U TRAP SHOTGUN

Gauge: 12, 2-3/4" chambers. **Barrel:** 30", 32" (Imp. Mod. & Full or choke tubes). **Weight:** About 8-1/2 lbs. **Stock:** Four stock dimensions or adjustable stock available; all have palm swell grips. Checkered European walnut. **Features:** Satin nickel receiver. Selective mechanical trigger, adjustable for position. Ventilated step rib. Introduced 1980. Imported from Germany by Krieghoff International, Inc.

Price: K-80 O/U (30", 32", Imp. Mod. & Full), from	$7,375.00
Price: K-80 Unsingle (32", 34", Full), Standard, from	$7,950.00
Price: K-80 Combo (two-barrel set), Standard, from	$10,475.00

Krieghoff K-20 O/U Shotgun

Similar to the K-80 except built on a 20-gauge frame. Designed for skeet, sporting clays and field use. Offered in 20, 28 and .410, 28" and 30" barrels. Imported from Germany by Krieghoff International Inc.

Price: K-20, 20 gauge, from	$8,150.00
Price: K-20, 28 gauge, from	$8,425.00
Price: K-20, .410, from	$8,425.00

LEBEAU - COURALLY BOSS-VEREES O/U

Gauge: 12, 20, 2-3/4" chambers. **Barrel:** 25" to 32". **Weight:** To customer specifications. **Stock:** Exhibition-quality French walnut. **Features:** Boss-type sidelock with automatic ejectors; single or double triggers; chopper lump barrels. A custom gun built to customer specifications. Imported from Belgium by Wm. Larkin Moore.

Price: From	$96,000.00

LJUTIC LM-6 SUPER DELUXE O/U SHOTGUN

Gauge: 12. **Barrel:** 28" to 34", choked to customer specs for live birds, trap, International Trap. **Weight:** To customer specs. **Stock:** To customer specs. Oil finish, hand checkered. **Features:** Custom-made gun. Hollow-milled rib, pull or release trigger, pushbutton opener in front of trigger guard. From Ljutic Industries.

Price: Super Deluxe LM-6 O/U	$17,995.00
Price: Over/Under Combo (interchangeable single barrel, two trigger guards, one for single trigger, one for doubles)	$24,995.00
Price: Extra over/under barrel sets, 29"-32"	$5,995.00

LUGER CLASSIC O/U SHOTGUNS

Gauge: 12, 3" and 3-1/2" chambers. **Barrel:** 26", 28", 30"; imp. cyl. mod. and full choke tubes. **Weight:** 7-1/2 lbs. **Length:** 45" overall (28" barrel) **Stock:** Select-grade European walnut, hand-checkered grip and forend. **Features:** Gold, single selective trigger; automatic ejectors. Introduced 2000.

Price: Classic (26", 28" or 30" barrel; 3-1/2" chambers)	$919.00
Price: Classic Sporting (30" barrel; 3" chambers)	$964.00

MAROCCHI CONQUISTA SPORTING CLAYS O/U SHOTGUNS

Gauge: 12, 2-3/4" chambers. **Barrel:** 28", 30", 32" (ContreChoke tubes); 10mm concave vent rib. **Weight:** About 8 lbs. **Stock:** 14-1/2"-14-7/8"x2-3/16"x1-7/16"; American walnut with checkered grip and forend; Sporting Clays butt pad. **Sights:** 16mm luminescent front. **Features:** Lower monoblock and frame profile. Fast lock time. Ergonomically-shaped trigger adjustable for pull length. Automatic selective ejectors. Coin-finished receiver, blued barrels. Five choke tubes, hard case. Available as true left-hand model-opening lever operates from left to right; stock has left-hand cast. Introduced 1994. Imported from Italy by Precision Sales International.

Price: Grade I, right-hand	$1,490.00
Price: Grade I, left-hand	$1,615.00
Price: Grade II, right-hand	$1,828.00
Price: Grade II, left-hand	$2,180.00
Price: Grade III, right-hand, from	$3,093.00
Price: Grade III, left-hand, from	$3,093.00

Marocchi Conquista TRAP O/U Shotgun

Similar to Conquista Sporting Clays model except 30" or 32" barrels choked Full & Full, stock dimensions of 14-1/2"-14-7/8"x1-11/16"x1-9/32"; weighs about 8-1/4 lbs. Introduced 1994. Imported from Italy by Precision Sales International.

Price: Grade I, right-hand	$1,490.00
Price: Grade II, right-hand	$1,828.00
Price: Grade III, right-hand, from	$3,093.00

Marocchi Conquista Skeet O/U Shotgun

Similar to Conquista Sporting Clays except 28" (Skeet & Skeet) barrels, stock dimensions of 14-3/8"-14-3/4"x2-3/16"x1-1/2". Weighs about 7-3/4 lbs. Introduced 1994. Imported from Italy by Precision Sales International.

Price: Grade I, right-hand	$1,490.00
Price: Grade II, right-hand	$1,828.00
Price: Grade III, right-hand, from	$3,093.00

MAROCCHI MODEL 99 SPORTING TRAP AND SKEET

Gauge: 12, 2-3/4", 3" chambers. **Barrel:** 28", 30", 32". **Stock:** French walnut. **Features:** Boss Locking system, screw-in chokes, low recoil, lightweight monoblock barrels and ribs. Imported from Italy by Precision Sales International.

Price: Grade I	$2,350.00
Price: Grade II	$2,870.00
Price: Grade II Gold	$3,025.00
Price: Grade III	$3,275.00
Price: Grade III Gold	$3,450.00
Price: Blackgold	$4,150.00
Price: Lodestar	$5,125.00
Price: Brittania	$5,125.00
Price: Diana	$6,350.00

Marocchi Conquista Sporting Clay

Merkel Model 2001EL

Merkel Model 2001EL

MAROCCHI CONQUISTA
USA MODEL 92 SPORTING CLAYS O/U SHOTGUN

Gauge: 12, 3" chambers. **Barrel:** 30"; back-bored, ported (ContreChoke Plus tubes); 10 mm concave ventilated top rib, ventilated middle rib. **Weight:** 8 lbs. 2 oz. **Stock:** 14-1/4"-14-5/8"x 2-1/8"x1-3/8"; American walnut with checkered grip and forend; Sporting Clays butt pad. **Features:** Low profile frame; fast lock time; automatic selective ejectors; blued receiver and barrels. Comes with three choke tubes. Ergonomically shaped trigger adjustable for pull length without tools. Barrels are back-bored and ported. Introduced 1996. Imported from Italy by Precision Sales International.
Price: **$1,490.00**

MERKEL MODEL 2001EL O/U SHOTGUN

Gauge: 12, 20, 3" chambers, 28, 2-3/4" chambers. **Barrel:** 12-28"; 20, 28 ga.-26-3/4". **Weight:** About 7 lbs. (12 ga.). **Stock:** Oil-finished walnut; English or pistol grip. **Features:** Self-cocking Blitz boxlock action with cocking indicators; Kersten double cross-bolt lock; silver-grayed receiver with engraved hunting scenes; coil spring ejectors; single selective or double triggers. Imported from Germany by GSI, Inc.
Price: 12, 20 .... **$7,295.00**
Price: 28 ga. **$7,295.00**
Price: Model 2000EL (scroll engraving, 12, 20 or 28)......... **$5,795.00**

MERKEL MODEL 303EL O/U SHOTGUN

Similar to Model 2001 EL except Holland & Holland-style sidelock action with cocking indicators; English-style Arabesque engraving. Available in 12, 20, 28 gauge. Imported from Germany by GSI, Inc.
Price: **$19,995.00**

Merkel Model 2002 EL O/U Shotgun

Similar to Model 2001 EL except dummy sideplates, Arabesque engraving with hunting scenes; 12, 20, 28 gauge. Imported from Germany by GSI, Inc.
Price: **$10,995.00**

PERAZZI MX8 OVER/UNDER SHOTGUNS

Gauge: 12, 2-3/4" chambers. **Barrel:** 28-3/8" (Imp. Mod. & Extra Full), 29-1/2" (choke tubes). **Weight:** 7 lbs., 12 oz. **Stock:** Special specifications. **Features:** Has single selective trigger; flat 7/16" x 5/16" vent. rib. Many op-tions available. Imported from Italy by Perazzi U.S.A., Inc.
Price: Sporting **$10,800.00**
Price: Trap Double Trap (removable trigger group) **$9,560.00**
Price: Skeet **$9,560.00**

Price: SC3 grade (variety of engraving patterns) .... **$16,200+**
Price: SCO grade (more intricate engraving, gold inlays)..... **$26,000+**

PERAZZI MX12 HUNTING OVER/UNDER

Gauge: 12, 2-3/4" chambers. **Barrel:** 26-3/4", 27-1/2", 28-3/8", 29-1/2" (Mod. & Full); choke tubes available in 27-5/8", 29-1/2" only (MX12C). **Weight:** 7 lbs., 4 oz. **Stock:** To customer specs; Interchangeable. **Features:** Single selective trigger; coil springs used in action; schnabel forend tip. Imported from Italy by Perazzi U.S.A., Inc.
Price: From **$10,841.00**
Price: MX12C (with choke tubes), from **$11,612.00**

Perazzi MX20 Hunting Over/Under

Similar to the MX12 except 20 ga. frame size. Non-removable trigger group. Available in 20, 28, .410 with 2-3/4" or 3" chambers. 26" standard, and choked Mod. & Full. Weight is 6 lbs., 6 oz. Imported from Italy by Perazzi U.S.A., Inc.
Price: From **$10,841.00**
Price: MX20C (as above, 20 ga. only, choke tubes), from **$11,612.00**

PERAZZI MX8/MX8 SPECIAL TRAP, SKEET

Gauge: 12, 2-3/4" chambers. **Barrel:** Trap-29-1/2" (Imp. Mod. & Extra Full), 31-1/2" (Full & Extra Full). Choke tubes optional. Skeet-27-5/8" (Skeet & Skeet). **Weight:** About 8-1/2 lbs. (Trap); 7 lbs., 15 oz. (Skeet). **Stock:** Interchangeable and custom made to customer specs. **Features:** Has detachable and interchangeable trigger group with flat V springs. Flat 7/16" ventilated rib. Many options available. Imported from Italy by Perazzi U.S.A., Inc.
Price: From **$10,841.00**
Price: MX8 Special (adj. four-position trigger), from **$11,476.00**
Price: MX8 Special Combo (o/u and single barrel sets), from . **$15,127.00**

Perazzi MX8 Special Skeet O/U Shotgun

Similar to the MX8 Skeet except has adjustable four-position trigger, Skeet stock dimensions. Imported from Italy by Perazzi U.S.A., Inc.
Price: From **$10,841.00**

Perazzi MX8/20 Over/Under Shotgun

Similar to the MX8 except has smaller frame and has a removable trigger mechanism. Available in trap, Skeet, sporting or game models with fixed chokes or choke tubes. Stock is made to customer specifications. Introduced 1993. Imported from Italy by Perazzi U.S.A., Inc.
Price: From **$10,841.00**

PERAZZI MX10 OVER/UNDER SHOTGUN

Gauge: 12, 2-3/4" chambers. **Barrel:** 29.5", 31.5" (fixed chokes). **Weight:** NA. **Stock:** Walnut; cheekpiece adjustable for elevation and cast. **Features:** Adjustable rib; vent. side rib. Externally selective trigger. Available in single barrel, combo, over/under trap, Skeet, pigeon and sporting models. Introduced 1993. Imported from Italy by Perazzi U.S.A., Inc.
Price: MX200410 .... **$13,608.00**

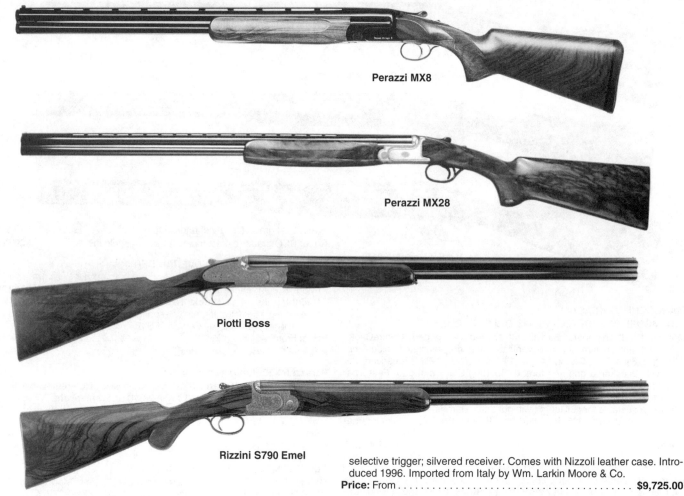

Perazzi MX8

Perazzi MX28

Piotti Boss

Rizzini S790 Emel

PERAZZI MX28, MX410 GAME O/U SHOTGUNS
Gauge: 28, 2-3/4" chambers, .410, 3" chambers. **Barrel:** 26" (Imp. Cyl. & Full). **Weight:** NA. **Stock:** To customer specifications. **Features:** Made on scaled-down frames proportioned to the gauge. Introduced 1993. Imported from Italy by Perazzi U.S.A., Inc.
Price: From $19,120.00

PIOTTI BOSS OVER/UNDER SHOTGUN
Gauge: 12, 20. **Barrel:** 26" to 32", chokes as specified. **Weight:** 6.5 to 8 lbs. **Stock:** Dimensions to customer specs. Best quality figured walnut. **Features:** Essentially a custom-made gun with many options. Introduced 1993. Imported from Italy by Wm. Larkin Moore.
Price: From $48,000.00

REMINGTON MODEL 332 O/U SHOTGUN
Gauge: 12, 3" chambers. **Barrel:** 26", 28", 30". **Weight:** 7.75 lbs. **Length:** 42"-47" **Stock:** Satin-finished American walnut. **Sights:** Twin bead. **Features:** Light-contour, vent rib, Rem chock barrel, blued, traditional M-32 experience with M-300 Ideal performance, standard auto ejectors, set trigger. Proven boxlock action.
Price: $1,624.00

RIZZINI S790 EMEL OVER/UNDER SHOTGUN
Gauge: 20, 28, .410. **Barrel:** 26", 27.5" (Imp. Cyl. & Imp. Mod.). **Weight:** About 6 lbs. **Stock:** 14"x1-1/2"x2-1/8". Extra-fancy select walnut. **Features:** Boxlock action with profuse engraving; automatic ejectors; single selective trigger; silvered receiver. Comes with Nizzoli leather case. Introduced 1996. Imported from Italy by Wm. Larkin Moore & Co.
Price: From $9,725.00

RIZZINI S792 EMEL OVER/UNDER SHOTGUN
Similar to S790 EMEL except dummy sideplates with extensive engraving coverage. Nizzoli leather case. Introduced 1996. Imported from Italy by Wm. Larkin Moore & Co.
Price: From $9,075.00

RIZZINI UPLAND EL OVER/UNDER SHOTGUN
Gauge: 12, 16, 20, 28, .410. **Barrel:** 26", 27-1/2", Mod. & Full, Imp. Cyl. & Imp. Mod. choke tubes. **Weight:** About 6.6 lbs. **Stock:** 14-1/2"x1-1/2"x2-1/4". **Features:** Boxlock action; single selective trigger; ejectors; profuse engraving on silvered receiver. Comes with fitted case. Introduced 1996. Imported from Italy by Wm. Larkin Moore & Co.
Price: From $3,350.00

Rizzini Artemis Over/Under Shotgun
Same as Upland EL model except dummy sideplates with extensive game scene engraving. Fancy European walnut stock. Fitted case. Introduced 1996. Imported from Italy by Wm. Larkin Moore & Co.
Price: From $2,100.00

RIZZINI S782 EMEL OVER/UNDER SHOTGUN
Gauge: 12, 2-3/4" chambers. **Barrel:** 26", 27.5" (Imp. Cyl. & Imp. Mod.). **Weight:** About 6.75 lbs. **Stock:** 14-1/2"x1-1/2"x2-1/4". Extra fancy select walnut. **Features:** Boxlock action with dummy sideplates, extensive engraving with gold inlaid game birds, silvered receiver, automatic ejectors, single selective trigger. Nizzoli leather case. Introduced 1996. Imported from Italy by Wm. Larkin Moore & Co.
Price: From $11,450.00

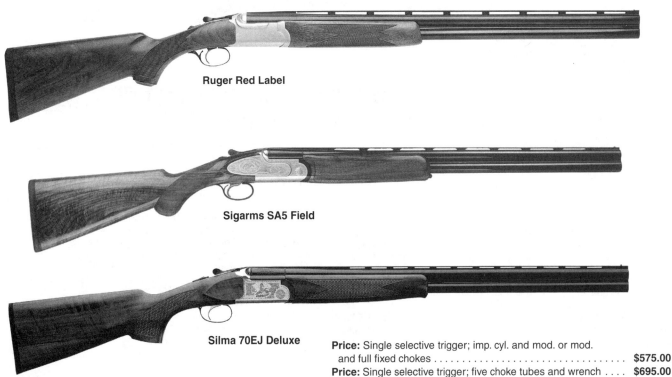

Ruger Red Label

Sigarms SA5 Field

Silma 70EJ Deluxe

RUGER RED LABEL O/U SHOTGUN

Gauge: 12, 20, 3" chambers; 28 2-3/4" chambers. **Barrel:** 26", 28" (Skeet [two], Imp. Cyl., Full, Mod. screw-in choke tubes). Proved for steel shot. **Weight:** About 7 lbs. (20 ga.); 7-1/2 lbs. (12 ga.). **Length:** 43" overall (26" barrels). **Stock:** 14"x1-1/2"x2-1/2". Straight grain American walnut or black synthetic. Checkered pistol grip and forend, rubber butt pad. **Features:** Stainless steel receiver. Single selective mechanical trigger, selective automatic ejectors; serrated free-floating vent. rib. Comes with two Skeet, one Imp. Cyl., one Mod., one Full choke tube and wrench. Made in U.S. by Sturm, Ruger & Co.
Price: Red Label with pistol grip stock **$1,489.00**
Price: English Field with straight-grip stock **$1,489.00**
Price: All-Weather Red Label with black
synthetic stock. . . . . **$1,489.00 to $1,545.00**
Price: Factory engraved All-Weather models . . . . **$1,650.00 to $1,725.00**

Ruger Engraved Red Label O/U Shotgun

Similar to Red Label except scroll engraved receiver with 24-carat gold game bird (pheasant in 12 gauge, grouse in 20 gauge, woodcock in 28 gauge, duck on All-Weather 12 gauge). Introduced 2000.
Price: Engraved Red Label (12 gauge, 30" barrel) **$1,725.00**
Price: Engraved Red Label (12, 20 and 28 gauge in 26"
and 28" barrels). **$1,650.00**
Price: Engraved Red Label, All-Weather (synthetic stock, 12 gauge only;
26" and 28" brls.) **$1,650.00**
Price: Engraved Red Label, All-Weather (synthetic stock, 12 gauge only,
30" barrel) **$1,650.00**

SARSILMAZ OVER/UNDER SHOTGUN

Gauge: 12, 3" chambers. **Barrel:** 26", 28"; fixed chokes or choke tubes. **Weight:** NA. **Length:** NA. **Stock:** Oil-finished hardwood. **Features:** Double or single selective trigger, wide ventilated rib, chrome-plated parts, blued finish. Introduced 2000. Imported from Turkey by Armsport Inc.
Price: Double triggers; mod. and full or imp. cyl. and mod. fixed
chokes. **$499.95**

Price: Single selective trigger; imp. cyl. and mod. or mod.
and full fixed chokes **$575.00**
Price: Single selective trigger; five choke tubes and wrench **$695.00**

SIGARMS SA5 OVER/UNDER SHOTGUN

Gauge: 12, 20, 3" chamber. **Barrel:** 26-1/2", 27" (Full, Imp. Mod., Mod., Imp. Cyl., Cyl. choke tubes). **Weight:** 6.9 lbs. (12 gauge), 5.9 lbs. (20 gauge). **Stock:** 14-1/2" x 1-1/2" x 2-1/2". Select grade walnut; checkered 20 l.p.i. at grip and forend. **Features:** Single selective trigger, automatic ejectors; hand-engraved detachable sideplated; matte nickel receiver, rest blued; tapered bolt lock-up. Introduced 1997. Imported by SIGARMS, Inc.
Price: Field, 12 gauge. **$2,670.00**
Price: Sporting Clays **$2,800.00**
Price: Field 20 gauge **$2,670.00**

SILMA MODEL 70EJ DELUXE

Gauge: 12 (3-1/2" chambers), 20, .410 (3" chambers), 28 (2-3/4" chambers). **Barrel:** 28" (12 and 20 gauge, fixed and tubed, 28 and .410 fixed), 26" (12 and 20 fixed). **Weight:** 7.6 lbs 12 gauge, 6.9 lbs, 20, 28 and .410. **Stock:** Checkered select European walnut, pistol grip, solid rubber recoil pad. **Features:** Monobloc construction, chrome-moly blued steel barrels, raised vent rib, automatic safety and ejectors, single selective trigger, gold plated, bead front sight. Brushed, engraved receiver. Introduced 2002. Clays models introduced 2003. Imported from Italy by Legacy Sports International.
Price: 12 gauge **$1,020.00**
Price: 20 gauge **$945.00**
Price: 28, .410 . . . . **$1,060.00**

Silma Model 70 EJ Superlight

Similar to Silma 70EJ Deluxe except 12 gauge, 3" chambers, alloy receiver, weighs 5.6 lbs.
Price: 12, 20 multichokes (IC, M, F) **$1,105.00**

Silma Model 70 EJ Standard

Similar to Silma 70EJ Deluxe except 12 and 20 gauge only, standard walnut stock, light engraving, silver-plated trigger.
Price: 12 gauge **$940.00**
Price: 20 gauge **$865.00**
Price: Sporting Clays model **$1,305.00**

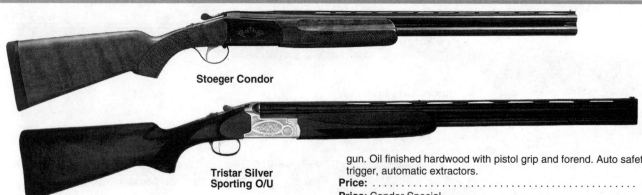

Stoeger Condor

Tristar Silver Sporting O/U

SKB MODEL 85TSS OVER/UNDER SHOTGUN

Gauge: 12, 20, .410 - 3"; 28, 2-3/4". **Barrel:** Chrome lined 26", 28", 30", 32" (w/choke tubes). **Weight:** 7 lbs., 7 oz. to 8 lbs, 14 oz. **Stock:** Hand-checkered American walnut with matte finish, schnabel or grooved forend. Target stocks available in various styles. **Sights:** Metal bead front or HiViz competition sights. **Features:** Low profile boxlock action with Greener-style cross bolt; single selective trigger; manual safety. Back-bored barrels with lengthened forcing cones. Introduced 2004. Imported from Japan by G.U. Inc.

Price: Sporting Clays, 12 or 20 . . . . **$1,949.00**
Price: Sporting Clays, 28 . . . . **$1,949.00**
Price: Sporting Clays set, 12 and 20 . . . . **$3,149.00**
Price: Skeet, 12 or 20 . . . . **$1,949.00**
Price: Skeet, 28 or .410 . . . . **$2,129.00 to $2,179.00**
Price: Skeet, three-barrel set, 20, 28, .410 . . . . **$4,679.00**
Price: Trap, standard or Monte Carlo **$1,499.00**
Price: Trap adjustable comb **$2,129.00**

SKB MODEL 585 OVER/UNDER SHOTGUN

Gauge: 12 or 20, 3"; 28, 2-3/4"; .410, 3". **Barrel:** 12 ga.-26", 28", 30", 32", 34" (Inter-Choke tubes); 20 ga.-26", 28" (Inter-Choke tube); 28-26", 28" (Inter-Choke tubes); .410-26", 28" (Inter-Choke tubes). Ventilated side ribs. **Weight:** 6.6 to 8.5 lbs. **Length:** 43" to 51-3/8" overall. **Stock:** 14-1/8"x1-1/2"x2-3/16". Hand checkered walnut with high-gloss finish. Target stocks available in standard and Monte Carlo. **Sights:** Metal bead front (field), target style on Skeet, trap, Sporting Clays. **Features:** Boxlock action; silver nitride finish with Field or Target pattern engraving; manual safety, automatic ejectors, single selective trigger. All 12 gauge barrels are back-bored, have lengthened forcing cones and longer choke tube system. Sporting Clays models in 12 gauge with 28" or 30" barrels available with optional 3/8" step-up target-style rib, matte finish, nickel center bead, white front bead. Introduced 1992. Imported from Japan by G.U., Inc.

Price: Field **$1,499.00**
Price: Two-barrel Field Set, 12 & 20 . . . . **$2,399.00**
Price: Two-barrel Field Set, 20 & 28 or 28 & .410 . . . . **$2,469.00**

SKB Model 585 Gold Package

Similar to Model 585 Field except gold-plated trigger, two gold-plated game inlays, schnabel forend. Silver or blue receiver. Introduced 1998. Imported from Japan by G.U. Inc.

Price: 12, 20 ga. **$1,689.00**
Price: 28, .410 . . . . **$1,749.00**

SKB Model 505 Shotguns

Similar to Model 585 except blued receiver, standard bore diameter, standard Inter-Choke system on 12, 20, 28, different receiver engraving. Imported from Japan by G.U. Inc.

Price: Field, 12 (26", 28"), 20 (26", 28") **$1,229.00**

STOEGER CONDOR SPECIAL

Gauge: 12, 20, 2-3/4" 3" chambers. **Barrel:** 26", 28". **Weight:** 7.7 lbs. **Sights:** Brass bead. **Features:** IC and M screw-in choke trubes with each gun. Oil finished hardwood with pistol grip and forend. Auto safety, single trigger, automatic extractors.

Price: **$390.00**
Price: Condor Special **$440.00**
Price: Supreme Deluxe w/SS and red bar sights **$500.00**

TRADITIONS CLASSIC SERIES O/U SHOTGUNS

Gauge: 12, 3"; 20, 3"; 16, 2-3/4"; 28, 2-3/4"; .410, 3". **Barrel:** 26" and 28". **Weight:** 6 lbs., 5 oz. to 7 lbs., 6 oz. **Length:** 43" to 45" overall. **Stock:** Walnut. **Features:** Single-selective trigger; chrome-lined barrels with screw-in choke tubes; extractors (Field Hunter and Field I models) or automatic ejectors (Field II and Field III models); rubber butt pad; top tang safety. Imported from Fausti of Italy by Traditions.

Price: (Field Hunter - blued receiver; 12 or 20 ga.; 26" bbl. has I.C. and mod. tubes, 28" has mod. and full tubes) **$669.00**
Price: (Field I - blued receiver; 12, 20, 28 ga. or .410; fixed chokes [26" has I.C. and mod., 28" has mod. and full]) **$619.00**
Price: (Field II - coin-finish receiver; 12, 16, 20, 28 ga. or .410; gold trigger; choke tubes) **$789.00**
Price: (Field III - coin-finish receiver; gold engraving and trigger; 12 ga.; 26" or 28" bbl.; choke tubes) **$999.00**
Price: (Upland II - blued receiver; 12 or 20 ga.; English-style straight walnut stock; choke tubes) **$839.00**
Price: (Upland II - blued receiver, gold engraving; 20 ga.; high-grade pistol grip walnut stock; choke tubes) **$1,059.00**
Price: (Upland III - blued, gold engraved receiver, 12 ga. Round pistol grip stock, choke tubes) **$1,059.00**
Price: (Sporting Clay II - silver receiver; 12 ga.; ported barrels with skeet, i.c., mod. and full extended tubes) **$959.00**
Price: (Sporting Clay III - engraved receivers, 12 and 20 ga., walnut stock, vent rib, extended choke tubes) **$1,189.00**

TRADITIONS MAG 350 SERIES O/U SHOTGUNS

Gauge: 12, 3-1/2". **Barrels:** 24", 26" and 28". **Weight:** 7 lbs. to 7 lbs., 4 oz. **Length:** 41" to 45" overall. **Stock:** Walnut or composite with Mossy Oak® Break-Up™ or Advantage® Wetlands ™ camouflage. **Features:** Black matte, engraved receiver; vent rib; automatic ejectors; single-selective trigger; three screw-in choke tubes; rubber recoil pad; top tang safety. Imported from Fausti of Italy by Traditions.

Price: (Mag Hunter II - 28" black matte barrels, walnut stock, includes I.C., Mod. and Full tubes) **$799.00**
Price: (Turkey II - 24" or 26" camo barrels, Break-Up camo stock, includes Mod., Full and X-Full tubes) **$889.00**
Price: (Waterfowl II - 28" camo barrels, Advantage Wetlands camo stock, includes I.C., Mod. and Full tubes) **$899.00**

TRISTAR SILVER SPORTING O/U

Gauge: 12, 2-3/4" chambers, 20 3" chambers. **Barrel:** 28", 30" (Skeet, Imp. Cyl., Mod., Full choke tubes). **Weight:** 7-3/8 lbs. **Length:** 45-1/2" overall. **Stock:** 14-3/8"x1-1/2"x2-3/8". Figured walnut, cut checkering; Sporting Clays quick-mount buttpad. **Sights:** Target bead front. **Features:** Boxlock action with single selective trigger, automatic selective ejectors; special broadway channeled rib; vented barrel rib; chrome bores. Chrome-nickel finish on frame, with engraving. Introduced 1990. Imported from Italy by Tristar Sporting Arms Ltd.

Price: **$799.00**

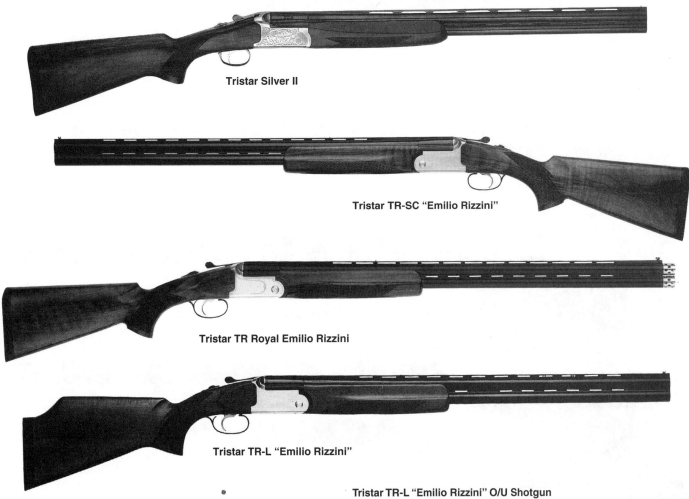

Tristar Silver II

Tristar TR-SC "Emilio Rizzini"

Tristar TR Royal Emilio Rizzini

Tristar TR-L "Emilio Rizzini"

Tristar Silver II Shotgun

Similar to the Silver I except 26" barrel (Imp. Cyl., Mod., Full choke tubes, 12 and 20 ga.), 28" (Imp. Cyl., Mod., Full choke tubes, 12 ga. only), 26" (Imp. Cyl. & Mod. fixed chokes, 28 and .410), automatic selective ejectors. Weight is about 6 lbs., 15 oz. (12 ga., 26").

Price: **$669.00**

TRISTAR TR-SC "EMILIO RIZZINI" OVER/UNDER

Gauge: 12, 20, 3" chambers. **Barrel:** 28", 30" (Imp. Cyl., Mod., Full choke tubes). **Weight:** 7-1/2 lbs. **Length:** 46" overall (28" barrel). **Stock:** 1-1/2"x2-3/ 8"x14-3/8". Semi-fancy walnut; pistol grip with palm swell; semi-beavertail forend; black Sporting Clays recoil pad. **Features:** Silvered boxlock action with Four Locks locking system, auto ejectors, single selective (inertia) trigger, auto safety. Hard chrome bores. Vent. 10mm rib with target-style front and mid-rib beads. Introduced 1998. Imported from Italy by Tristar Sporting Arms, Ltd.

Price: Sporting Clay model **$1,047.00**
Price: 20 ga. **$1,127.00**

Tristar TR-Royal "Emilio Rizzini" O/U Shotgun

Similar to the TR-SC except has special parallel stock dimensions (1-1/2"x1-5/8"x14-3/8") to give low felt recoil; Rhino ported, extended choke tubes; solid barrel spacer; has "TR-Royal" gold engraved on the silvered receiver. Available in 12 gauge (28", 30") 20 and 28 gauge (28" only). Introduced 1999. Imported from Italy by Tristar Sporting Arms, Ltd.

Price: 12, 20, 28 ga. **$1,319.00**

Tristar TR-L "Emilio Rizzini" O/U Shotgun

Similar to the TR-SC except has stock dimensions designed for female shooters (1-1/2" x 3" x 13-1/2"). Standard grade walnut. Introduced 1998. Imported from Italy by Tristar Sporting Arms, Ltd.

Price: **$1,063.00**

TRISTAR TR-I, II "EMILIO RIZZINI" O/U SHOTGUN

Gauge: 12, 20, 3" chambers (TR-I); 12, 16, 20, 28, .410 3" chambers. **Barrel:** 12 ga., 26" (Imp. Cyl. & Mod.), 28" (Mod. & Full); 20 ga., 26" (Imp. Cyl. & Mod.), fixed chokes. **Weight:** 7-1/2 lbs. **Stock:** 1-1/2"x2-3/8"x14-3/8". Walnut with palm swell pistol grip, hand checkering, semi-beavertail forend, black recoil pad. **Features:** Boxlock action with blued finish, Four Locks locking system, gold single selective (inertia) trigger system, automatic safety, extractors. Introduced 1998. Imported from Italy by Tristar Sporting Arms, Ltd.

Price: TR-I. **$779.00**
Price: TR-II (automatic ejectors, choke tubes) 12, 16 ga. **$919.00**
Price: 20, 28 ga., .410 . . . . **$969.00**

Tristar TR-Mag "Emilio Rizzini" O/U Shotgun

Similar to TR-I, 3-1/2" chambers; choke tubes; 24" or 28" barrels with three choke tubes; extractors; auto safety. Matte blue finish on all metal, non-reflective wood finish. Introduced 1998. Imported from Italy by Tristar Sporting Arms, Ltd.

Price: **$799.00**
Price: Mossy Oak® Break-Up camo. **$969.00**
Price: Mossy Oak® Shadow Grass camo **$969.00**
Price: 10 ga., Mossy Oak® camo patterns **$1,132.10**

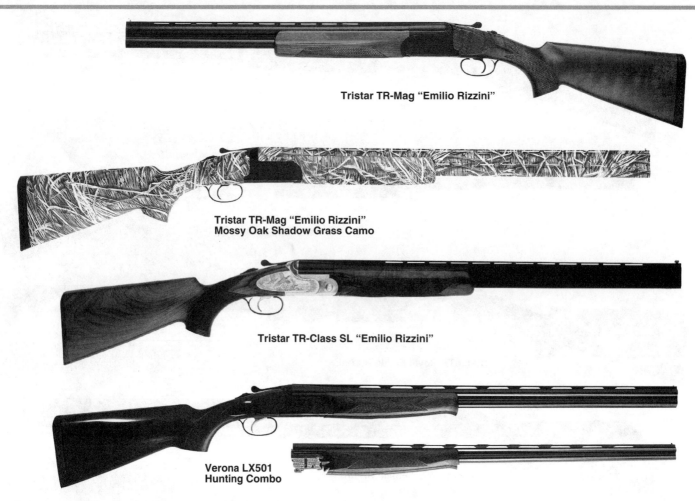

Tristar TR-Mag "Emilio Rizzini"

Tristar TR-Mag "Emilio Rizzini"
Mossy Oak Shadow Grass Camo

Tristar TR-Class SL "Emilio Rizzini"

Verona LX501
Hunting Combo

TRISTAR TR-CLASS SL EMILIO RIZZINI O/U
Gauge: 12, 2-3/4" chambers. **Barrel:** 28", 30". **Weight:** 7-3/4 lbs. **Stock:** Fancy walnut, hand checkering, semi-beavertail forend, black recoil pad, gloss finish. **Features:** Boxlock action with silvered, engraved sideplates; Four Lock locking system; automatic ejectors; hard chrome bores; vent tapered 7mm rib with target-style front bead. hand-fitted gun. Introduced 1999. Imported from Italy by Tristar Sporting Arms, Ltd.
Price: **$1,775.00**

TRISTAR WS/OU 12 SHOTGUN
Gauge: 12, 3-1/2" chambers. **Barrel:** 28" or 30" (imp. cyl., mod., full choke tubes). **Weight:** 6 lbs., 15 oz. **Length:** 46" overall. **Stock:** 14-1/8"x1-1/8"x2-3/8". European walnut with cut checkering, black vented recoil pad, matte finish. **Features:** Boxlock action with single selective trigger, automatic selective ejectors; chrome bores. Matte metal finish. Imported by Tristar Sporting Arms Ltd.
Price: **$645.00**

VERONA LX501 HUNTING O/U SHOTGUNS
Gauge: 12, 20, 28, .410 (2-3/4", 3" chambers). **Barrel:** 28"; 12, 20 ga. have Interchoke tubes, 28 ga. and .410 have fixed Full & Mod. **Weight:** 6-7 lbs. **Stock:** Matte-finished walnut with machine-cut checkering. **Features:** Gold-plated single-selective trigger; ejectors; engraved, blued receiver; non-automatic safety; coil spring-operated firing pins. Introduced 1999. Imported from Italy by B.C. Outdoors.
Price: 12 and 20 ga. **$878.08**
Price: 28 ga. and .410 . . . . **$926.72**
Price: .410 . . . . **$907.01**
Price: Combos 20/28, 28/.410 . . . . **$1,459.20**

Verona LX692 Gold Hunting O/U Shotgun
Similar to Verona LX501 except engraved, silvered receiver with false sideplates showing gold-inlaid bird hunting scenes on three sides; Schnabel forend tip; hand-cut checkering; black rubber butt pad. Available in 12 and 20 gauge only, five InterChoke tubes. Introduced 1999. Imported from Italy by B.C. Outdoors.
Price: **$1,295.00**
Price: LX692G Combo 28/.410 . . . . **$2,192.40**

Verona LX680 Sporting O/U Shotgun
Similar to Verona LX501 except engraved, silvered receiver; ventilated middle rib; beavertail forend; hand-cut checkering; available in 12 or 20 gauge only with 2-3/4" chambers. Introduced 1999. Imported from Italy by B.C. Outdoors.
Price: **$1,159.68**

Verona LX680 Skeet/Sporting/Trap O/U Shotgun
Similar to Verona LX501 except skeet or trap stock dimensions; beavertail forend, palm swell on pistol grip; ventilated center barrel rib. Introduced 1999. Imported from Italy by B.C. Outdoors.
Price: **$1,736.96**

Verona LX692 Gold Sporting O/U Shotgun
Similar to Verona LX680 except false sideplates have gold-inlaid bird hunting scenes on three sides; red high-visibility front sight. Introduced 1999. Imported from Italy by B.C. Outdoors.
Price: Skeet/Sporting **$1,765.12**
Price: Trap (32" barrel, 7-7/8 lbs.) **$1,594.80**

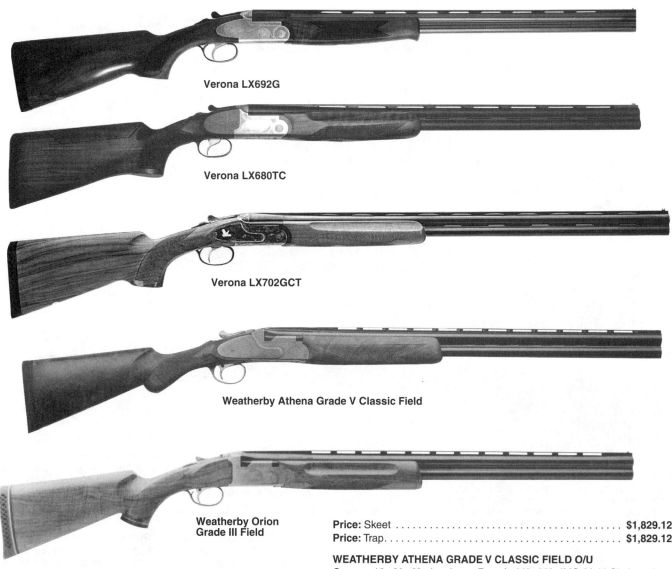

Verona LX692G

Verona LX680TC

Verona LX702GCT

Weatherby Athena Grade V Classic Field

Weatherby Orion
Grade III Field

VERONA LX680 COMPETITION TRAP
Gauge: 12. **Barrel:** 30" O/U, 32" single bbl. **Weight:** 8-3/8 lbs. combo, 7 lbs. single. **Stock:** Walnut. **Sights:** White front, mid-rib bead. **Features:** Interchangeable barrels switch from O/U to single configurations. 5 Briley chokes in combo, 4 in single bbl. extended forcing cones, parted barrels 32" with raised rib. By B.C. Outdoors.
Price: Trap Single (LX680TGTSB) $1,736.96
Price: Trap Combo (LX680TC) $2,553.60

VERONA LX702 GOLD TRAP COMBO
Gauge: 20/28, 2-3/4"chamber. **Barrel:** 30". **Weight:** 7 lbs. **Stock:** Turkish walnut with beavertail forearm. **Sights:** White front bead. **Features:** 2-barrel competition gun. Color case-hardened side plates and receiver with gold inlaid pheasant. Ventilated rib between barrels. 5 interchokes. Imported from Italy by B.C. Outdoors.
Price: Combo $2,467.84
Price: 20 ga. $1,829.12

Verona LX702 Skeet/Trap O/U Shotgun
Similar to Verona LX702. Both are 12 gauge and 2-3/4" chamber. Skeet has 28" barrel and weighs 7-3/4 lbs. Trap has 32" barrel and weighs 7-7/8 lbs. By B.C. Outdoors.

Price: Skeet $1,829.12
Price: Trap $1,829.12

WEATHERBY ATHENA GRADE V CLASSIC FIELD O/U
Gauge: 12, 20, 3" chambers. **Barrel:** 26", 28", IMC Multi-Choke tubes. **Weight:** 12 ga., 7-1/4-8 lbs.; 20 ga. 6-1/2-7-1/4 lbs. **Stock:** Oil-finished American Claro walnut with fine-line checkering, rounded pistol grip and slender forend. **Features:** Old English recoil pad. Sideplate receiver has rose and scroll engraving.
Price: $3,037.00

Weatherby Athena Grade III Classic Field O/U
Similar to Athena Grade V, has Grade III Claro walnut with oil finish, rounded pistol grip, slender forend; silver nitride/gray receiver has rose and scroll engraving with gold-overlay upland game scenes. Introduced 1999. Imported from Japan by Weatherby.
Price: 12, 20, 28 ga. $2,173.00

WEATHERBY ORION GRADE III FIELD O/U SHOTGUNS
Gauge: 12, 20, 3" chambers. **Barrel:** 26", 28", IMC Multi-Choke tubes. **Weight:** 6-1/2 to 8 lbs. **Stock:** 14-1/4"x1-1/2"x2-1/2". American walnut, checkered grip and forend. Rubber recoil pad. **Features:** Selective automatic ejectors, single selective inertia trigger. Top tang safety, Greener cross bolt. Has silver-gray receiver with engraving and gold duck/pheasant. Imported from Japan by Weatherby.
Price: Orion III, Field, 12, IMC, 26", 28" $1,955.00
Price: Orion III, Field, 20, IMC, 26", 28" $1,955.00

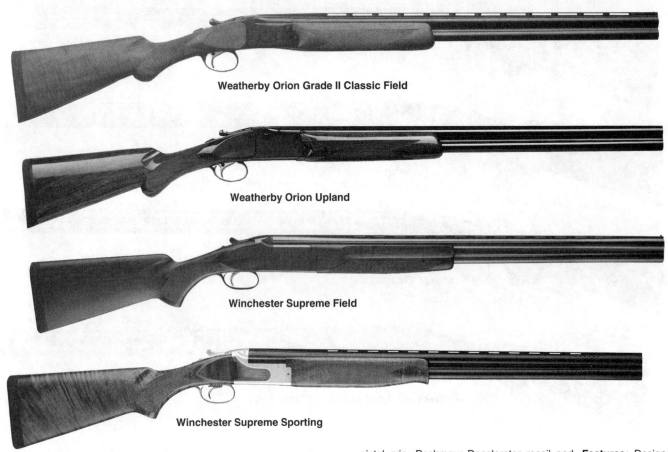

Weatherby Orion Grade II Classic Field

Weatherby Orion Upland

Winchester Supreme Field

Winchester Supreme Sporting

Weatherby Orion Grade II Classic Field O/U

Similar to Orion III Classic Field except stock has high-gloss finish, and bird on receiver is not gold. Available in 12 gauge, 26", 28", 30" barrels, 20 gauge, 26" 28", both with 3" chambers, 28 gauge, 26", 2-3/4" chambers. All have IMC choke tubes. Imported from Japan by Weatherby.

Price: **$1,622.00**

Weatherby Orion Upland O/U

Similar to Orion Grade I. Plain blued receiver, gold W on trigger guard; rounded pistol grip, slender forend of Claro walnut with high-gloss finish; black butt pad. Available in 12 and 20 gauge with 26" and 28" barrels. Introduced 1999. Imported from Japan by Weatherby.

Price: **$1,299.00**

WEATHERBY ORION SSC O/USHOTGUN

Gauge: 12, 3" chambers. **Barrel:** 28", 30", 32" (Skeet, SC1, Imp. Cyl., SC2, Mod. IMC choke tubes). **Weight:** About 8 lbs. **Stock:** 14-3/4"x2-1/4"x1-1/2". Claro walnut with satin oil finish; schnabel forend tip; Sporter-style pistol grip; Pachmayr Decelerator recoil pad. **Features:** Designed for Sporting Clays competition. Has lengthened forcing cones and back-boring; ported barrels with 12mm grooved rib with mid-bead sight; mechanical trigger is adjustable for length of pull. Introduced 1998. Imported from Japan by Weatherby.

Price: SSC (Super Sporting Clays). **$2,059.00**

WINCHESTER SELECT O/U SHOTGUNS

Gauge: 12, 2-3/4", 3" chambers. **Barrel:** 28", 30", Invector Plus choke tubes. **Weight:** 7 lbs. 6 oz. to 7 lbs. 12. oz. **Length:** 45" overall (28" barrel). **Stock:** Checkered walnut stock. **Features:** Chrome-plated chambers; back-bored barrels; tang barrel selector/safety; deep-blued finish. Introduced 2000. From U.S. Repeating Arms. Co.

Price: Select Field (26" or 28" barrel, 6mm ventilated rib) **$1,438.00**
Price: Select Energy. **$1,871.00**
Price: Select Eleganza **$2,227.00**
Price: Select Energy Trap **$1,871.00**
Price: Select Energy Trap adjustable **$2,030.00**
Price: Select Energy Sporting adjustable **$2,030.00**

Variety of models for utility and sporting use, including some competitive shooting.

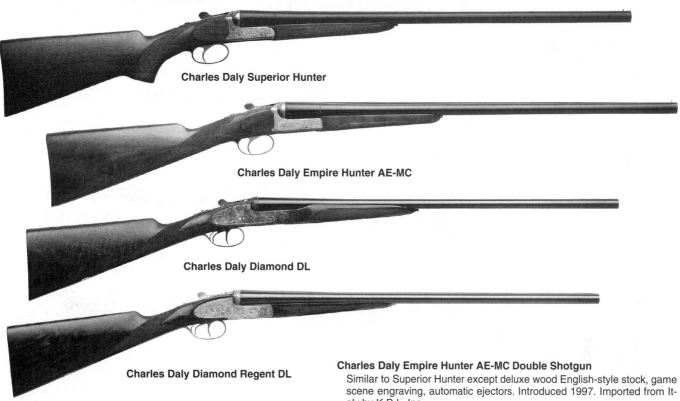

Charles Daly Superior Hunter

Charles Daly Empire Hunter AE-MC

Charles Daly Diamond DL

Charles Daly Diamond Regent DL

RRIETA SIDELOCK DOUBLE SHOTGUNS

auge: 12, 16, 20, 28, .410. **Barrel:** Length and chokes to customer specs. **Weight:** To customer specs. **Stock:** To customer specs. Straight English with checkered butt (standard), or pistol grip. Select European walnut with oil finish. **Features:** Essentially custom gun with myriad options. H&H pattern hand-detachable sidelocks, selective automatic ejectors, double triggers (hinged front) standard. Some have self-opening action. Finish and engraving to customer specs. Imported from Spain by Wingshooting Adventures.

rice: Model 557, auto ejectors, from	$3,250.00
rice: Model 570, auto ejectors, from	$3,950.00
rice: Model 578, auto ejectors, from	$4,350.00
rice: Model 600 Imperial, self-opening, from	$6,050.00
rice: Model 601 Imperial Tiro, self-opening, from	$6,950.00
rice: Model 801, from	$9,135.00
rice: Model 802, from	$9,135.00
rice: Model 803, from	$6,930.00
rice: Model 871, auto ejectors, from	$5,060.00
rice: Model 872, self-opening, from	$12,375.00
rice: Model 873, self-opening, from	$8,200.00
rice: Model 874, self-opening, from	$9,250.00
rice: Model 875, self-opening, from	$14,900.00

HARLES DALY SUPERIOR HUNTER AND SUPERIOR MC DOUBLE HOTGUN

auge: 12, 20, 3" chambers, 28, 2-3/4" chambers. **Barrel:** 28" (Mod. & Full) 26" (Imp. Cyl. & Mod.). **Weight:** About 7 lbs. **Stock:** Checkered walnut pis-tol grip buttstock, splinter forend. **Features:** Silvered, engraved receiv-er; chrome-lined barrels; gold single trigger; automatic safety; extractors; gold bead front sight. Introduced 1997. Imported from Italy by K.B.I., Inc.

rice: Superior Hunter, 28 gauge and .410 .... $1,029.00
rice: Superior Hunter MC 26"-28" $1,059.00

Charles Daly Empire Hunter AE-MC Double Shotgun

Similar to Superior Hunter except deluxe wood English-style stock, game scene engraving, automatic ejectors. Introduced 1997. Imported from Italy by K.B.I., Inc.

Price: 12 or 20 .... $1,349.00

CHARLES DALY DIAMOND DL DOUBLE SHOTGUN

Gauge: 12, 20, .410, 3" chambers, 28, 2-3/4" chambers. **Barrel:** 28" (Mod. & Full), 26" (Imp. Cyl. & Mod.), 26" (Full & Full, .410). **Weight:** About 5-7 lbs. **Stock:** Select fancy European walnut, English-style butt, beavertail forend; hand-checkered, hand-rubbed oil finish. **Features:** Drop-forged action with gas escape valves; demiblock barrels with concave rib; selec-tive automatic ejectors; hand-detachable double safety sidelocks with hand-engraved rose and scrollwork. Hinged front trigger. Color case-hard-ened receiver. Introduced 1997. Imported from Spain by K.B.I., Inc.

Price: .... **Special order only**

CHARLES DALY DIAMOND REGENT DL DOUBLE SHOTGUN

Gauge: 12, 20, .410, 3" chambers, 28, 2-3/4" chambers. **Barrel:** 28" (Mod. & Full), 26" (Imp. Cyl. & Mod.), 26" (Full & Full, .410). **Weight:** About 5-7 lbs. **Stock:** Special select fancy European walnut, English-style butt, splinter forend; hand-checkered; hand-rubbed oil finish. **Features:** Drop-forged action with gas escape valves; demiblock barrels of chrome-nickel steel with concave rib; selective automatic-ejectors; hand-detachable, double-safety H&H sidelocks with demi-relief hand engraving; H&H pat-tern easy-opening feature; hinged trigger; coin finished action. Introduced 1997. Imported from Spain by K.B.I., Inc.

Price: Special Custom Order .... **NA**

CHARLES DALY FIELD II, AE-MC HUNTER DOUBLE SHOTGUN

Gauge: 12, 20, 28, .410 (3" chambers; 28 has 2-3/4"). **Barrel:** 32" (Mod. & Mod.), 28, 30" (Mod. & Full), 26" (Imp. Cyl. & Mod.) .410 (Full & Full). **Weight:** 6 lbs. to 11.4 lbs. **Stock:** Checkered walnut pistol grip and forend. **Features:** Silvered, engraved receiver; gold single selective trigger in 10-, 12, and 20 ga.; double triggers in 28 and .410; automatic safety; extractors; gold bead front sight. Introduced 1997. Imported from Spain by K.B.I., Inc.

Price: 28 ga., .410-bore $729.00
Price: 12 or 20 AE-MC $799.00

Charles Daly Field Hunter

EAA/Baikal IZH-43 Bounty Hunter

EAA/Baikal MP-213

Fabarm Classic Lion

Fabarm Classic Lion Elite

DAKOTA PREMIER GRADE SHOTGUNS

Gauge: 12, 16, 20, 28, .410. **Barrel:** 27". **Weight:** NA. **Length:** NA. **Stock:** Exhibition-grade English walnut, hand-rubbed oil finish with straight grip and splinter forend. **Features:** French grey finish; 50 percent coverage engraving; double triggers; selective ejectors. Finished to customer specifications. Made in U.S. by Dakota Arms.
Price: 12, 16, 20 gauge **$13,950.00**
Price: 28 gauge and .410 . . . . **$15,345.00**

Dakota Legend Shotgun

Similar to Premier Grade except has special selection English walnut, full-coverage scroll engraving, oak and leather case. Made in U.S. by Dakota Arms.
Price: 12, 16, 20 gauge **$18,000.00**
Price: 28 gauge and .410 . . . . **$19,800.00**

EAA BAIKAL BOUNTY HUNTER IZH43K SHOTGUN

Gauge: 12, 3-inch chambers. **Barrel:** 18-1/2", 20", 24", 26", 28", three choke tubes. **Weight:** 7.28 lbs. **Overall length:** NA. **Stock:** Walnut, checkered forearm and grip. **Features:** Machined receiver; hammer-forged barrels with chrome-line bores; external hammers; double triggers (single, selective trigger available); rifle barrel inserts optional. Imported by European American Armory.
Price: . . . . **$379.00 to 399.00**

EAA BAIKAL IZH43 BOUNTY HUNTER SHOTGUN

Gauge: 12, 3-inch chambers. **Barrel:** 20", 24", 26", 28"; imp., mod. and full choke tubes. **Stock:** Hardwood or walnut; checkered forend and grip.

Features: Hammer forged barrel; internal hammers; extractors; engraved receiver; automatic tang safety; non-glare rib. Imported by European American Armory.
Price: IZH-43 Bounty Hunter (12 gauge, 2-3/4" chambers, 20" brl., dbl. triggers, hardwood stock) **$329.00**
Price: IZH-43 Bounty Hunter (20 gauge, 3" chambers, 20" bbl., dbl. triggers, walnut stock) **$359.00**

E.M.F. HARTFORD MODEL COWBOY SHOTGUN

Gauge: 12. **Barrel:** 20". **Weight:** NA. **Length:** NA. **Stock:** Checkered walnut. **Sights:** Center bead. **Features:** Exposed hammers; color-case hardened receiver; blued barrel. Introduced 2001. Imported from Spain by E.M.F. Co. Inc.
Price: **$625.00**

FABARM CLASSIC LION DOUBLE SHOTGUN

Gauge: 12, 3" chambers. **Barrel:** 26", 28", 30" (Cyl., Imp. Cyl., Mod., Imp. Mod., Full choke tubes). **Weight:** 7.2 lbs. **Length:** 44.5"-48.5. **Stock:** English-style or pistol grip oil-finished European walnut. **Features:** Boxlock action with double triggers, automatic ejectors, automatic safety. Introduced 1998. Imported from Italy by Heckler & Koch, Inc.
Price: Grade I **$1,499.0**
Price: Grade II **$2,099.0**
Price: Elite (color-case hardened type finish, 44.5") **$1,689.0**

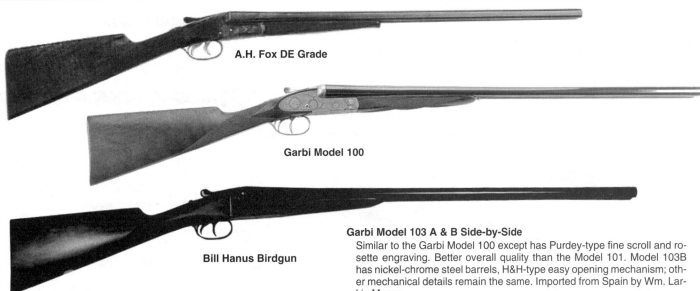

A.H. Fox DE Grade

Garbi Model 100

Bill Hanus Birdgun

FOX, A.H., SIDE-BY-SIDE SHOTGUNS

Gauge: 16, 20, 28, .410. **Barrel:** Length and chokes to customer specifications. Rust-blued Chromox or Krupp steel. **Weight:** 5-1/2 to 6-3/4 lbs. **Stock:** Dimensions to customer specifications. Hand-checkered Turkish Circassian walnut with hand-rubbed oil finish. Straight, semi or full pistol grip; splinter, schnabel or beavertail forend; traditional pad, hard rubber buttplate or skeleton butt. **Features:** Boxlock action with automatic ejectors; double or Fox single selective trigger. Scalloped, rebated and color case-hardened receiver; hand finished and hand-engraved. Grades differ in engraving, inlays, grade of wood, amount of hand finishing. Add $1,500 for 28 or .410-bore. Introduced 1993. Made in U.S. by Connecticut Shotgun Mfg.

Price: CE Grade $11,000.00
Price: XE Grade $12,500.00
Price: DE Grade $15,000.00
Price: FE Grade $20,000.00
Price: Exhibition Grade. $30,000.00
Price: 28/.410 CE Grade $12,500.00
Price: 28/.410 XE Grade $14,000.00
Price: 28/.410 DE Grade $16,500.00
Price: 28/.410 FE Grade. $21,500.00
Price: 28/.410 Exhibition Grade $30,000.00

GARBI MODEL 100 DOUBLE

Gauge: 12, 16, 20, 28. **Barrel:** 26", 28", choked to customer specs. **Weight:** 5-1/2 to 7-1/2 lbs. **Stock:** 14-1/2"x2-1/4"x1-1/2". European walnut. Straight grip, checkered butt, classic forend. **Features:** Sidelock action, automatic ejectors, double triggers standard. Color case-hardened action, coin finish optional. Single trigger; beavertail forend, etc. optional. Five other models are available. Imported from Spain by Wm. Larkin Moore.

Price: From $4,850.00

Garbi Model 200 Side-by-Side

Similar to the Garbi Model 100 except has heavy-duty locks, magnum proofed. Very fine Continental-style floral and scroll engraving, well figured walnut stock. Other mechanical features remain the same. Imported from Spain by Wm. Larkin Moore.

Price: $11,200.00

Garbi Model 101 Side-by-Side

Similar to the Garbi Model 100 except is hand engraved with scroll engraving, select walnut stock. Better overall quality than the Model 100. Imported from Spain by Wm. Larkin Moore.

Price: From $6,250.00

Garbi Model 103 A & B Side-by-Side

Similar to the Garbi Model 100 except has Purdey-type fine scroll and rosette engraving. Better overall quality than the Model 101. Model 103B has nickel-chrome steel barrels, H&H-type easy opening mechanism; other mechanical details remain the same. Imported from Spain by Wm. Larkin Moore.

Price: Model 103A, from $8,000.00
Price: Model 103B, from 11,800.00

HANUS BIRDGUN

Gauge: 16, 20, 28. **Barrel:** 27", 20 and 28 ga.; 28", 16 ga. (Skeet 1 & Skeet 2). **Weight:** 5 lbs., 4 oz. to 6 lbs., 4 oz. **Stock:** 14-3/8"x1-1/2"x2-3/8", with 1/4" cast-off. Select walnut. **Features:** Boxlock action with ejectors; splinter forend, straight English grip; checkered butt; English leather-covered handguard and AyA snap caps included. Made by AyA. Introduced 1998. Imported from Spain by Bill Hanus Birdguns.

Price: $2,495.00

ITHACA CLASSIC DOUBLES SKEET GRADE SxS

Gauge: 20, 28, 2-3/4" chambers, .410, 3". **Barrel:** 26", 28", 30", fixed chokes. **Weight:** 5 lbs., 14 oz. (20 gauge). **Stock:** 14-1/2"x2-1/4"x1-3/8". High-grade American black walnut, hand-rubbed oil finish; splinter or beavertail forend, straight or pistol grip. **Features:** Double triggers, ejectors; color case-hardened, engraved action body with matted top surfaces. Introduced 1999. Made in U.S. by Ithaca Classic Doubles.

Price: From $5,999.00

Ithaca Classic Doubles Grade 4E Classic SxS Shotgun

Gold-plated triggers, jeweled barrel flats and hand-turned locks. Feather crotch and flame-grained black walnut hand-checkered 28 lpi with fleur de lis pattern. Action body engraved with three game scenes and bank note scroll, color case-hardened. Introduced 1999. Made in U.S. by Ithaca Classic Doubles.

Price: From $7,500.00

Ithaca Classic Doubles Grade 7E Classic SxS Shotgun

Engraved with bank note scroll and flat 24k gold game scenes: gold setter and gold pointer on opposite action sides, American bald eagle inlaid on bottom plate. Hand-timed, polished, jeweled ejectors and locks. Exhibition grade American black walnut stock and forend with eight-panel fleur de lis borders. Introduced 1999. Made in U.S. by Ithaca Classic Doubles.

Price: From $11,000.00

Ithaca Classic Doubles Grade 5E SxS Shotgun

Completely hand-made, it is based on the early Ithaca engraving patterns of master engraver William McGraw. The hand engraving is at 90% coverage in deep chiseled floral scroll with game scenes in 24kt inlays. Stocks are of high-grade Turkish and American walnut and are hand-checkered. Available in 12, 16, 20, 28 gauges and .410 bore including two barrel combination sets in 16/20 ga. and 28/.410 bore. Introduced 2003. Made in U.S.A. by Ithaca Classic Doubles.

Price: From $8,500.00

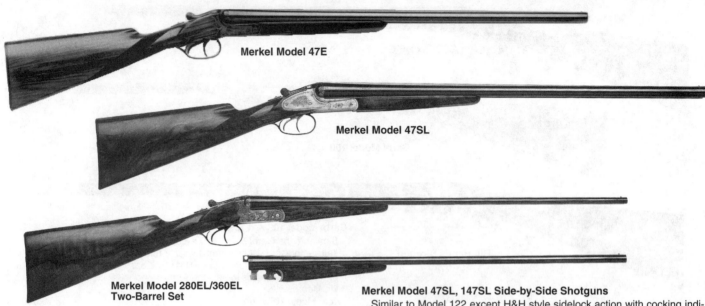

Merkel Model 47E

Merkel Model 47SL

Merkel Model 280EL/360EL
Two-Barrel Set

Ithaca Classic Doubles Grade 6e Side-by-Side Shotgun
Features hand engraving of fine English scroll coupled with game scenes and 24kt gold inlays. Stock are hand-made of best quality American, Turkish or English walnut with hand checkering. All metal work is finished in traditional bone and charcoal color case hardening and deep rust blue. Available in 12, 16, 20, 28 gauges and .410 bore. Introduced 2003. Made in U.S.A. by Ithaca Classic Doubles.
Price: From **$9,999.00**

Ithaca Classic Doubles Sousa Grade Side-by-Side Shotgun
Presentation grade American black walnut, hand-carved and checkered; hand-engraving with 24-karat gold inlays; tuned action and hand-applied finishes. Made in U.S. by Ithaca Classic Doubles.
Price: From **$18,000.00**

LEBEAU - COURALLY BOXLOCK SIDE-BY-SIDE SHOTGUN
Gauge: 12, 16, 20, 28, .410-bore. **Barrel:** 25" to 32". **Weight:** To customer specifications. **Stock:** French walnut. **Features:** Anson & Deely-type action with automatic ejectors; single or double triggers. Essentially a custom gun built to customer specifications. Imported from Belgium by Wm. Larkin Moore.
Price: From **$25,500.00**

LEBEAU - COURALLY SIDELOCK SIDE-BY-SIDE SHOTGUN
Gauge: 12, 16, 20, 28, .410-bore. **Barrel:** 25" to 32". **Weight:** To customer specifications. **Stock:** Fancy French walnut. **Features:** Holland & Holland-type action with automatic ejectors; single or double triggers. Essentially a custom gun built to customer specifications. Imported from Belgium by Wm. Larkin Moore.
Price: From **$56,000.00**

MERKEL MODEL 47E, 147E SIDE-BY-SIDE SHOTGUNS
Gauge: 12, 3" chambers, 16, 2-3/4" chambers, 20, 3" chambers. **Barrel:** 12, 16 ga.-28"; 20 ga.-26-3/4" (Imp. Cyl. & Mod., Mod. & Full). **Weight:** About 6-3/4 lbs. (12 ga.). **Stock:** Oil-finished walnut; straight English or pistol grip. **Features:** Anson & Deeley-type boxlock action with single selective or double triggers, automatic safety, cocking indicators. Color case-hardened receiver with standard Arabesque engraving. Imported from Germany by GSI.
Price: Model 47E (H&H ejectors) **$3,295.00**
Price: Model 147E (as above with ejectors) **$3,995.00**

Merkel Model 47SL, 147SL Side-by-Side Shotguns
Similar to Model 122 except H&H style sidelock action with cocking indicators, ejectors. Silver-grayed receiver and sideplates have Arabesque engraving, engraved border and screws (Model 47S), or fine hunting scene engraving (Model 147S). Imported from Germany by GSI.
Price: Model 47SL **$5,995.00**
Price: Model 147SL **$7,995.00**
Price: Model 247SL (English-style engraving, large scrolls) **$7,995.00**
Price: Model 447SL (English-style engraving, small scrolls) . . . **$9,995.00**

Merkel Model 280EL, 360EL Shotguns
Similar to Model 47E except smaller frame. Greener cross bolt with double under-barrel locking lugs, fine engraved hunting scenes on silver-grayed receiver, luxury-grade wood, Anson and Deely box-lock action. H&H ejectors, single-selective or double triggers. Introduced 2000. From Merkel.
Price: Model 280EL (28 gauge, 28" barrel, imp. cyl. and mod. chokes) 4 mod. chokes) **$5,795.00**
Price: Model 360EL (.410, 28" barrel, mod. and full chokes). **$5,795.00**
Price: Model 280/360EL two-barrel set (28 and .410 gauge as above) **$8,295.00**

Merkel Model 280SL and 360SL Shotguns
Similar to Model 280EL and 360EL except has sidelock action, double triggers, English-style Arabesque engraving. Introduced 2000. From Merkel.
Price: Model 280SL (28 gauge, 28" barrel, imp. cyl. and mod. chokes) **$8,495.00**
Price: Model 360SL (.410, 28" barrel, mod. and full chokes) **$8,495.00**
Price: Model 280/360SL two-barrel set **$11,995.00**

PIOTTI KING NO. 1 SIDE-BY-SIDE
Gauge: 12, 16, 20, 28, .410. **Barrel:** 25" to 30" (12 ga.), 25" to 28" (16, 20, 28, .410). To customer specs. Chokes as specified. **Weight:** 6-1/2 lbs. to 8 lbs. (12 ga. to customer specs.). **Stock:** Dimensions to customer specs. Finely figured walnut; straight grip with checkered butt with classic splinter forend and hand-rubbed oil finish standard. Pistol grip, beavertail forend. **Features:** Holland & Holland pattern sidelock action, automatic ejectors. Double trigger; non-selective single trigger optional. Coin finish standard, color case-hardened optional. Top rib; level, file-cut; concave, ventilated optional. Very fine, full coverage scroll engraving with small floral bouquets. Imported from Italy by Wm. Larkin Moore.
Price: From **$29,600.00**

SHOTGUNS — SIDE-BY-SIDES

Piotti Lunik

Rizzini Sidelock

Ruger Gold Label

SKB Model 385

Piotti King Extra Side-by-Side
Similar to the Piotti King No. 1 except with upgraded engraving. Choice of any type of engraving, including bulino game scene engraving and game scene engraving with gold inlays. Engraved and signed by a master engraver. Other mechanical specifications remain the same. Imported from Italy by Wm. Larkin Moore.
Price: From $35,000.00

Piotti Lunik Side-by-Side
Similar to the Piotti King No. 1 in overall quality. Has Renaissance-style large scroll engraving in relief. Best quality Holland & Holland-pattern sidelock ejector double with chopper lump (demi-bloc) barrels. Other mechanical specifications remain the same. Imported from Italy by Wm. Larkin Moore.
Price: From $30,900.00

PIOTTI PIUMA SIDE-BY-SIDE
Gauge: 12, 16, 20, 28, .410. **Barrel:** 25" to 30" (12 ga.), 25" to 28" (16, 20, 28, .410). **Weight:** 5-1/2 to 6-1/4 lbs. (20 ga.). **Stock:** Dimensions to customer specs. Straight grip stock with walnut checkered butt, classic splinter forend, hand-rubbed oil finish are standard; pistol grip, beavertail forend, satin luster finish optional. **Features:** Anson & Deeley boxlock ejector double with chopper lump barrels. Level, file-cut rib, light scroll and rosette engraving, scalloped frame. Double triggers; single non-selective optional. Coin finish standard, color case-hardened optional. Imported from Italy by Wm. Larkin Moore.
Price: From $14,800.00

RIZZINI SIDELOCK SIDE-BY-SIDE
Gauge: 12, 16, 20, 28, .410. **Barrel:** 25" to 30" (12, 16, 20 ga.), 25" to 28" (28, .410). To customer specs. Chokes as specified. **Weight:** 6-1/2 lbs. to 8 lbs. (12 ga. to customer specs). **Stock:** Dimensions to customer specs. Finely figured walnut; straight grip with checkered butt with classic splinter forend and hand-rubbed oil finish standard. Pistol grip, beavertail forend. **Features:** Sidelock action, auto ejectors. Double triggers or non-selective

single trigger standard. Coin finish standard. Imported from Italy by Wm. Larkin Moore.
Price: 12, 20 ga., from $66,900.00
Price: 28, .410 bore, from $75,500.00

RUGER GOLD LABEL SIDE-BY-SIDE SHOTGUN
Gauge: 12, 3" chambers. **Barrel:** 28" with skeet tubes. **Weight:** 6-1/2 lbs. **Length:** 45". **Stock:** American walnut straight or pistol grip. **Sights:** Gold bead front, full length rib, serrated top. **Features:** Spring-assisted break-open, SS trigger, auto eject. 5 interchangeable screw-in choke tubes, combination safety/barrel selector with auto safety reset.
Price: $1,950.00

SKB MODEL 385 SIDE-BY-SIDE
Gauge: 12, 20, 3" chambers; 28, 2-3/4" chambers. **Barrel:** 26" (Imp. Cyl., Mod., Skeet choke tubes). **Weight:** 6-3/4 lbs. **Length:** 42-1/2" overall. **Stock:** 14-1/8"x1-1/2"x2-1/2" American walnut with straight or pistol grip stock, semi-beavertail forend. **Features:** Boxlock action. Silver nitrided receiver with engraving; solid barrel rib; single selective trigger, selective automatic ejectors, automatic safety. Introduced 1996. Imported from Japan by G.U. Inc.
Price: $2,159.00
Price: Field Set, 20, 28 ga., 26" or 28", English or pistol grip . . . $3,059.00

SKB Model 385 Sporting Clays
Similar to the Field Model 385 except 12 gauge only; 28" barrel with choke tubes; raised ventilated rib with metal middle bead and white front. Stock dimensions 14-1/4"x1-7/16"x1-7/8". Introduced 1998. Imported from Japan by G.U. Inc.
Price: $2,159.00
Price: Sporting Clays set, 20, 28 ga. $3,059.00

SKB Model 485 Side-by-Side
Similar to the Model 385 except has dummy sideplates, raised ventilated rib with metal middle bead and white front, extensive upland game scene engraving, semi-fancy American walnut English or pistol grip stock. Imported from Japan by G.U. Inc.
Price: $2,769.00
Price: Field set, 20, 28 ga., 26". $2,769.00

Stoeger Uplander

Stoeger Silverado Coach

Traditions Uplander V

Tristar Rota Model 411

STOEGER UPLANDER SIDE-BY-SIDE SHOTGUN
Gauge: 16, 28, 2-3/4 chambers. 12, 20, .410, 3" chambers. **Barrel:** 26", 28". **Weight:** 7.3 lbs. **Sights:** Brass bead. **Features:** Double trigger, IC, M fixed choke tubes with gun.
Price: . . . . . (With fixed chokes) **$335.00**; (With screw-in chokes) **$350.00**
Price: With English stock . . . . **$335.00 to $350.00**
Price: Upland Special **$375.00**
Price: Upland Supreme with SST, red bar sights **$445.00**
Price: Upland Short Stock (Youth) **$335.00**

STOEGER COACH GUN SIDE-BY-SIDE SHOTGUN
Gauge: 12, 20, .410, 2-3/4", 3" chambers. **Barrel:** 20". **Weight:** 6-1/2 lbs. **Stock:** Brown hardwood, classic beavertail forend. **Sights:** Brass bead. **Features:** IC & M fixed chokes, tang auto safety, auto extractors, black plastic butt plate. 12 ga. and 20 ga. also with English style stock.
Price: . . . . $320.00; (Nickel) **$375.00**
Price: Silverado . . . . **$375.00**; (With English stock) **$375.00**

TRADITIONS ELITE SERIES SIDE-BY-SIDE SHOTGUNS
Gauge: 12, 3"; 20, 3"; 28, 2-3/4"; .410, 3". **Barrel:** 26". **Weight:** 5 lbs., 12 oz. to 6-1/2 lbs. **Length:** 43" overall. **Stock:** Walnut. **Features:** Chrome-lined barrels; fixed chokes (Elite Field III ST, Field I DT and Field I ST) or choke tubes (Elite Hunter ST); extractors (Hunter ST and Field I models) or au-tomatic ejectors (Field III ST); top tang safety. Imported from Fausti of Italy by Traditions.
Price: (Elite Field I DT - 12, 20, 28 ga. or .410; I.C. and Mod. fixed chokes [F and F on .410]; double triggers) . . . . **$789.00 to $969.00**
Price: (Elite Field I ST - 12, 20, 28 ga. or .410; same as DT but with single trigger). **$969.00 to $1,169.00**
Price: (Elite Field III ST - 28 ga. or .410; gold-engraved receiver; high-grade walnut stock) **$2,099.00**
Price: (Elite Hunter ST - 12 or 20 ga.; blued receiver; I.C. and Mod. choke tubes) **$999.00**

TRADITIONS UPLANDER SERIES SIDE-BY-SIDE SHOTGUNS
Gauge: 12, 3"; 20, 3". **Barrel:** 26", 28". **Weight:** 6-1/4 lbs. to 6-1/2 lbs. **Length:** 43"-45" overall. **Stock:** Walnut. **Features:** Barrels threaded for choke tubes (Improved Cylinder, Modified and Full); top tang safety, ex-tended trigger guard. Engraved silver receiver with side plates and lavish gold inlays. From Traditions.
Price: Uplander III Silver 12, 20 ga. **$2,699.00**
Price: Uplander V Silver 12, 20 ga. **$3,199.00**

TRISTAR ROTA MODEL 411 SIDE-BY-SIDE
Gauge: 12, 16, 20, .410, 3" chambers; 28, 2-3/4". **Barrel:** 12 ga., 26", 28"; 16, 20, 28 ga., .410-bore, 26"; 12 and 20 ga. have three choke tubes, 16, 28 (Imp. Cyl. & Mod.), .410 (Mod. & Full) fixed chokes. **Weight:** 6-1/2 to 7-1/4 lbs. **Stock:** 14-3/8" l.o.p. Standard walnut with pistol grip, splinter-style forend; hand checkered. **Features:** Engraved, color case-hardened box-lock action; double triggers, extractors; solid barrel rib. Introduced 1998. Imported from Italy by Tristar Sporting Arms, Ltd.
Price: **$849.00**

Tristar Rota Model 411D Side-by-Side
Similar to Model 411 except automatic ejectors, straight English-style stock, single trigger. Solid barrel rib with matted surface; chrome bores; color case-hardened frame; splinter forend. Introduced 1999. Imported from Italy by Tristar Sporting Arms, Ltd.
Price: **$1,110.00**

Tristar Rota Model 411R Coach Gun Side-by-Side
Similar to Model 411 except in 12 or 20 gauge only with 20" barrels and fixed chokes (Cyl. & Cyl.). Double triggers, extractors, choke tubes. Intro-duced 1999. Imported from Italy by Tristar Sporting Arms, Ltd.
Price: **$745.00**

Tristar Rota Model 411F Side-by-Side
Similar to Model 411 except silver, engraved receiver, ejectors, IC, M and F choke tubes, English-style stock, single gold trigger, cut checkering. Im-ported from Italy by Tristar Sporting Arms Ltd.
Price: **$1,608.00**

TRISTAR DERBY CLASSIC SIDE-BY-SIDE
Gauge: 12. **Barrel:** 28" Mod. & Full fixed chokes. **Features:** Sidelock ac-tion, engraved, double trigger, auto ejectors, English straight stock. Made in Europe for Tristar Sporting Arms Ltd.
Price: **$1,059.00**

Variety of designs for utility and sporting purposes, as well as for competitive shooting.

Browning BT-99 Trap

EAA/Baikal IZH-18

EAA/Baikal IZH-18Max

H&R 928 Ultra Slug Hunter Deluxe

BERETTA DT10 TRIDENT TRAP TOP SINGLE SHOTGUN
Gauge: 12, 3" chamber. **Barrel:** 34"; five Optima Choke tubes (full, full, imp. modified, mod. and imp. cyl.). **Weight:** 8.8 lbs. **Stock:** High-grade walnut; adjustable. **Features:** Detachable, adjustable trigger group; Optima Bore for improved shot pattern and reduced recoil; slim Optima Choke tubes; raised and thickened receiver for long life. Introduced 2000. Imported from Italy by Beretta USA.
Price: **$8,500.00**

BRNO ZBK 100 SINGLE BARREL SHOTGUN
Gauge: 12 or 20. **Barrel:** 27.5". **Weight:** 5.5 lbs. **Length:** 44" overall. **Stock:** Beech. **Features:** Polished blue finish; sling swivels. Announced 1998. Imported from The Czech Republic by Euro-Imports.
Price: **$185.00**

BROWNING BT-99 TRAP SHOTGUN
Gauge: 12, 2-3/4" chamber. **Barrel:** 32" or 34"; Invector choke system (full choke tube only included); High Post Rib; back-bored. **Weight:** 8 lbs., 10 oz. (34" bbl.). **Length:** 50-1/2" overall (34" bbl.). **Stock:** Conventional or adjustable-comb. **Features:** Re-introduction of the BT-99 Trap Shotgun. Full beavertail forearm; checkered walnut stock; ejector; rubber butt pad. Re-introduced 2001. Imported by Browning.
Price: Conventional stock, 32" or 34" barrel **$1,290.00**
Price: Adj.-comb stock, 32" or 34" barrel **$1,558.00**
Price: Micro (for small-framed shooters) **$1,290.00**

BROWNING GOLDEN CLAYS SHOTGUN
Gauge: 12, 3" chamber. **Barrel:** 32", 34" with Full, Improved Modified, Modified tubes. **Weight:** 8 lbs. 14 oz. to 9 lbs. **Length:** 49" to 51" overall. **Stock:** Adjustable comb; Walnut with high gloss finish; cut checkering. GraCoil recoil reduction system. Imported from Japan by Browning.
Price: 34" bbl. **$3,407.00**
Price: 32" bbl. **$3,407.00**

CHIPMUNK 410 YOUTH SHOTGUN
Gauge: .410. **Barrel:** 18-1/4" tapered, blue. **Weight:** 3.25 lbs. **Length:** 33". **Stock:** Walnut. **Features:** Manually cocking single shot bolt, blued receiver.
Price: **$225.95**

EAA BAIKAL IZH-18 SINGLE BARREL SHOTGUN
Gauge: 12 (2-3/4" and 3" chambers), 20 (2-3/4" and 3"), 16 (2-3/4"), .410 (3"). **Barrel:** 26-1/2", 28-1/2"; modified or full choke (12 and 20 gauge); full only (16 gauge); improved cylinder (20 gauge) and full or improved modified (.410). **Stock:** Walnut-stained hardwood; rubber recoil pad. **Features:** Hammer-forged steel barrel; machined receiver; cross-block safety; cocking lever with external cocking indicator; optional automatic ejector, screw- in chokes and rifle barrel. Imported by European American Armory.
Price: IZH-18 (12, 16, 20 or .410) **$109.00**
Price: IZH-18 (20 gauge w/imp. cyl. or .410 w/imp. mod.) **$109.00**

EAA BAIKAL IZH-18MAX SINGLE BARREL SHOTGUN
Gauge: 12, 3"; 20, 3"; 410, 3". **Barrel:** 24" (.410), 26" (.410 or 20 ga.) or 28" (12 ga.). **Weight:** 6.4 to 6.6 lbs. **Stock:** Walnut. **Features:** Polished nickel receiver; ventilated rib; I.C., Mod. and Full choke tubes; titanium-coated trigger; internal hammer; selectable ejector/extractor; rubber butt pad; decocking system. Imported by European American Armory.
Price: (12 or 20 ga., choke tubes). **$229.00**
Price: (.410, full choke only) **$239.00**
Price: Sporting, 12 ga., ported, Monte Carlo stock **$219.00**

HARRINGTON & RICHARDSON SB2-980 ULTRA SLUG
Gauge: 12, 20, 3" chamber. **Barrel:** 22" (20 ga. Youth) 24", fully rifled. **Weight:** 9 lbs. **Length:** NA. **Stock:** Walnut-stained hardwood. **Sights:** None furnished; comes with scope mount. **Features:** Uses the H&R 10 gauge action with heavy-wall barrel. Monte Carlo stock has sling swivels; comes with black nylon sling. Introduced 1995. Made in U.S. by H&R 1871, LLC.
Price: **$259.00**

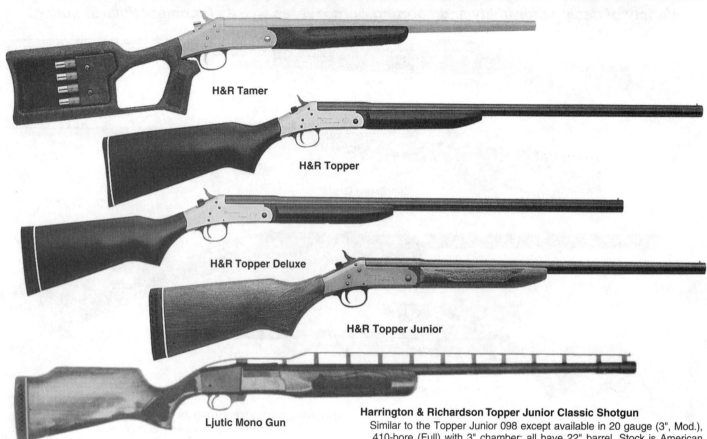

H&R Tamer

H&R Topper

H&R Topper Deluxe

H&R Topper Junior

Ljutic Mono Gun

Harrington & Richardson Model 928 Ultra Slug Hunter Deluxe

Similar to the SB2-980 Ultra Slug except uses 12 gauge action and 12 gauge barrel blank bored to 20 gauge, then fully rifled with 1:28" twist. Has hand-checkered camo laminate Monte Carlo stock and forend. Comes with Weaver-style scope base, offset hammer extension, ventilated recoil pad, sling swivels and nylon sling. Introduced 1997. Made in U.S. by H&R 1871 LLC.

Price: **$315.00**

HARRINGTON & RICHARDSON TAMER SHOTGUN

Gauge: .410, 3" chamber. **Barrel:** 20" (Full). **Weight:** 5-6 lbs. **Length:** 33" overall. **Stock:** Thumbhole grip of high density black polymer. **Features:** Uses H&R Topper action with matte electroless nickel finish. Stock holds four spare shotshells. Introduced 1994. From H&R 1871, LLC.

Price: **$164.00**

HARRINGTON & RICHARDSON TOPPER MODEL 098

Gauge: 12, 16, 20, 28 (2-3/4"), .410, 3" chamber. **Barrel:** 12 ga.-28" (Mod.); 16 ga.- 28" (Full.); 20 ga.-26" (Mod.); 28 ga.-26" (Mod.); .410 bore- 26" (Full). **Weight:** 5-6 lbs. **Stock:** Black-finish hardwood with full pistol grip; semi-beavertail forend. **Sights:** Gold bead front. **Features:** Break-open action with side-lever release, automatic ejector. Satin nickel frame, blued barrel. Reintroduced 1992. From H&R 1871, LLC.

Price: **$145.00**
Price: Topper Junior 098 (as above except 22" barrel, 20 ga. (Mod.), .410-bore (Full), 12-1/2" length of pull) **$152.00**

Harrington & Richardson Topper Deluxe Model 098

Similar to the standard Topper 098 except 12 gauge only with 3-1/2" chamber, 28" barrel with choke tube (comes with Mod. tube, others optional). Satin nickel frame, blued barrel, black-finished wood. Introduced 1992. From H&R 1871, LLC.

Price: **$169.00**

Harrington & Richardson Topper Junior Classic Shotgun

Similar to the Topper Junior 098 except available in 20 gauge (3", Mod.), .410-bore (Full) with 3" chamber; all have 22" barrel. Stock is American black walnut with cut-checkered pistol grip and forend. Ventilated rubber recoil pad. Blued barrel, blued frame. Introduced 1992. From H&R 1871, LLC.

Price: **$184.00**

Ithaca Classic Doubles Knickerbocker Trap Gun

A reissue of the famous Ithaca Knickerbocker Trap Gun. Built on a custom basis only. Introduced 2003. Made in U.S.A. by Ithaca Classic Doubles.

Price: From **$9,000.00**

KRIEGHOFF K-80 SINGLE BARREL TRAP GUN

Gauge: 12, 2-3/4" chamber. **Barrel:** 32" or 34" Unsingle. Fixed Full or choke tubes. **Weight:** About 8-3/4 lbs. **Stock:** Four stock dimensions or adjustable stock available. All hand-checkered European walnut. **Features:** Satin nickel finish. Selective mechanical trigger adjustable for finger position. Tapered step vent. rib. Adjustable point of impact.

Price: Standard grade full Unsingle, from **$7,950.00**

KRIEGHOFF KX-5 TRAP GUN

Gauge: 12, 2-3/4" chamber. **Barrel:** 34"; choke tubes. **Weight:** About 8-1/2 lbs. **Stock:** Factory adjustable stock. European walnut. **Features:** Ventilated tapered step rib. Adjustable position trigger, optional release trigger. Fully adjustable rib. Satin gray electroless nickel receiver. Fitted aluminum case. Imported from Germany by Krieghoff International, Inc.

Price: **$4,200.00**

LJUTIC MONO GUN SINGLE BARREL

Gauge: 12 only. **Barrel:** 34", choked to customer specs; hollow-milled rib, 35-1/2" sight plane. **Weight:** Approx. 9 lbs. **Stock:** To customer specs. Oil finish, hand checkered. **Features:** Totally custom made. Pull or release trigger; removable trigger guard contains trigger and hammer mechanism; Ljutic pushbutton opener on front of trigger guard. From Ljutic Industries.

Price: Std., med. or Olympic rib, custom bbls., fixed choke. **$5,795.00**
Price: As above with screw-in choke barrel **$6,095.00**
Price: Stainless steel mono gun **$6,795.00**

Mossberg SSi One

New England Firearms Camo Turkey

New England Firearms Tracker II

New England Firearms Special Purpose

Ljutic LTX Pro 3 Deluxe Mono Gun
Deluxe, lightweight version of the Mono Gun with high quality wood, up-grade checkering, special rib height, screw-in chokes, ported and cased.
Price: $8,995.00
Price: Stainless steel model $9,995.00

MOSSBERG SSi-ONE 12 GAUGE SLUG SHOTGUN
Gauge: 12, 3" chamber. **Barrel:** 24", fully rifled. **Weight:** 8 pounds. **Length:** 40" overall. **Stock:** Walnut, fluted and cut checkered; sling-swivel studs; drilled and tapped for scope base. **Sights:** None (scope base supplied). **Features:** Frame accepts interchangeable rifle barrels (see Mossberg SSi-One rifle listing); lever-opening, break-action design; ambidextrous, top-tang safety; internal eject/extract selector. Introduced 2000. From Mossberg.
Price: **$480.00**

Mossberg SSi-One Turkey Shotgun
Similar to SSi-One 12 gauge Slug Shotgun, but chambered for 12 ga., 3-1/2" loads. Includes Accu-Mag Turkey Tube. Introduced 2001. From Mossberg.
Price: **$459.00**

NEW ENGLAND FIREARMS CAMO TURKEY SHOTGUNS
Gauge: 10, 3-1/2"; 12, 20, 3" chamber. **Barrel:** 24"; extra-full, screw-in choke tube (10 ga.); fixed full choke (12, 20). **Weight:** NA. **Stock:** American hardwood, green and black camouflage finish with sling swivels and ventilated recoil pad. **Sights:** Bead front. **Features:** Matte metal finish; stock counterweight to reduce recoil; patented transfer bar system for hammer-down safety; includes camo sling and trigger lock. Accepts other factory-fitted barrels. Introduced 2000. From New England Firearms.
Price: . . . . 10 ga. **$278.00**; 12 ga., **$189.00**
Price: 20 ga. youth model (22" bbl.) **$189.00**

NEW ENGLAND FIREARMS TRACKER II SLUG GUN
Gauge: 12, 20, 3" chamber. **Barrel:** 24" (Cyl.), rifle bore. **Weight:** 5-1/4 lbs. **Length:** 40" overall. **Stock:** Walnut-finished hardwood with full pistol grip, recoil pad. **Sights:** Blade front, fully adjustable rifle-type rear. **Features:** Break-open action with side-lever release; blued barrel, color case-hardened frame. Introduced 1992. From New England Firearms.
Price: Tracker II **$187.00**

NEW ENGLAND FIREARMS SPECIAL PURPOSE SHOTGUNS
Gauge: 10, 3-1/2" chamber. **Barrel:** 28" (Full), 32" (Mod.). **Weight:** 9.5 lbs. **Length:** 44" overall (28" barrel). **Stock:** American hardwood with walnut or matte camo finish; ventilated rubber recoil pad. **Sights:** Bead front. **Features:** Break-open action with side-lever release; ejector. Matte finish on metal. Introduced 1992. From New England Firearms.
Price: Walnut-finish wood sling and swivels **$215.00**
Price: Camo finish, sling and swivels **$278.00**
Price: Camo finish, 32", sling and swivels **$272.00**
Price: Black matte finish, 24", Turkey Full choke tube,
sling and swivels **$251.00**

NEW ENGLAND FIREARMS SURVIVOR
Gauge: .410/45 Colt, 3" chamber. **Barrel:** 22" (Mod.); 20" (.410/45 Colt, rifled barrel, choke tube). **Weight:** 6 lbs. **Length:** 36 overall. **Stock:** Black polymer with thumbhole/pistol grip, sling swivels; beavertail forend. **Sights:** Bead front. **Features:** Buttplate removes to expose storage for extra ammunition; forend also holds extra ammunition. Black or nickel finish. Introduced 1993. From New England Firearms.
Price: .410/45 Colt, black **$203.00**
Price: .410/45 Colt, nickel **$221.00**

New England Firearms Survivor

New England Firearms Standard Pardner

Rossi Single-Shot

Rossi Matched Pair

Ruger KTS-1234-BRE

NEW ENGLAND FIREARMS STANDARD PARDNER

Gauge: 12, 20, .410, 3" chamber; 16, 28, 2-3/4" chamber. **Barrel:** 12 ga.-28" (Full, Mod.), 32" (Full); 16 ga.-28" (Full), 32" (Full); 20 ga.-26" (Full, Mod.); 28 ga.-26" (Mod.); .410-bore-26" (Full). **Weight:** 5-6 lbs. **Length:** 43" overall (28" barrel). **Stock:** Walnut-finished hardwood with full pistol grip. **Sights:** Bead front. **Features:** Transfer bar ignition; break-open action with side-lever release. Introduced 1987. From New England Firearms.

Price: **$132.00**
Price: Youth model (12, 20, 28 ga., .410, 22" barrel, recoil pad). . **$141.00**

ROSSI SINGLE-SHOT SHOTGUN

Gauge: 12, 20, 2-3/4" chamber; .410, 3" chamber. **Barrel:** 28" full, 22" Youth. **Weight:** 5 lbs. **Stock:** Stained hardwood. **Sights:** Bead. **Features:** Break-open, positive ejection, internal transfer bar, trigger block.

Price: **$101.00**

ROSSI MATCHED PAIR SINGLE-SHOT SHOTGUN/RIFLE

Gauge: .410, 20 or 12. **Barrel:** 22" (18.5" Youth), 28" (23"full). **Weight:** 4-6 lbs **Stock:** Hardwood (brown or black finish). **Sights:** Bead front. **Features:** Break-open internal transfer bar manual external safety; blued or stainless steel finish; sling-swivel studs; includes matched 22 LR or 22 Mag. barrel with fully adjustable front and rear sight. Trigger block system. Introduced 2001. Imported by BrazTech/Taurus.

Price: Blue **$139.95**
Price: Stainless steel **$169.95**

RUGER KTS-1234-BRE TRAP MODEL SINGLE-BARREL SHOTGUN

Gauge: 12, 2-3/4" chamber. **Barrel:** 34". **Weight:** 9 lbs. **Length:** 50-1/2" overall. **Stock:** Select walnut checkered; adjustable pull length 13"-15". **Features:** Fully adjustable rib for pattern position; adjustable stock comb cast for right- or left-handed shooters; straight grooves the length of barrel to keep wad from rotating for pattern improvement. Full and modified choke tubes supplied. Gold inlaid eagle and Ruger name on receiver. Introduced 2000. From Sturm Ruger & Co.

Price: **$2,850.00**

Savage 210F Master Shot Slug Warrior

Stoeger Single-Shot

Tar-Hunt RSG-20 Mountaineer

Thompson/Center Encore Rifled Slug

Thompson/Center Encore Turkey

SAVAGE MODEL 210F SLUG WARRIOR

Gauge: 12, 3" chamber; 2-shot magazine. **Barrel:** 24" 1:35" rifling twist. **Weight:** 7-1/2 lbs. **Length:** 43.5" overall. **Stock:** Glass-filled polymer with positive checkering. **Features:** Based on the Savage Model 110 action; 60 bolt lift; controlled round feed; comes with scope mount. Introduced 1996. Made in U.S. by Savage Arms.

Price: **$458.00**
Price: (Camo) **$495.00**

STOEGER SINGLE-SHOT SHOTGUN

Gauge: 12, 20, .410, 2-3/4", 3" chambers. **Barrel:** 26", 28". **Weight:** 5.4 lbs. **gth:** 40-1/2" to 42-1/2" overall. **Sights:** Brass bead. **Features:** .410, full fixed choke tubes, rest M, screw-in. .410 12 ga. hardwood pistol-grip stock and forend. 20 ga. 26" bbl., hardwood forend.

Price: Blue; Youth **$109.00**
Price: Youth with English stock **$119.00**

TAR-HUNT RSG-12 PROFESSIONAL RIFLED SLUG GUN

Gauge: 12, 16 & 20, 2-3/4" or 3" chamber, 1-shot magazine. **Barrel:** 23", fully rifled with muzzle brake. **Weight:** 7-3/4 lbs. **Length:** 41-1/2" overall. **Stock:** Matte black McMillan fiberglass with Pachmayr Decelera-tor pad. **Sights:** None furnished; comes with Leupold windage or Weaver bases. **Features:** Uses rifle-style action with two locking lugs; two-position safety; Shaw barrel; single-stage, trigger; muzzle brake. Many options available.

Right- and left-hand models at same prices. Introduced 1991. Made in U.S. by Tar-Hunt Custom Rifles, Inc.
Price: 12 ga. Professional model, right- or left-hand;
Elite 16 ga. **$2,395.00**
Price: Millennium/10th Anniversary models (limited to 25 guns): NP-3 nickel/Teflon metal finish, black McMillan
Fibergrain stock, Jewell adj. trigger. **$2,300.00**

Tar-Hunt RSG-20 Mountaineer Slug Gun

Similar to the RSG-12 Professional except chambered for 20 gauge (3" shells); 23" Shaw rifled barrel, with muzzle brake; two-lug bolt; one-shot blind magazine; matte black finish; McMillan fiberglass stock with Pach-mayr Decelerator pad; receiver drilled and tapped for Rem. 700 bases. Weighs 6-1/2 lbs. Introduced 1997. Made in U.S. by Tar-Hunt Cus-tom Ri-fles, Inc.
Price: **$2,395.00**

THOMPSON/CENTER ENCORE RIFLED SLUG GUN

Gauge: 20, 3" chamber. **Barrel:** 26", fully rifled. **Weight:** About 7 pounds. **Length:** 40-1/2" overall. **Stock:** Walnut with walnut forearm. **Sights:** Steel, click-adjustable rear and ramp-style front, both with fiber optics. **Features:** Encore system features a variety of rifle, shotgun and muzzle-loading rifle barrels interchangeable with the same frame. Break-open de-sign operates by pulling up and back on trigger guard spur. Composite stock and forearm available. Introduced 2000.
Price: **$665.00**

THOMPSON/CENTER ENCORE TURKEY GUN

Gauge: 12 ga. **Barrel:** 24". **Features:** All-camo finish, high definition Real-tree Hardwoods HD camo.
Price: **$740.00**

Designs for utility, suitable for and adaptable to competitions and other sporting purposes.

Benelli M3 Convertible

Benelli M1 Tactical

Benelli M1 Practical

Fabarm Tactical

BENELLI M3 CONVERTIBLE SHOTGUN

Gauge: 12, 2-3/4", 3" chambers, 5-shot magazine. **Barrel:** 19-3/4" (Cyl.). **Weight:** 7 lbs., 4oz. **Length:** 41" overall. **Stock:** High-impact polymer with sling loop in side of butt; rubberized pistol grip on stock. **Sights:** Open rifle, fully adjustable. Ghost ring and rifle type. **Features:** Combination pump/auto action. Alloy receiver with inertia recoil rotating locking lug bolt; matte finish; automatic shell release lever. Introduced 1989. Imported by Benelli USA. Price with pistol grip, open rifle sights.

Price: With standard stock, open rifle sights **$1,135.00**
Price: With ghost ring sight system, standard stock **$1,185.00**
Price: With ghost ring sights, pistol grip stock. **$1,200.00**

BENELLI M1 TACTICAL SHOTGUN

Gauge: 12, 2-3/4", 3" chambers, 5-shot magazine. **Barrel:** 18.5" IC, M, F choke tubes. **Weight:** 6.7 lbs. **Length:** 39.75" overall. **Stock:** Black polymer. **Sights:** Rifle type with ghost ring system, tritium night sights optional. **Features:** Semi-auto intertia recoil action. Cross-bolt safety; bolt release button; matte-finish metal. Introduced 1993. Imported from Italy by Benelli USA.

Price: With rifle sights, standard stock **$945.00**
Price: With ghost ring rifle sights, standard stock **$1,015.00**
Price: With ghost ring sights, pistol grip stock. **$1,030.00**
Price: With rifle sights, pistol grip stock. **$960.00**
Price: MI Entry, 14" barrel (law enforcement only) . . **$980.00 to $1,060.00**

Benelli M1 Practical

Similar to M1 Field Shotgun, Picatinny receiver rail for scope mounting, nine-round magazine, 26" compensated barrel and ghost ring sights. Designed for IPSC competition.

Price: **$1,265.00**

CROSSFIRE SHOTGUN/RIFLE

Gauge/Caliber: 12, 2-3/4" Chamber: 4-shot/223 Rem. (5-shot). **Barrel:** 20" (shotgun), 18" (rifle). **Weight:** About 8.6 lbs. **Length:** 40" overall. **Stock:** Composite. **Sights:** Meprolight night sights. Integral Weaver-style scope rail. **Features:** Combination pump-action shotgun, rifle; single selector, single trigger; dual action bars for both upper and lower actions; ambidextrous selector and safety. Introduced 1997. Made in U.S. From Hesco.

Price: About **$1,895.00**
Price: With camo finish **$1,995.00**

FABARM TACTICAL SEMI-AUTOMATIC SHOTGUN

Gauge: 12, 3" chamber. **Barrel:** 20". **Weight:** 6.6 lbs. **Length:** 41.2" overall. **Stock:** Polymer or folding. **Sights:** Ghost ring (tritium night sights optional). **Features:** Gas operated; matte receiver; twin forged action bars; over-sized bolt handle and safety button; Picatinny rail; includes cylinder bore choke tube. New features include polymer pistol grip stock. Introduced 2001. Imported from Italy by Heckler & Koch Inc.

Price: **$999.00**

Fabarm FP6

Mossberg Model 500 Persuader

Mossberg Model 500 Persuader

Mossberg Ghost Ring

Mossberg Model HS410

FABARM FP6 PUMP SHOTGUN

Gauge: 12, 3" chamber. **Barrel:** 20" (Cyl.); accepts choke tubes. **Weight:** 6.6 lbs. **Length:** 41.25" overall. **Stock:** Black polymer with textured grip, grooved slide handle. **Sights:** Blade front. **Features:** Twin action bars; anodized finish; free carrier for smooth reloading. Introduced 1998. New features include ghost-ring sighting system, low profile Picatinny rail, and pistol grip stock. Imported from Italy by Heckler & Koch, Inc.

Price: (Carbon fiber finish) **$499.00**
Price: With flip-up front sight, Picatinny rail with rear sight, oversize safety button **$499.00**

MOSSBERG MODEL 500 PERSUADER SECURITY SHOTGUNS

Gauge: 12, 20, .410, 3" chamber. **Barrel:** 18-1/2", 20" (Cyl.). **Weight:** 7 lbs. **Stock:** Walnut-finished hardwood or black synthetic. **Sights:** Metal bead front. **Features:** Available in 6- or 8-shot models. Top-mounted safety, double action slide bars, swivel studs, rubber recoil pad. Blue, Parkerized, Marinecote finishes. Mossberg Cablelock included. From Mossberg.

Price: 12 ga., 18-1/2", blue, wood or synthetic stock, 6-shot **$353.00**
Price: Cruiser, 12 ga., 18-1/2", blue, pistol grip, heat shield **$357.00**
Price: As above, 20 ga. or .410 bore. **$345.00**

Mossberg Model 500, 590 Mariner Pump

Similar to the Model 500 or 590 Security except all metal parts finished with Marinecote metal finish to resist rust and corrosion. Synthetic field stock; pistol grip kit included. Mossberg Cablelock included.

Price: 6-shot, 18-1/2" barrel **$497.00**
Price: 9-shot, 20" barrel **$513.00**

Mossberg Model 500, 590 Ghost-Ring Shotguns

Similar to the Model 500 Security except has adjustable blade front, adjustable Ghost-Ring rear sight with protective "ears." Model 500 has 18.5" (Cyl.) barrel, 6-shot capacity; Model 590 has 20" (Cyl.) barrel, 9-shot capacity. Both have synthetic field stock. Mossberg Cablelock included. Introduced 1990. From Mossberg.

Price: 500 parkerized **$468.00**
Price: 590 parkerized **$543.00**
Price: 590 parkerized Speedfeed stock **$586.00**

Mossberg Model HS410 Shotgun

Similar to the Model 500 Security pump except chambered for 20 gauge or .410 with 3" chamber; has pistol grip forend, thick recoil pad, muzzle brake and has special spreader choke on the 18.5" barrel. Overall length is 37.5", weight is 6.25 lbs. Blue finish; synthetic field stock. Mossberg Cablelock and video included. Introduced 1990.

Price: HS 410 . . . . **$355.00**

Tactical Response TR-870

Winchester Model 1300 Defender

Winchester Model 1300 Marine

Winchester Model 1300 Camp Defender®

MOSSBERG MODEL 590 SHOTGUN
Gauge: 12, 3" chamber. **Barrel:** 20" (Cyl.). **Weight:** 7-1/4 lbs. **Stock:** Synthetic field or Speedfeed. **Sights:** Metal bead front. **Features:** Top-mounted safety, double slide action bars. Comes with heat shield, bayonet lug, swivel studs, rubber recoil pad. Blue, Parkerized or Marinecote finish. Mossberg Cablelock included. From Mossberg.
Price: Blue, synthetic stock.................................. **$417.00**
Price: Parkerized, synthetic stock......................... **$476.00**
Price: Parkerized, Speedfeed stock **$519.00**

TACTICAL RESPONSE TR-870 STANDARD MODEL SHOTGUN
Gauge: 12, 3" chamber, 7-shot magazine. **Barrel:** 18" (Cyl.). **Weight:** 9 lbs. **Length:** 38" overall. **Stock:** Fiberglass-filled polypropolene with non-snag recoil absorbing butt pad. Nylon tactical forend houses flashlight. **Sights:** Trak-Lock ghost ring sight system. Front sight has tritium insert. **Features:** Highly modified Remington 870P with Parkerized finish. Comes with nylon three-way adjustable sling, high visibility non-binding follower, high performance magazine spring, Jumbo Head safety, and Side Saddle extended 6-shot shell carrier on left side of receiver. Introduced 1991. From Scattergun Technologies, Inc.
Price: Standard model **$815.00**
Price: FBI model.. **$770.00**
Price: Patrol model....................................... **$595.00**
Price: Border Patrol model **$605.00**
Price: K-9 model (Rem. 11-87 action)................. **$995.00**
Price: Urban Sniper, Rem. 11-87 action **$1,290.00**

Price: Louis Awerbuck model **$705.00**
Price: Practical Turkey model **$725.00**
Price: Expert model **$1,350.00**
Price: Professional model............................... **$815.00**
Price: Entry model **$840.00**
Price: Compact model **$635.00**
Price: SWAT model...................................... **$1,195.00**

WINCHESTER MODEL 1300 DEFENDER PUMP GUN
Gauge: 12, 20, 3" chamber, 5- or 8-shot capacity. **Barrel:** 18" (Cyl.). **Weight:** 6-3/4 lbs. **Length:** 38-5/8" overall. **Stock:** Walnut-finished hardwood stock and ribbed forend, synthetic or pistol grip. **Sights:** Metal bead front or TRUGLO® fiber-optic. **Features:** Cross-bolt safety, front-locking rotary bolt, twin action slide bars. Black rubber butt pad. From U.S. Repeating Arms Co.
Price: 8-Shot (black synthetic stock, TRUGLO® sight)........ **$343.00**
Price: 8-Shot Pistol Grip (pistol grip synthetic stock) **$343.00**

Winchester Model 1300 Coastal Pump Gun
Same as the Defender 8-Shot except has bright chrome finish, nickel-plated barrel, bead front sight. Phosphate coated receiver for corrosion resistance.
Price: **$576.00**

Winchester Model 1300 Camp Defender®
Same as the Defender 8-Shot except has hardwood stock and forearm, fully adjustable open sights and 22" barrel with WinChoke® choke tube system (cylinder choke tube included). Weighs 6-7/8 lbs. Introduced 2001. From U.S. Repeating Arms Co.
Price: Camp Defender®.................................. **$392.00**

Mossberg Model 500

Similar/Identical Pattern Guns

The same basic assembly/disassembly steps for the Mossberg Model 500 also apply to the following guns:

Mossberg Model 500 AGVD	**Mossberg Model 500 AHT**
Mossberg Model 500 AHTD	**Mossberg Model 500 ALD**
Mossberg Model 500 ALDR	**Mossberg Model 500 ALMR**
Mossberg Model 500 ALS	**Mossberg Model 500 APR**
Mossberg Model 500 ASG	**Mossberg Model 500 ATP6**
Mossberg Model 500 ATP8	**Mossberg Model 500 ATP8-SP**
Mossberg Model 500 CLD	**Mossberg Model 500 CLDR**
Mossberg Model 500 CLS	**Mossberg Model 500 500E**
Mossberg Model 500 EGV	**Mossberg Model 500 EL**
Mossberg Model 500 ELR	**Mossberg Model 500 ETV**
Mossberg Model 500 Medallion	**Mossberg Model 500 Security Series**
Mossberg Model 500 Trophy Slugster	**Mossberg Model 500 Mariner**
Mossberg Model 500 590	**Mossberg Model 590 Mariner**
Mossberg Model 500 600E	**New Haven Model 600 AST Slugster**

Data:	Mossberg Model 500
Origin:	United States
Manufacturer:	O.F. Mossberg & Sons, North Haven, Connecticut
Gauges:	12, 16, 20, and 410
Magazine capacity:	4 rounds
Overall length:	48 inches (with 28-inch barrel)
Barrel length:	18-1/2 to 32 inches
Weight:	6 to 7-1/4 pounds

Since its introduction in 1961, the Model 500 has been offered in a wide variety of sub-models, ranging from a full trap-type gun with a high rib and Monte Carlo stock to the "Slugster," a hunting version available with an 18 1/2-inch barrel. The Model 500 series of guns is still in production, and variations have been made for several large retail firms bearing their brand names. All of these guns are mechanically identical, and the instructions will apply.

Disassembly:

1. Open the action, and unscrew the takedown knob, located at the front of the forend, until it stops. Remove the barrel toward the front.

2. If necessary, the knob can be removed by inserting a tool inside the rear of the barrel loop to immobilize the C-clip. The knob can then be unscrewed and taken off toward the front.

3. Move the bolt back to its forward position, and push out the cross pin at the lower rear of the receiver.

4. Remove the trigger housing downward.

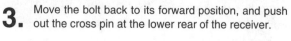

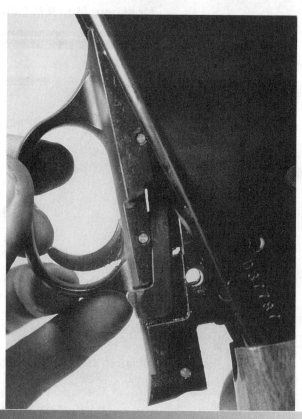

5. Removal of the trigger group will release the right and left shell stops for detachment from their recesses inside the receiver. The left shell stop will usually fall free as the trigger housing is removed, and can be taken out downward.

6. Move the right shell stop inward, withdrawing its post from the wall of the receiver, and take it out downward.

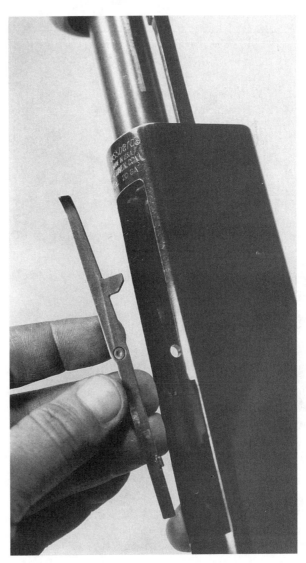

7. Restrain the hammer, pull the trigger, and ease the hammer down to the fired position. Insert a tool at the rear of the housing to slightly depress the hammer spring, and push out the cross pin at the rear of the housing. The spring is under some tension, so control it. Remove the hammer spring and follower toward the rear.

8. Remove the hammer strut toward the rear.

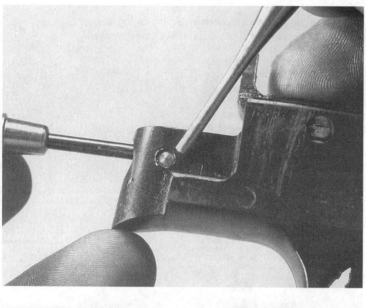

9. Push out the trigger pin.

10. Remove the trigger and its spring upward, disengaging it from the rear tip of the disconnector.

11. Push out the hammer pivot toward the left.

12. Remove the hammer upward. Note that the two cross pins in the hammer are bearing pins, and their removal is not necessary in normal disassembly.

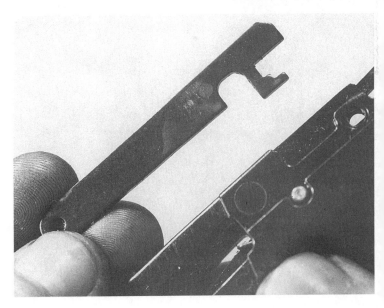

13. Move the disconnector toward the rear, then remove it upward.

14. Push out the slide latch pivot pin toward the left.

15. Remove the combination disconnector and slide latch spring upward.

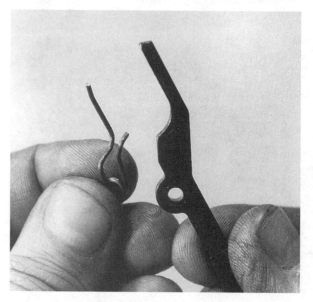

16. Lift the slide latch at the front, swing it over toward the right and remove it from the housing, along with its attached release spring.

17. The slide latch release spring is easily detached from the front of the slide latch.

18. Pushing out the small cross pin at the front of the trigger housing will release the sear and its torsion spring for removal upward and toward the rear. The spring is under tension, so restrain it as the pin is removed.

19. Move the bolt and slide assembly toward the rear until the sides of the slide piece align with the exit cuts on the inside of the receiver. Lift the slide piece at the front, disengaging it from the bolt, and remove it from the bottom of the receiver. Move the forend and slide bar assembly out toward the front and remove it. (Note: This applies to late guns only. See step 24.)

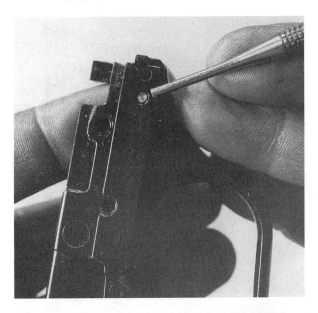

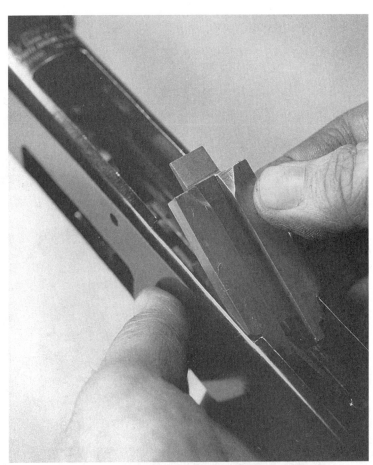

20. Remove the bolt from the front of the receiver.

21. Swing the carrier out, squeeze the rear arms of the carrier to move the pivot studs out of their holes in the receiver, and remove the carrier. Note that the safety must be in the on-safe position (pushed to the rear) during this operation, to clear the arms of the carrier.

22. Insert a screwdriver through the ejection port, and remove the large screw that retains the ejector. Remove the ejector toward the right.

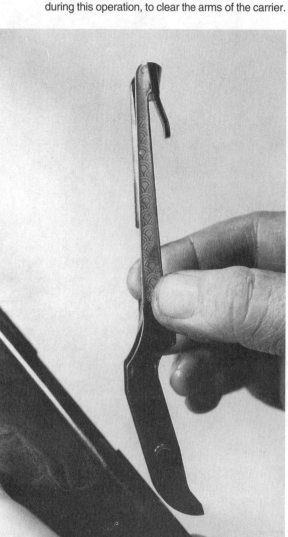

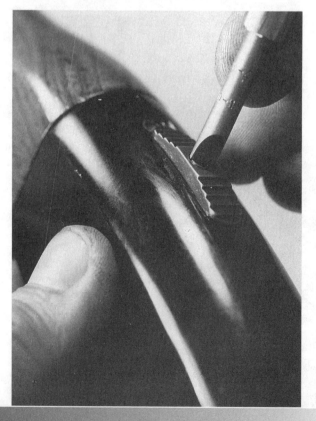

23. Back out the screw in the center of the safety button. Remove the safety button, the detent ball, and detent spring upward, and take out the safety block from inside the receiver.

24. The magazine spring and follower can be removed only by taking off the magazine tube, which is threaded into the receiver. A large screw slot is provided at the front of the tube, and a tool can be made from steel plate to fit the curve of the slot. Note that if the gun is an early one, removal of the magazine tube will be necessary before the action slide can be taken off, as the earlier versions have a stop ring on the tube.

25. Remove the buttplate, and use a B-Square stock tool or a long-shanked screwdriver to back out the stock bolt. Remove the bolt, washer, and stock toward the rear.

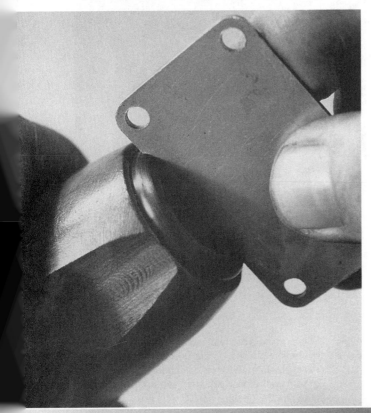

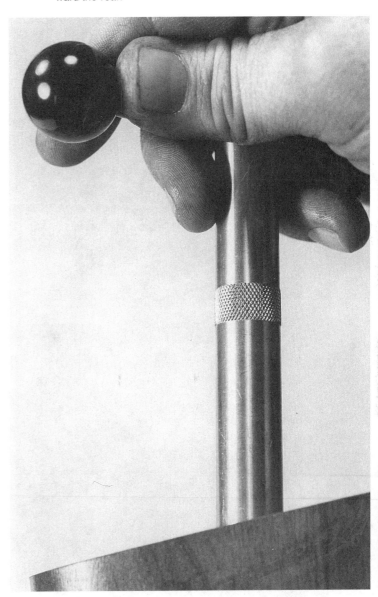

26. Use a small piece of steel plate of the proper size and thickness to fit the notches in the front of the slide tube nut, and unscrew the nut counter-clockwise (front view). Slide the tube and slide bar assembly out toward the rear.

27. The firing pin is retained in the bolt by a vertical pin on the left side at the rear, and the pin is drifted out upward. Remove the firing pin toward the rear.

28. Drift out the locking block cross pin, and remove the locking block from the bolt. Note that the cross pin is splined at the center for tight seating, and a firm support will be required when driving it out.

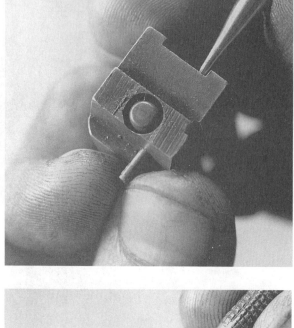

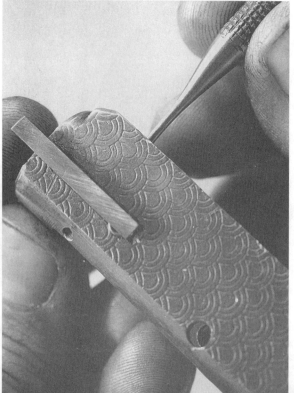

29. The extractors are retained on each side of the bolt by vertical pins which are driven out upward, and the extractors and their coil springs are taken off toward each side. Keep them separate, as they are not interchangeable.

Reassembly Tips:

1. When installed inside the front of the trigger housing, the sear and its spring must be assembled as shown (the cross pin has been temporarily inserted for purposes of illustration). Remember that before the hammer is installed, the sear must be lifted to the vertical position.

2. This top view of the trigger housing, before installation of the hammer, trigger, and disconnector, shows the proper engagement of the two torsion springs with the slide latch.

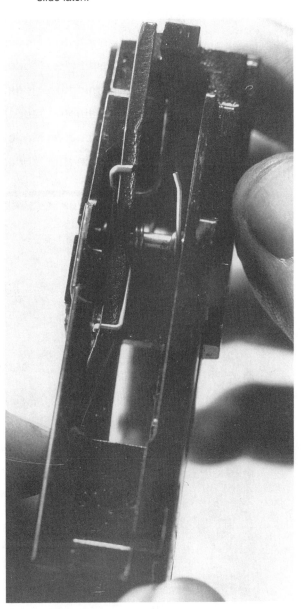

3. When replacing the safety block inside the receiver, note that it must be installed with its lower projection at the rear, as shown. (The safety button has been temporarily attached for purpose of illustration.)

Remington Model 870

Similar/Identical Pattern Guns

The same basic assembly/disassembly steps for the Reimington Model 870 also apply to the following guns:

Remington Model 870 LT-20	**Remington Model 870ADL**
Remington Model 870AP	**Remington Model 870BDL**
Remington Model 870D	**Remington Model 870DL**
Remington Model 870F	**Remington Model 870SA**
Remington Model 870SF	**Remington Model 870 SP**
Remington Model 870TB	**Remington Sportsman Pump**

Data:	Remington Model 870
Origin:	United States
Manufacturer:	Remington Arms Company
Gauges:	12, 16, and 20
Magazine capacity:	4 rounds
Overall length:	48-1/2 inches (with 28-inch barrel)
Barrel length:	26 to 30 inches
Weight:	6-1/4 to 7-1/2 pounds

Introduced in 1950 to replace the Model 31, the Remington 870 has been made in a wide variety of sub-models, but all have the same basic mechanism. The trigger group design is particularly notable, having made its first appearance in the Model 11-48 autoloader, and used with only slight variation in every Remington rifle and shotgun (auto or slide action) made since. The Model 870 is a simple and reliable gun, and is still in production today.

Disassembly:

1. Open the action, and unscrew the magazine cap and remove it. Pull the barrel straight out toward the front.

2. Insert a screwdriver to pry the magazine spring retainer from inside the front of the magazine tube. Move the screwdriver to pry the retainer in equal increments, to avoid warping it. Caution: The magazine spring is under tension, so control the retainer and ease it out Remove the spring and follower toward the front.

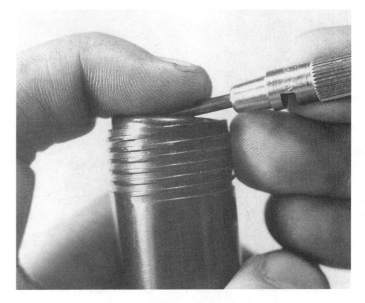

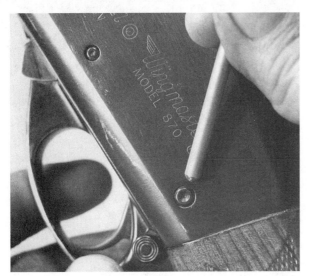

3. Move the action slide back to the front, bringing the bolt to the closed position, and set the safety in the on-safe position. Push out the large and small cross pins at the lower edge of the receiver toward either side.

4. Remove the trigger group downward, tilting it slightly as it emerges to clear the arm of the slide lock on the left side.

5. Restrain the carrier by resting a thumb on the carrier dog, and push out the carrier pivot, which is also the front cross pin sleeve.

6. Slowly release the tension of the carrier spring, and remove the carrier upward and toward the front. Remove the carrier spring and plunger from the right side of the trigger housing. Note that the carrier dog and its washer/plate are retained on the right rear wing of the carrier by a cross pin that is riveted in place. If removal is necessary for repair, be sure the wing of the carrier is well supported.

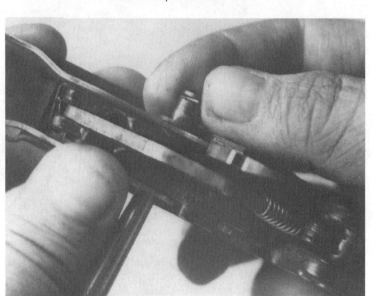

7. Move the safety to the off-safe position, restrain the hammer, pull the trigger, and ease the hammer down to the fired position. Keeping the trigger pulled to the rear, push out the rear cross pin sleeve toward the left and remove it.

8. Removal of the rear cross pin sleeve will allow the top of the trigger to move to the rear beyond its normal position, easing the tension of the combination sear and trigger spring. This spring is now easily detached from its studs on the sear and trigger and is removed upward.

9. Drift out the trigger cross pin.

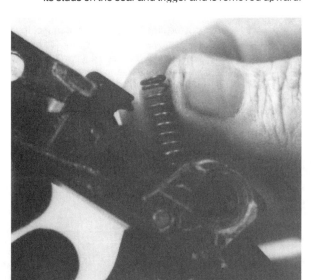

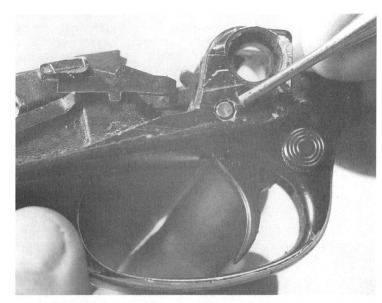

10. Remove the trigger and its attached connectors upward. It will be necessary to tilt the trigger slightly to clear the left connector arm past the shelf on the housing. The cross pin that retains the connectors on the trigger is riveted in place, and should be removed only for repair. If removal is necessary, be sure the top of the trigger is supported firmly, and take care not to deform the upper extension of the trigger.

11. The sear cross pin is accessible by angling a drift punch on the right side into the top of the carrier spring hole, and the sear pin is nudged out toward the left for removal with smooth-jawed pliers. The sear is then removed upward.

12. The hammer pivot is also the pivot and retainer for the slide latch/disconnector, and the pin is riveted on the right side over a washer which is set into a recess. Unless absolutely necessary for repair, this system should be left in place. If it must be removed, be sure the assembly is well supported on the left side when driving out the cross pin, and take care not to deform the slide latch. Use a drift that will enter the depression at the center of the cross pin. While driving out the pin, restrain the hammer spring plunger, as the spring will be released as the pin clears the slide latch. When the pin is out, ease the spring out slowly, and remove the plunger, spring, hammer, slide latch, and the round-wire slide latch spring.

13. Push out the small cross pin at the rear of the housing, and remove the safety spring upward, along with the safety detent ball, if it can be shaken out. Remove the safety button toward either side. If the ball can't be taken out upward, wait until the button is removed, then use a small tool to push the ball downward, for removal through the button tunnel. Take care that the small ball isn't lost.

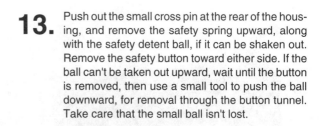

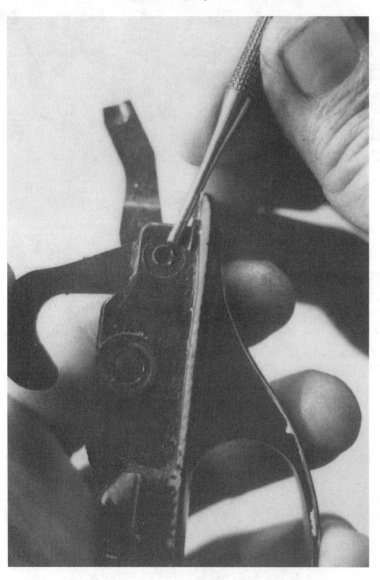

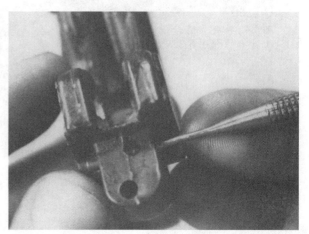

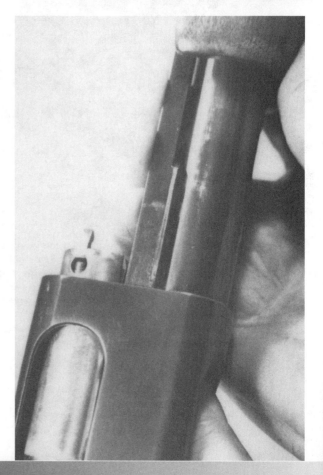

14. Insert a fingertip through the underside of the receiver to depress the left shell stop, and move the bolt and slide assembly out toward the front.

15. As soon as the slide bars are clear of the receiver, the bolt and locking slide are easily detached from the bars.

16. The locking slide is easily removed from the bottom of the bolt.

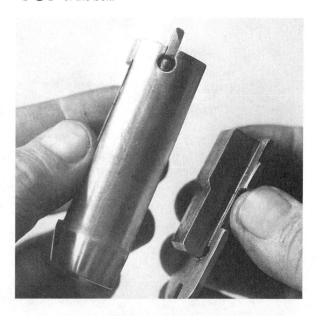

17. Drift out the vertical pin at the rear of the bolt downward, and remove the firing pin and its return spring toward the rear.

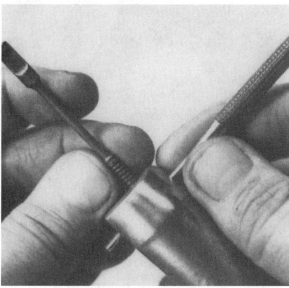

18. Remove the locking block downward.

19. Insert a small screwdriver between the extractor and its plunger, depress the plunger toward the rear, and remove the extractor from its recess. Caution: Control the plunger, and ease out the plunger and spring for removal toward the front.

20. The right and left shell stops are lightly staked in their shallow recesses at the rear, and can usually be freed by inserting a tool beneath the rear tail of each one and prying them gently inward. If the stakes are particularly heavy, angle a drift punch into the cross pin holes from inside the receiver, and nudge them slightly toward the rear to clear the stakes. Keep the right and left shell stops separate, as they are not interchangeable.

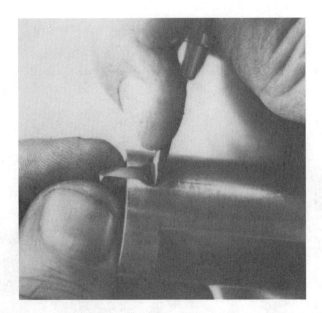

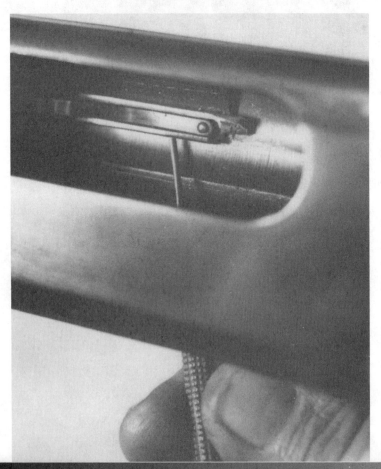

21. The ejector and its housing are attached to the inside left wall of the receiver by two riveted pins, through to the outside, and this assembly should not be disturbed unless necessary for repair. If replacement is necessary, this is a job for a competent gunsmith, or the factory.

22. Removal of the action slide assembly from the forend is much easier with a B-Square wrench made especially for this purpose. If the wrench is not available, a section of steel plate cut to the right dimensions can be used. The forend tube nut is unscrewed counter-clockwise (front view), and the tube and action bar assembly is taken out of the forend toward the rear.

23. Remove the buttplate, and use a B-Square Model 870 stock tool or a long-shanked screwdriver to back out the stock mounting bolt. Remove the bolt, lock washer, and washer toward the rear. Take off the buttstock toward the rear, and remove the stock bearing plate from the rear of the receiver.

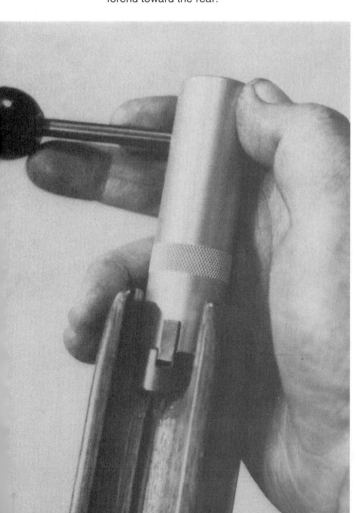

YRARBIL CILBUP ELADNARU
TEERTS HT6S 0363
8504-42608 DU ELADNARU

1. When replacing the shell stops, the upper extensions at the front must be inserted first, then the rear of the parts moved into the recesses on each side. Note that the stop with the recessed section goes on the left side. Temporarily inserting the front trigger group cross pin will help to hold the stops in alignment as they are re-staked in place. This can be done with an angled punch, but is much easier if a B-Square Remington staking tool is used, as shown.

2. When replacing the trigger assembly in the housing, be sure the forward tip of the left connector is above the rear tail of the slide latch, as shown.

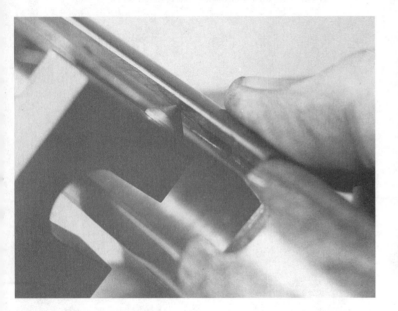

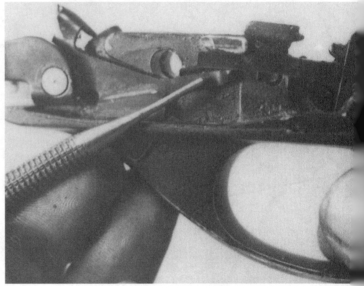

3. When replacing the carrier assembly, be sure the step at the rear of the carrier dog engages the top of the carrier spring plunger, as shown.

When replacing the bolt and slide assembly in the receiver, you must depress the shell stops in sequence as the assembly is moved toward the rear. Depress the right, then the left shell stop, in that order.

URBANDALE PUBLIC LIBRARY
3520 86TH STREET
URBANDALE, IA 50322-4056